Traders Versus the State

Traders Versus the State

Anthropological Approaches to Unofficial Economies

EDITED BY

Gracia Clark

Westview Press

BOULDER & LONDON

Westview Special Studies in Applied Anthropology

Published in 1988 in the United States of America by Westview Press, Inc., 5500 Central Avenue, Boulder, Colorado 80301, and in the United Kingdom by Westview Press, Inc., 13 Brunswick Centre, London WC1N 1AF, England

Library of Congress Cataloging-in-Publication Data
Traders versus the state.
  (Westview special studies in applied anthropology)
  Bibliography: p.
  1. Informal sector (Economics)—Cross-cultural studies.   2. Black market—Cross-cultural studies.
3. Economic anthropology. I. Clark, Gracia.
II. Series
GN448.2.T73 1988   306'.3   88-20788
ISBN 0-8133-7619-X

Printed and bound in the United States of America

The paper used in this publication meets the requirements of the American National Standard for Permanence of Paper for Printed Library Materials Z39.48-1984.

10   9   8   7   6   5   4   3   2   1

Contents

Tables and Figures

TABLES

FIGURES

Acknowledgments

This book began with the enthusiasm and encouragement expressed by M. Estellie Smith and Mona Etienne as discussants on a panel of the same name at the American Anthropological Association 1986 meetings, and by the contributors who participated in that panel. Florence Babb and Hanna Lessinger were especially supportive with publishing advice. Lillian Trager also provided valuable comments on those papers.

It was edited in large part with resources generously provided by the Center for Afro-American and African Studies, University of Michigan. Rachel Cohen and Shalane Sheley gave essential word-processing advice throughout the process. Steven Mandeville-Gamble prepared the camera-ready copy, drawing on considerable reserves of energy and patience. Finally, I would like to thank all the contributors for their promptness and cooperative spirit at every stage.

Gracia Clark

Introduction

Gracia Clark
University of Michigan

Relations between state institutions and market or street traders attract growing attention in theory and policy discussions because of the emerging significance of these relations to contemporary economic and political systems. Traders are among the most visible of a diverse set of commercial, service and production workers operating outside state registration or regulation. Although continuity with pre-capitalist activities is evident, international integration and new technology have changed and expanded these unofficial activities, rather than freezing or shrinking them. Current economic crisis conditions seem to be stimulating further multiplication of such work, in both Third World and post-industrial countries. It represents a substantial proportion of the real economy, in either GNP or labor force terms. Efforts to understand or control economic relations therefore must give unofficial economies their share of attention.

Unofficial or black market traders threaten or defy state control of the national economy. This control is problematic for relatively new governments struggling to gain control over internal and international linkages, but also for established government struggling to retain such control. Whether illegal or simply extralegal, traders' highly visible activities advertise the inadequacy of official distribution channels and the existence of fundamental problems related to migration, employment and pricing. They may supply needs for food, consumer goods and incomes which recognised sectors are unable or unwilling to meet, but in the ideal economy these functions would not be necessary.

Dramatic, even violent confrontations, replicated in many parts of the world, provide substantial evidence of hostility and tension between specific sets of traders and government functionaries. Arrests, confiscations, demolitions and deportations, as well as direct policy statements, testify to the desire of many governments to reduce or eliminate unofficial trade. Less dramatic tactics of restrictive licensing and taxation are even more widespread.

Traders' active counter-strategies validate presenting their relations with the state in terms of antagonism, a term presuming agency on both sides, rather than of victimization. In the cases presented here, traders have responded with demonstrations, strikes, party politics, legal and ritual maneuvers, and group and individual negotiations. More indirect confrontations, from simple evasion and persistence to the innovation and expansion of trading roles, also reflect traders' pursuit of independent agendas.

This collection of case analyses shows that, while none displays all of these features, they appear frequently enough to suggest patterns of conflict. Both state and traders' strategies display recurrent themes, emphasized and combined differently in specific contexts. These papers identify labor mobility, employment, urban food supply, political legitimacy, taxation and land use as sources of tension in many parts of the world. These issues may be primary, secondary, or relatively trivial in a given case, depending on which resources are most hotly contested in the specific local historical context. The resulting contrasts highlight significant aspects of local political and economic formations, including their placement within international systems.

Conflict, whether overt or covert, clearly does not require either monolithic or homogenous adversaries on either side. If it did, very few conflicts of any kind would last long today. As these papers show, the confronting categories of state and traders are complexly constituted from diverse segments or interest groups that do not always work smoothly together, to say the least. These divisions deeply affect the nature and course of conflict between them, without necessarily reducing it. Traders are divided by gender and ethnic group, as well as by commercial characteristics such as wealth, location or commmodity. These divisions shape the goals attractive to them and the effectiveness of their tactics. Likewise, parts of the state apparatus, such as civil servants, soldiers, or local police, have specific interests and strengths in carrying out or evading policies.

Antagonism between traders and the state arises despite, and partly because of, substantial linkages and mutual dependence between specific groups of traders and agencies of the state. This interdependence only fuels the continuing hostility, since neither can afford to ignore the other. Actors within each half control access to certain resources important to the others.

THEORETICAL ISSUES

Controversies over the degree of these economic linkages and their benign or malignant character lie at the root of much of the recent argument over the terminology of "informal sector" and "petty commodity mode of production," to name the two most influential alternatives (Moser 1978). Analysts like Moser and Hart (1973) try to identify specific linkage relations or organisational features which they can plausibly argue are typical of the group as a whole. On the basis on this single relation or coherent set of relations, they go on to diagnose the economic position or development potential of the entire group. These implicit or explicit ideal types are repeatedly contradicted by the heterogeneity even within a subdivision such as traders, so consistently as to call into question the whole project of typification on such a basis. Without endorsing the premise, however, one can acknowledge the great expansion in understanding of the selected linkage and organisational relations that research inspired by these two competing approaches has produced.

The concept of the informal sector was pioneered by Hart (1973) and enthusiastically adopted by the ILO (1972) and others (McGee 1978). The classic definition, later modified in response to some contradictions, describes activities with minimal linkages to the "formal" industrial or bureaucratic sector. Organisational characteristics used to define enterprises as informal include low capital, meagre physical facilities, easy and frequent entry and exit, reliance on kinship or other non-contractural working relations and lack of written records. These features both reflect lack of access to major resources of capital or training and enable informal entrepreneurs to retain autonomy from formal or state control, evading most taxation and surplus extraction.

These same characteristics also give informal enterprises the potential for rapid expansion of employment and wide distribution of income, justifying recommendations of public policy support for this sector from the early advocates mentioned above. Once further studies revealed that many enterprises with the defining characteristics in fact had subordinating linkages to the formal sector and apparent severe constraints on their income and employment expansion, these analysts renounced this terminology. It persists, however, among other analysts who still emphasize the accumulative intent and entrepreneurial possibilities of enterprises of this type.

By contrast, analysts favoring petty commodity terminology consider subordination through industrial and international linkages more typical of small-scale production and commerce. According to this model, although petty commodity traders (and producers) retain control of their working capital, these linkages ensure low capital accumulation. These structural constraints make trading a dead end for participants and planners alike (Moser 1978, Williams 1976). The development prognosis is correspondingly gloomy, with policy support of minimal long-term benefit. These analysts can point to many concrete cases of increasing subordination over time, with a greater percentage of traders depending on outside capital through credit and commission sales. Some analysts take these overtly dependent relations as typical for the sector as a whole. They consider petty trading a form of "disguised wage labor", like subcontracting in production, that in itself worsens participants' subordination (Scott 1979; King 1979; Gerry 1979; Moser 1980; Babb 1987).

The wide range of variation undoubtedly found challenges the basic distinctions of both approaches, between industrial/bureaucratic enterprises and either informal or petty commodity enterprises. Specific organisational features, such as kinship recruitment, small size or unstable organisation, can be found in both formal and informal enterprise (Peattie 1980; Green 1981). The frequent evidence of disarray and personalism in state agencies and corporations, apparently spreading in response to economic crisis, makes informal/formal sector distinctions even more problematic. Counter-examples to the petty commodity approach are also plentiful. The lack of accumulation and international subordination considered typical there are all too frequent among state and large-scale private enterprises not plausibly distinct from mainstream capitalism. At the same time, relative personal autonomy and the chance of accumulation remain a factor attracting erstwhile waged workers into trade. Trager suggests that variation between the analysts' home regions explains some theoretical divergences (Trager 1987). For example, subcontracting and capital accumulation seem more common in South America and West Africa, respectively. But rather extreme heterogeneity clearly remains within regions and even within single towns and cities.

These debates take the form of arguments over which kind of relation is truly typical of traders worldwide, but their failure to reach a satisfying conclusion suggests a need to redefine the question. The very heterogeneity of both linkages and organisational relations, constantly remarked by these observers among others, seems more typical than any given relation. Escaping from this theoretical dead end would seem to require restating the issue in such a way as to make wide variation consistent with the process analysed, rather than contradictory to any proposed analysis.

Rather than any specific form or level of dependence or independence, a more consistent unifying feature emerges in the terms of the struggle which has constructed these specific relations. As case studies accumulate, relations to the state-sponsored apparatus of banking, registration, regulation, licensing, and taxation appear useful to locating a wide variety of enterprises within their national and international economic contexts and explaining their response to changing political and economic conditions. An adversarial relation to the state produces a historically specific configuration of wins and losses, compromises and withdrawals, which changes over both time and space to support the specific relations that vary so widely. As remarked earlier, this adversarial status implies both a relation and a degree of relative separation, much like the concept of marginality. Terms like unofficial or underground economy or black market address the contrast with state-sponsored or protected activity. They are spreading in use, although the authors in this volume use even these general terms sparingly (Trager 1987; Hansen n.d.).

The term unofficial economy avoids an overly restrictive focus on illegality that creates problems comparable to those with the term informal. The concept of an illegal or black market economy lumps illegal trading and small-scale production together with violent criminal activities usually considered intrinsically immoral by state and society alike. Activities such as theft, extortion, corruption and bribery are usually conceptually distinguished from illegal or extralegal trade and production, not least by traders themselves.

On the other hand, the connection is not purely generated by unconsidered terminology. Official propaganda and public opinion frequently also conflate illegal traders with thieves and prostitutes, to legitimise attacks on traders. In some cases the same people are undeniably involved in both types of activity, either opportunistically or through mafia-type organisations (Hart 1973, Green 1981, also J. Smart). Traders' illegal status not only makes them seek or succumb to such connections, but the criminalisation of productive and commercial activities essential to the survival of the poor is a significant aspect of destabilising and intensifying the oppression of the lowest levels of society.

In many cases, including some described here, trading enterprises are legal or illegal depending on location or licensing. Property and working relations may be virtually identical, and the same enterprise changes status with few other associated changes. While illegality is far from a trivial issue for some of these traders, it seems unreasonable to place them on opposite sides of a primary division. The boundary between legal and illegal trading sometimes shifts so rapidly and reversibly that legal status seems to function as a disputed asset rather than an enterprise characteristic. For example, in the Hong Kong district discussed by J. Smart here, traders in the illegal location were eventually legalised, while those in the legal market found themselves evicted for a building project, not to mention those who had legal places but traded in the illegal area.

The amount of energy traders devote to obtaining and protecting their legal status and extending effective recognition to more legal rights, as documented in these studies, argues convincingly against considering their legal status irrelevant. Their frequent evident desire for legalisation also argues against romanticizing them as the antithesis of the state. Traders evidently value specific state relations that they feel improve enterprise survival and long-term profit levels. The attraction of closer or more distant relations to the state depends upon the relations affecting local commercial needs and the efficacy and orientation of the local state.

The concept of unofficial trade bridges not only the legal or illegal status of individuals or categories of traders, but variations in the level of hostility or rapprochement with the state. Relations with some states, and still more often some segments of the state apparatus, can be justly classified as benign neglect, toleration, or even promotion, showing little of the open conflict depicted here (E. Smith). But even legal or tolerated traders still lack the full protection of the state, when compared to stores, factories and other enterprises with more official status. For example, traders in legally recognised markets in Ghana and India were summarily deregularised and evicted. Although they paid taxes or rents, they received little or no compensation for their stall rights, compared to procedures governing more general kinds of property rights, such as land ownership. Hong Kong made a similar distinction in awarding resettlement rights to traders and householders in squatter clearance areas (Clark, Lessinger, A. Smart).

RELATIONS AT ISSUE

The unified voice of these papers arises from taking a certain set of relations seriously, rather than from defining them as the same. Relations linking and dividing traders and state institutions, and various constituents of each group, become problematic because they consider all involved parties as actors. Explicit and implicit alliances determine the alternative strategies available and successful in a given context. A comparative focus emerges on demonstrations and negotiations, arrests and demolitions, but parallels and divergences become equally illuminating. Issues which are not the primary focus of conflict in a given paper frequently emerge as secondary issues on closer examination, or on other occasions in the same location. The configuration of issues and strategies proves quite revealing about contradictions in the larger process of state formation.

<u>Migration</u>

Migration issues focus trader/state tensions where urban/rural relations remain highly problematic. Kerner's paper on the recent "Hard Work" campaign in Tanzania presents a national policy aimed at physically reversing unauthorised rural/urban migration. Traders and other unofficial workers were arrested and deported to rural areas. Regional variations in implementation reflected the state's dominant local problem in control of the countryside. Plantation labor supply, export crop production, gender subordination or border controls appeared as local "beneficiaries" of the exercise. The "housecleaning exercise" in Ghana displayed a secondary concern with urban/rural migration. Women traders were also exhorted to return to honest labor on the farm, although not physically sent there (Clark).

Mushrooming numbers of street and market traders draw attention embarrassingly to the rural problems that lead to uncontrollable urban/rural migration. In the cases described by Babb, Kerner and Lessinger, specific combinations of problems with access to land, excruciatingly low incomes and unacceptable working conditions keep farmers and farm workers migrating to the cities despite difficult urban conditions. Publicly accepting their presence in the cities would require publicly acknowledging the depth of rural distress. Kerner depicts a government attributing widespread unofficial activity to laziness and parasitism, with the assumption of adequate rural wages and conditions, in order to divert attention from serious rural problems. Babb describes very similar propaganda in Peru and suggests similar motives. By providing some urban employment, trading supports some freedom of movement, enabling rural people to "vote with their feet."

Where governments construct legal barriers to control urban migration and settlement, traders' oppositional status is

directly linked to their association and identification with illegal
"squatter" communities. Babb discusses the Peruvian
situation, with parallels throughout Latin America, but the
cases from India and Hong Kong also show direct parallels
(Lessinger, A. Smart and J. Smart). Squatter settlements in
East and Southern Africa had a similar pattern of illegal trade
and housing provision (Nelson 1979; Parpart 1986; Mbilinyi
1985). In these cases men and women migrants had markedly
different legal statuses.

The high percentage of recent or illegal migrants in
unofficial trade, due to considerable barriers to their entry into
official occupations, makes migration a secondary issue in
almost every case. International migration has special
prominence in the cases of Hong Kong and Washington, DC,
where internal migration is less of a problem (A. and J. Smart
and Spalter-Roth). Although the articles here address other
episodes, Ghana and Nigeria have each carried out massive
explusion of each others' citizens since independence, aimed
specifically at unofficial workers and traders.

<u>Segmented Labor Market</u>

Unofficial trade also articulates with employment
structures, gaps and policies at the national level. Social
groups excluded from jobs in industry or the civil service
become identified with the unofficial economy, so that ethnic
and gender tensions find expression in commercial policies
(Robertson 1984). In four of these eight chapters the traders in
question are predominantly female, reflecting women's
exclusion from full-status urban jobs (Babb and Kerner).
Exclusion from smallholder export crop production also
concentrates women in trading (Eames and Clark). In the
African cases, hostile commercial policies take on a strong
element of gender hostility. Loss of economic control over
traders is equated with loss of sexual control over women.

Even ostensibly gender-neutral policies can affect women
traders disproportionately because of their specific economic or
social position. In Washington, DC, male street harassment
made locational issues more critical to women traders, who
needed to band together for protection. Male traders also
harassed them for economic motives, but also more often had
the resources to meet new licensing and equipment costs
(Spalter-Roth). Lessinger has described elsewhere how Indian
women's strong association with home and privacy provokes
tension or hostility when their trading brings them into public
space (Lessinger, 1986).

Subordinated ethnic groups, such as blacks in Washington,
DC and Indians in Peru, also face restricted entrance to the
urban economy. As in Mexico, in Peru market trading is
strongly associated with Indian ethnic identity, and especially
with Indian women (Chinas 1973). Ethnic prejudices and
tensions find their expression in attitudes towards traders, as in
urban/rural relations generally, but also provide a basis for
popular support for traders. Peruvian politicans courting
Indian and lower class votes adopted trading policy as a
symbolic and practical issue attractive to their constituents.
    In Nigeria, the strength of indigenous political institutions,
upon whom local administrations still depended, provided a
comparable arena for expression of gender solidarity (Eames).
Women leaders within the local chiefly hierarchy, firmly
identified as traders' representatives because of the sexual
division of labor, had powerful ritual/constitutional sanctions
against the male town chief. Women leaders in the Ghanaian
case, not strictly identified with trade because women also
farmed actively, failed to come to women traders' defense
(Clark).

Unmet Needs

    Street and market trading provide evidence of serious
problems in the officially recognised urban economy as well as
the rural economy. With or without ethnic and gender
barriers, it usually can absorb only a small proportion of the
actual residents at respectable levels of subsistence. Unofficial
economic activities testify not only to rural problems, but to
controversial urban conditions of low wages and restricted
opportunities preventing full absorption into waged work. In
Peru, stagnant industrialisation and abysmal wages and
conditions in domestic service swell the ranks of illegal traders
(Babb). In Tanzania, as in Zambia, Ghana and Uganda,
increasing numbers of government and industrial workers, even
at the upper levels, must supplement their wages with
unofficial incomes to survive (Kerner; Hansen, n.d.; Green,
1981). Attributing these supplemental activities, often illegal,
to individual immorality obscures the underlying structural
problems generating them.
    While undermining state control over its workers and
policies on the one hand, unofficial trading preserves state
institutions on the other hand by defusing potential civil unrest.
The marginal social groups already discussed are to some
degree placated and subordinated by employment at minimal
incomes. Unofficial institutions like marketplace systems also
incorporate marginal parts of the country or region as sources

of foodstuffs, export crops and labor. By settling for indirect access, the state incorporates areas where direct access would be too costly or difficult, such as highland Peru or rural West Africa (Babb, Clark).

In a context of grossly inadequate official channels, the unofficial economy likewise enables the state to retain some access even to waged and salaried workers, in industry or government service. Large employers such as the state itself lose many working hours from employees committed to unofficial trading, but without second incomes these workers would depart or rebel. When unofficial marketing channels provide second incomes, and supply food and consumer goods at lower cost, wages can remain within official revenues. Even elites may rely on unofficial channels for luxury goods to preserve their middle-class status (Hansen, n.d.).

As an employer, the state has a direct interest in price levels in the unofficial economy, leading to direct intervention. Unofficial prices are strategic to the intensely contested issue of relative wage and price levels, especially when most worker needs are met unofficially. The "wage subsidy" function of the unofficial economy depends on low income levels in unofficial trade (and production) and low prices for farmers. The balance of power between the state and suppliers, whether local farmers or multinational firms, proves critical to the success of those efforts.

State Credibility

Several of the papers here show the short-lived impact of enforcement alone, when substantial demands remain unmet. In Ghana, the government succeeded in shutting down unofficial urban food supply channels at enormous social cost, but could not provide any viable alternative (Clark). Hong Kong street vendors survived raids twice or three times daily because of the pressing demand for their products, mainly among waged workers (J. Smart). If the inability to eradicate unofficial trading undermines the legitimacy of state institutions like the police, the inability to challenge it economically undermines the legitimacy of the official economy.

Ineffectual interventions in local foodstuffs marketing show states' limited control over the farm population. The price controls attempted in Ghana would have made traders the enforcers of low farm prices. Instead, farmers simply kept food off the market until the urban-based state abandoned the effort (Clark). Direct sales from farmers to urban dwellers had equally little success in Ghana and Peru (Babb). State staple marketing boards in Tanzania also faced substantial

competition from unofficial trade (Kerner). Basically, the
official economy is unable or unwilling to provide an equivalent
level of service to the producer or the consumer.

Price controls in imports and manufactures founder on the
rock of dependency. Traders are often held responsible (in
Peru, Ghana and Tanzania) for price rises in imported and
manufactured commodities that arise from worsening terms of
international trade and foreign exchange shortages (Babb,
Clark and Kerner). Even where states successfully attack local
traders, they cannot keep prices down or supplies on hand
themselves.

Unofficial trading not only fills in gaps and shortcomings in
the official economy but depends on their persistence for its
survival. Unofficial traders operate in the spaces left or
wrested from state-sponsored economic activity. Many
enterprises rely on supplies, customers, capital or personnel
from the official sector. Substantial increases in enforcement
activities can put formerly tolerated or permitted unofficial
traders out of business for as long as the government can
sustain them (Clark and Spalter-Roth).

Closing such gaps positively would require increasing the
coverage of official channels of distribution to provide adequate
goods, jobs and wages to those presently marginalised.
Economic crisis and deepening stratification between and
within states reduce real wages and create a growing demand
for lower-cost food and consumer goods. This makes official
provision of affordable goods increasing difficult for Third World
countries, and accounts for the recent resurgence of unofficial
activity in industrialised countries (Spalter-Roth).

Taxation and licensing policies try to bring traders more
closely under the control of state agencies, and make their
resources available as public revenue. Public support for these
controls and taxes depends on the credibility of state and state-
recognised institutions. In the Nigerian case, increased
taxation was the major issue (Eames). Markets with official
recognition already contribute substantial revenues in stall
rents or daily ticket fees, but this does not necessarily protect
them from further tax demands. Along with other unofficial
workers, traders pay no income or sales taxes. Smugglers
among them also evade customs duties, often a major concern
(Green 1981, Kerner and Clark).

Licensing initiatives can reflect revenue concerns, but are
most often a disguised tactic for simply reducing numbers.
Land use is the real issue, as larger businesses with fixed
premises feel entitled to control surrounding public spaces. In
highly urbanised locations, here represented by Hong Kong and
Washington, DC, licensing was reluctantly substituted for

outlawing traders altogether, after appeals to employment considerations (J. Smart and Spalter-Roth). Numbers and locations were both restricted to limit competition. Cosmetic and sanitary issues likewise disguise class-based definitions of appropiate land use.

   In newly industrialising locations, such as India and Peru, land use is an issue of open political confrontation as competition for downtown sites occupied by traders intensifies. More capital-intensive land use promises higher government revenues, as well as higher returns on capital for politically dominant classes. Pressure from the local elite investors is partly balanced by populist pressure from workers who depend on unofficial trading for food and supplemental employment. Outcomes depend on the relative local strength of these forces, including the depth of divisions among traders. In India and Peru, existing sites won official status and legal protection, but new sites did not benefit (Babb and Lessinger). Cities in a position to place serious land pressures on street and market traders are also more likely to provide legal and electoral avenues for traders to seek protection. Electoral systems and patronage networks provide useful arenas for traders, but party allegiance often fails to provide lasting political access (Barnes 1985; Lewis 1976).

HISTORICAL TRENDS

   Historical analyses of Africa and Guatemala make the point that this kind of confrontation is hardly new (C. Smith 1984; Guyer 1987). It has been a consistently important aspect of constructing the relations between rural and urban parts of a national economy and between international capitalism and specific incorporated and subordinated communities. Guyer's collection portrays the longstanding state intervention in African urban food supply systems. Smith's article highlights the influence of local political and economic resistance on the rate and terms of articulation of pre-capitalist areas to the world system. Both authors stress the importance of active agency on the part of both local traders and the national or imperial governments they faced. Wide variations in marketing systems found from place to place represent different outcomes of parallel struggles. These outcomes reflect the agenda of neither the coloniser or the colonised in a simplistic way.
   This line of analysis turns the characteristic heterogeneity of unofficial trading into a fruitful, rather than a frustrating condition. It takes the mediating position of traders, between

national or international and local systems, as their defining characteristic, rather than any particular form of linkage or economic organisation currently found. Specific relations, such as periodic markets or subcontracting, arise from the degree to which and the ways in which this mediation has constructed local autonomy or subordination. The unofficial enterprises and the systems they help articulate change over time and place, but these actors remain recognisably in between.

The persistence and expansion of unofficial economies also becomes less surprising in this context, considering the continuing reproduction of heterogeneity within the international capitalist system. Inequality between parts of the system persists and intensifies, while continually changing its form. This process ensures a continuing need for mediation, and continuing conflict over the changing terms of articulation of various parts of the system. Under such conditions, unofficial economies must grow, to bridge these growing gaps, and constantly change and diversify in form. Despite the confused and confusing terminology sometimes used to define this category, the occupational and social strategies it includes remain distinctive or recognizable because of this historical continuity, as they keep growing in size.

The papers collected here take this line of analysis a step further by offering comparisons beyond the regional level. Paradoxically, focussing on local rather than regional processes clarifies the action of issues and relations that are of wider interest. The authors provide important insights into the workings of the specific social formations mediated by the traders they study. Their detailed accounts of trader/state conflicts reveal much about the nature of relations between state agencies and other parts of the economy linked to it through traders. At the same time, they provide insights into the oppositional dynamics at the root of unofficial economic growth in general.

REFERENCES

Babb, Florence
    1987   Marketers as Producers: The Labor Process and
            Proletarianization of Peruvian Market Women. In
            David Hakken and Johanna Lessinger, eds.
            Perspectives in US Marxist Anthropology.
            Boulder: Westview Press.

Barnes, Sandra
    1985   Patrons and Power. London: International African
            Institute and Manchester University Press.

Birkbeck, Chris
    1978   Self-Employed Proletarians in an Informal
            Factory: the Case of Cali's Garbage Dump. World
            Development 6:1173.

Bromley, Ray
    1978   Organization, Regulation and Exploitation in the
            So-called "Urban Informal Sector": The Street
            Traders of Cali, Columbia. World Development
            6:1033.

Chinas, Beverly
    1973   The Isthmus Zapotecs: Women's Roles in Cultural
            Context. New York: Holt, Rinehart and Winston.

Gerry, Chris
    1978   Petty Production and Capitalist Production in
            Dakar: The Crisis of the Self-employed. World
            Development 6:1147.

Green, Reginald
    1981   Magendo in the Political Economy of Uganda:
            Pathology, Parallel System or Dominant
            Sub-mode of Production? IDS Discussion Paper
            #164. Brighton: U. of Sussex.

Guyer, Jane
    1987   Feeding African Cities. London: International
            African Institute and Manchester University
            Press.

Hansen, Karen
    n.d.   The Black Market and Women Traders in Lusaka,
            Zambia. forthcoming in Jane Parpart and Kathy
            Staudt, eds. Women and the State in Africa.
            Boulder: Lynne Rienner.

Hart, J. Keith
    1973   Informal Income Opportunities and Urban
            Employment in Ghana. Journal of Modern
            African Studies 11:61.

ILO (International Labour Office)
   1972   Employment, Incomes and Equality: A Strategy
           for Increasing Productive Employment in Kenya.
           Geneva: ILO.

Lessinger, Hanna
   1986   Work and Modesty: The Dilemma of Women
           Market Traders in South India. Feminist Studies:
           Winter 1986.

Lewis, Barbara
   1976   The Limitations of Group Action Among
           Entrepreneurs: The Market Women of Abidjan,
           Ivory Coast. In Nancy Hafkin and Edna Bay, eds.
           Women in Africa. Stanford: Stanford University
           Press.

Mbilinyi, Marjorie
   1985   "City" and "Countryside"in Colonial Tanganyika.
           Economic and Political Weekly 20(43):WS-88.

McGee, T. G.
   1978   An invitation to the ball: dress formal or informal?
           In Rimmer, P.J. et. al. Food, Shelter and
           Transport in Southeast Asia and the Pacific.
           Canberra: Australian National University, Dept.
           of Human Geography.

Mintz, Sidney
   1971   Men, Women and Trade. Comparative Studies in
           Society and History 13:247

Moser, Caroline
   1978   Informal Sector or Petty Commodity Production:
           Dualism or Dependence in Urban Development?
           World Development 6:1041.

Nelson, Nici
   1979   How Men and Women Get By: The Sexual
           Division of Labour in the Informal Sector of a
           Nairobi Squatter Settlement. In Ray Bromley and
           Chris Gerry, eds. Casual Work and Poverty in
           Third World Cities. New York: John Wiley.

Parpart, Jane
    1986   Class and Gender on the Copperbelt: Women in
              Northern Rhodesian Copper Mining Communities,
              1926-1964. In Claire Robertson and Iris Berger,
              eds. Women and Class in Africa. New York:
              Africana.

Peattie, Lisa
    1980   Anthropological Perspectives on the Concepts of
              Dualism, the Informal Sector and Marginality in
              Developing Countries. International Regional
              Science Review 5:1.

Robertson, Claire
    1984   Sharing the Same Bowl. Bloomington: Indiana
              University Press.

Scott, Alison McEwan
    1979   Who Are the Self-Employed? In Ray Bromley
              and Chris Gerry, eds. Casual Work and Poverty
              in Third World Cities. New York: John Wiley.

Smith, Carol
    1984   Local History in Global Context: Social and
              Economic Transitions in Western Guatemala.
              Comparative Studies in Society and History
              26:193.

Trager, Lillian
    1987   A Re-examination of the Urban Informal Sector
              in West Africa. Canadian Journal of African
              Studies 21:238.

Williams, Gavin
    1976   There is No Theory of Petty-Bourgeois Politics.
              Review of African Political Economy 6:78.

1

"From the Field to the Cooking Pot": Economic Crisis and the Threat to Marketers in Peru[1]

Florence E. Babb
University of Iowa

In recent years, the Peruvian government has faced two related and pressing problems: rising food prices and a proliferation of urban marketers and street vendors. The way in which these problems have been linked together in an effort to stem Peru's economic crisis is revealing of national- and international-level interests. I will suggest that while it has served middle class interests to hold small marketers--among whom a majority are poor women--responsible for soaring food costs, closer examination shows that both high prices and the growth of petty commerce are responses to more fundamental economic problems of dependent capitalism in Peru. The Peruvian case may be understood in the more general context of the situation confronting many third world countries in which economic underdevelopment is accompanied by an expanding informal sector.

Of course, there is much that can be said for the irrationality of the present system of marketing in Peru--where 99 percent of retail activity is in the hands of small, independent[2] sellers (Esculies Larrabure et al. 1977 :181)--and we may imagine a situation in which economic planning might result in far smoother functioning of distribution. Certainly, many marketers would be delighted to leave their market stalls and places in the streets were there employment alternatives open to them. But to expect the state in its present form to accomplish successful reform of the system through curtailing petty trade overlooks certain critical factors. First, it ignores the role of the Peruvian government itself in generating and perpetuating the current economic crisis--and it never considers the broader international context of the crisis and the implications for Peru's food prices. Second, this view neglects some important features of the work of marketers within the present structure of underdevelopment in Peru, e.g., their capacity to keep down prices, their productive contribution to the process of bringing goods to consumers, and their self-sufficiency, which acts to offset the level of unemployment. If small-scale marketers provide essential services in Peru, and if petty commerce offers employment--however marginal--to members of society who might otherwise be unemployed, why then has the Peruvian government taken actions that appear to jeopardize the livelihood of marketers?

Following some brief background to the current economic crisis in Peru, I discuss the relationship of small marketers to food prices, counterposing the government policy position with my own view. Then, developments I observed in 1977 in the provincial city of Huaraz are presented to illustrate how national policy directives from Lima have resulted in tightening control of commerce at the local level. The last portion of the paper is based on revisits to Huaraz in 1982 and 1984, as well as reports which indicate that over the last decade, national efforts to curtail marketing activity have become an important aspect of repressive government action.

THE POLITICAL ECONOMIC SETTING

The Peruvian military coup which brought General Juan Velasco Alvarado to power in 1968 was met with early optimism as the expropriation of foreign interests and a program of agrarian reform were quickly introduced. Beginning in the 1970s, the military's concern to secure an adequate and cheap food supply for urban Peru made this a key element in domestic policy (Thorp and Bertram 1978; Fitzgerald 1979). In 1970, an agency, the Empresa Pública de Servicios Agropecuarios (EPSA), was created to control the marketing of basic foodstuffs, and in 1972 the production and marketing of all agricultural products came under state control. By the end of 1974 a Ministry of Food was established to regulate price structures on a regional basis, doing away with marketers' control of basic food prices.

The year 1975, however, marked a downturn in Peru's economy and the transition to power of the more conservative General Francisco Morales Bermúdez, who was willing to take increasingly harsh measures to try to manage the crisis. With the encouragement of international lending agencies, his government's policy was to reduce public spending, devalue the Peruvian sol, and hold down workers' wages while raising the official prices of primary food items. The result was growing impoverishment for Peru's working class, and even greater difficulty for the country's unemployed and marginally employed, who comprise the majority of the labor force. The

1980 civilian elections which brought back the president
unseated in 1968, Fernando Belaúnde Terry, and a "free
market" policy that applied to all but a few staple foods. This
has meant little relief for the impoverished population. On the
contrary, under the terms of the economic policy unveiled in
January 1981, and in subsequent economic "packages," the
price rises and other measures have been devastating. This has
sparked popular opposition, from a nationwide general strike to
numerous marches and protests.

In response to the economic crisis, foreign capital was
granted favorable terms once again in Peru (Bollinger 1980:12-
13; Latin American Working Group 1980:3). Actually, despite
the fanfare over Velasco's expropriations of international
concerns, Fitzgerald (1979:131) estimates that the profitability
of foreign capital before and after 1968 was substantially
higher than that of domestic capital. Hunt (1975:343-346)
agrees that Peru's relationship with Western capitalism
remained strong during the period of military rule, with foreign
capital continuing to play a major role. While it is difficult to
know precisely the degree of international control of the
Peruvian economy, it is certain that since 1975 the government
has been increasingly eager to renegotiate the terms of foreign
investment in the country, and by 1980 foreign capital was
thriving (Bollinger 1980; Petras and Havens 1979; Latin
American Working Group Newsletter 1980). It is too soon to
say what the current civilian government of Alan García Pérez
will mean for Peru's political economy. The results of the 1985
election demonstrate, at the very least, the strong
dissatisfaction felt by the majority of Peruvians who were
willing to shift their support to a major opposition party.

MARKETERS AND FOOD PRICES: TWO VIEWS

Much has been written in the last few years concerning the
commercialization of agricultural products in Peru, pleading for
the injured rights of the consumer in some cases and for the
legitimate interests of the producer in others. But the almost
invariable factor in the various inquiries has been the facile
blaming of the intermediary, presumed responsible for the
majority of problems inherent in this process that concerns
everybody: the provisioning of food. (Esculies Larrabure et al.
1977:9, my emphasis)

Under pressure from middle class and working class
consumers (and international interests as well), the Peruvian
government has directed considerable attention to controlling
food prices since the early 1970s. Much less attention has gone

to the problem of unemployment and underemployment which
Peru's least powerful constituencies face. Lack of employment
opportunities is most dramatic in Lima, but in provincial cities
like Huaraz, with little industry, the level of unemployment is
also high. Furthermore, unemployment is a special problem for
women, who have even fewer alternatives than men (Bunster
and Chaney 1985; Mercado 1978). The problem would be still
more severe were it not for the fact that a growing segment of
the population is counted among the self-employed--many in
petty commerce. In a limited but important way, small-scale
marketers reduce the national employment problem by
sustaining themselves during a time of economic hardship.
Just the same, the government has pointed the finger at
commercial intermediaries as a group, holding them
responsible--as the preceding quotation suggests--for the
troubles Peru has in provisioning its people with food at
affordable prices.

From the vantage point of urban consumers and their
representatives in government, there is a direct correspondence
between the number of marketers engaged in the distribution
process and the ultimate cost of food to buyers. Small retailers,
who make up the last link in the chain of intermediaries, are
often singled out for attack since they are both the most
numerous and the most visible to consumers. These small
marketers are viewed as providing an inessential service,
bringing goods to urban neighborhoods in very small quantities.
Their impoverished and sometimes unhygienic working
conditions are frequently viewed with alarm, at the same time
that these marketers are considered social parasites. Middle
class Peruvians bemoan the proliferation of the urban poor,
many of them recent migrants to the cities who have taken up
residence in squatter settlements, or pueblos jovenes, and who
now seek work wherever they can find it. Though they clearly
earn little enough in their retailing endeavors, for the urban
consumer their very presence represents an increment in the
price paid for primary foods.

This popularly held view of marketers and street vendors
(ambulantes) in Peru is shared by some writers who have
considered the problem. For example, in the work of Esculies
Larrabure et al. (1977), there is a sensitivity to the
socioeconomic forces which propel marketers to their work, and
a recognition of the essential nature of the work they do; yet
the authors are able to conclude that the reform of the
marketing system in Peru must begin with the elimination of
much of the wholesale and retail network and tighter control of
the rest. This position overlooks the role of the Peruvian
government in maintaining the present economic structure, the

grave unemployment problem that would result from the
proposed reform, and the positive contribution that marketers
make under conditions of national underdevelopment.

When Peru's economic troubles deepened in the mid-
seventies, the nation turned to international lending agencies
for assistance. As the country became more entrenched in debt
over the next few years, the International Monetary Fund
imposed severe conditions for the granting of further loans.
Peru's compliance with these conditions has been largely
responsible for the high cost of living relative to the low pay-
scale of working people in the country. Added to this, the
government's concern to favor development in the capital-
intensive formal sector has meant the neglect of the labor-
intensive informal sector in which petty marketers participate.
To the degree that the state has entered into the affairs of the
informal sector, it has generally done so in the interests of
urban consumers and the national and international elite. In
controlling the prices of staple foods, the Ministry of Food set
bounds on the "profits" marketers make. In the case of small
retailers, earnings rarely are enough to support a family, much
less reinvest in business.[3] But by working for so little reward,
marketers are in effect helping to keep prices at a more
tolerable level.

To appreciate the contribution that marketers make, it is
essential to assess the work they do within the framework of
the total production process (Babb 1987). The work of bringing
goods to the consumer is necessary to the realization of the
products' value, as the final step in the production process as a
whole, just as it is an indispensible social service. Moreover,
the work of marketers generally goes beyond the physical
transport of materials from one place to another to include, at
the least, the safeguarding, cleaning, sorting, preserving,
measuring, weighing, and packaging of goods. Many do even
more, adding value to the goods they sell by transforming raw
food to cooked food, unprocessed grains to flour, fresh pork to
smoked ham, whole vegetables to chopped vegetables in packets
for soup, and so on. All these activities should be regarded as
productive work for which the consumer pays the marketer,
and this must be figured into any plans for curtailing retail
trade.

Furthermore, the importance of marketers' self-sufficiency
during a period of high unemployment has been noted. Their
resourcefulness in making a living has the double advantage to
the government of quelling dissent--to a degree--and keeping on
hand a ready supply of workers who would enter the wage
labor force when called on. It is in this context that we must

view the role of marketers in Peru, and their relationship to present economic problems.

In arguing that our analysis must encompass the wider national and international situation which shapes the activity of marketers, the food supply, and food prices, I challenge the position taken by the government and encouraged in the media, which portrays marketers as cunning social parasites. Other researchers (e.g. Lele 1971:1; Bucklin 1972:5), writing about marketing in developed and underdeveloped economies, have noted the unwarranted antipathy of the public toward market intermediaries, who are often regarded as antisocial villains. In India, for example, this is traced to consumer and governmental ignorance of the fundamental importance of distribution to the total production process in society, and to the mistaken assumption that traditional markets cannot be successful channels for trade (Lele 1975:100-101).

The research of Harrison et al. (1974) on market systems in three Latin American countries has also emphasized the need to understand marketers as providers of socially useful services and as productive members of society. The authors (ibid.:23-24) offer the case of Bolivia, where policy-makers attempted without success to eliminate "unproductive" intermediaries.[4] Such interventions, they note, are sometimes the efforts of political leaders to create a show of concern for consumers at the expense of marketers (ibid.:90). This broad study concludes that, contrary to popular opinion, when the labor of marketers is assessed at the minimum wage level, there is little or no return on their capital (ibid.:42).

My observations in Peru are similar. In Huaraz, daily earnings of as little as US$.40-.50--or about half the wage for day laborers--were common in 1977, and by the early 1980s marketers reported even lower incomes. Marketers rarely earn enough to support themselves and their families, and most only manage to get by with other household resources. I turn now to examine why such economically marginal yet socially necessary workers in petty commerce have come under attack in Peru.

THE THREAT TO MARKETERS: THE CASE OF HUARAZ

Field research was undertaken in 1977 through a combination of participant observation and open-ended interviewing in and around the Andean city of Huaraz, located some 200 miles north of Lima. Huaraz is the commercial and administrative capital of the department of Ancash, and its population of about 45,000 is largely composed of bilingual

Quechua-Spanish speakers. Of the city's approximately 1,200
marketers counted in four markets in 1977, almost 80 percent
were women. Women were principally concentrated in the
retail sale of fruits and vegetables and cooked foods. Men
tended to be located in the sale of manufactured goods and in
larger scale retail or wholesale trade. There was substantial
overlap, however, in the areas of women's and men's trade.

Considerable time was spent in one of the four daily
markets in Huaraz, Mercado Central, to acquire an in-depth
understanding of the nature of market work. Many informal
interviews were carried out in the other three Huaraz markets,
especially in the sprawling open air marketplace known as La
Parada. In later phases of the fieldwork, I designed a
questionnaire for market women and their husbands and made
a census of shops along three city blocks. In addition to
interviews with some 300 marketers, conversations with
market officials, consumers, and producers were included in my
field data. During my 1982 and 1984 revisits, I reinterviewed
some marketers and spoke informally with many more. I also
consulted libraries and ministries, and discussed the current
situation of marketers with Peruvian researchers.

In Peru, 1977 was declared the "Year of Austerity" in
response to the economic and political demands of the
International Monetary Fund, in exchange for emergency loans.
That year saw rapidly rising food and fuel costs--conditions that
have grown steadily worse--and increasing state control over
the labor force. Here, I will describe the increasing regulation
of petty traders by the Peruvian government, the response of
the marketers themselves, and the implications these have for
our understanding of the economic crisis in the country. I will
refer to national-level policy affecting marketers generally, but
I will draw heavily on research conducted in Huaraz, in order
to show how marketers are meeting the threat to their means
of livelihood.

Marketers throughout Peru are regulated, taxed, and
supervised through a number of mechanisms.[5] In Huaraz, all
marketers must pay for identification cards showing they have
passed yearly medical exams, and marketers holding
permanent stalls must pay annual matriculation fees, based on
the size of their stalls and the type of goods they sell. Daily
fees are collected from all sellers, again in amounts varying by
the type and quantity of product sold. Other fees are collected
for the use of storage space, scales, and even the latrines.
Sellers of meat have veterinary and slaughtering fees to pay,
and the wholesalers have special fees for transporting goods in
and out of the city. During the time I was in Huaraz, the city
council called for significant increases in these fees; this call

was met by angry protest and the market unions' discussion of a possible strike. The council was forced to compromise in this case, though market taxation still increased.

As noted before, the wholesale and retail prices of basic foodstuffs were officially controlled in Peru during this period, and when marketers failed to comply with biweekly changes in prices issued by the Ministry of Food, they could be heavily fined. Fines were also given by the Inspectors of Hygiene and Weights and Measures for large and small violations. The authorities have the power to remove sellers from the markets if they cannot pay the fees and fines issued to them. Small retailers maintained--and I think they are correct--that they must pay a disproportionate share of such fees and fines, while larger violators, usually wholesalers, are less often apprehended and penalized.

These mechanisms for the control of marketers are already sufficient to make it difficult for many impoverished sellers to carry on their trade, but in recent years government control of marketing has been increasing. There has, in fact, been a national campaign against the broad category of commercial "intermediaries," in which the government portrays itself as the champion of urban consumers. As early as 1974, a program known as "De le chacra a la olla" ("From the field to the cooking pot") was launched in Lima with the announced goal of bringing goods directly from producers to consumers on a periodic basis (Shoemaker 1981:215-216). The efforts, while short-lived, were repeated in subsequent years. The effects of this campaign have been strongest in Lima, but they are felt in cities like Huaraz as well.

In 1977, an increasing number of articles began to appear in the Lima newspapers on the topic of producers' and wholesalers' markets being established to bring goods more cheaply to consumers. The Lima dailies La Prensa, El Commercio, and Expreso, all of which were government-controlled, invariably contained reports of actions taken for consumers and, often, against marketers. For example, on July 1 the Expreso ran the headline "Wholesalers' Stronghold Falls". Inside the issue, there were no fewer than three articles devoted to the government's decision to open several of Lima's wholesale markets to the public on a limited basis. The lead article was entitled "Starting Today: Food at Prices Below Official Rates", and was accompanied by one bearing a title denouncing intermediaries, "They Buy Sweet Potatoes for Two Soles...And Sell Them for Twelve!" Finally, a third article addressed housewives, "Prefect to Housewives: You Too are to Blame for Speculation!" This last article rebuked shoppers for not denouncing marketers they knew to be conducting illegal

activities (Expreso, July 1, 1977:3). These articles and many
others around this time implied that marketers, both
wholesalers and retailers, had an undifferentiated responsibility
for current high prices and the scarcity of certain items.

Two days after Expreso celebrated the direct sale of goods
from wholesalers to the public, La Prensa (July 3, 1977)
published an article announcing the effort was a failure. But
instead of criticizing the plan's conception, La Prensa declared
the sellers to be responsible due to their noncooperation.

Back in Huaraz, plans were underway for an Ancash
Regional Fair to take place in the outskirts of the city in late
July. The fair was to feature exhibits by artisans and, as a
special attraction, was to bring producers directly from their
fields to sell agricultural goods to the public--referred to by the
government slogan "From the field to the cooking pot." Despite
the fanfare, however, the producers' market was only a small
part of the fair; only one actual producer was included among
the ten people selling food at booths. This man, a producer of
wheat and barley, agreed that for producers it was better to
sell quickly to wholesalers and get back to work. Others at the
fair had been recruited from the Huaraz marketplace and were
paid to participate in the event. One man who normally sold
meat in a Huaraz market was hired by a nearby agricultural
cooperative to represent their organization at the fair. He
explained that the members of the cooperative preferred to
leave the job of selling to the public to marketers. Indeed, the
view that it was better to sell in large quantities to sure buyers
rather than slowly to the public was expressed to me by many
producers in the region.

The Regional Fair was not well attended, and those women
who came to shop for food were critical. Some had to pay for
transportation to and from the fair, and they were annoyed to
have to pay an entry fee as well. When they got there, they
found few sellers, little selection, and long lines. Furthermore,
primary foodstuffs were rationed, so if a woman wanted to
purchase more than, for example, three kilos of rice, she needed
to take her children along to receive extra portions. Several
women felt that the saving of a sol or two was not worth the
trouble of coming to the fair, and they spoke appreciatively of
the marketplace, which better served their needs.

The producers' market at the fair did not have any
significant impact in the city. After it was over, an official of
the Ministry of Food apologized for the low participation of
agricultural producers at the fair. Even so, the Mayor of
Huaraz expressed some interest in turning the fairgrounds into
a permanent market for producers and artisans. This
enterprising mayor also had a personal interest in building a

supermarket in the city, though he lacked funds for such a project. Clearly, if such plans as these were to materialize in Huaraz, the situation of small marketers might change considerably.

One marketer responded to the rumors of new markets and expressed a view shared by many others. He judged the notion of producers' markets to be a good idea for the public, but a very bad one for wholesalers and retailers. He explained, "In the first place, for us marketers it would mean marginalization. And secondly, what would we do, what work would we dedicate ourselves to? You could become a delinquent, a thief. The government has not thought this through carefully." This man went on to make the salient point that the idea of "from field to pot" was being implemented only in the area of food production, where the majority of people involved were weak, and not in the area of manufactured goods, where the truly powerful were. The government, he noted, cannot control the latter because they constitute the national bourgeoisie, who rule the country. He commented, moreover, that he could not see the advantage to agricultural producers in selling their own goods, since the goods must be divided among marketers in order to get them to the public while they are still fresh. If a producers' market were established, he said, he would try to buy out producers in the market and, furthermore, marketers as a group would be certain to launch a protest.

Another man, a former wholesaler now selling retail, had not heard about producers' markets before I mentioned them to him. When I asked how he would feel about one in Huaraz, he said he thought it would be good since food would cost less.[6] When I asked how it would affect sellers, he reconsidered and said they would not permit a producers' market to exist in the city. "The people would rise up," he said, and "the retailers would not accept it." He pointed to the high level of unemployment that would result if these markets were founded.

While marketers may be concerned about the future threat of new markets in which their jobs might be eliminated, the few showcase producer and wholesaler markets in Peru had limited success through 1977. We have seen that the producers and consumers interviewed regarded the work of small marketers as providing essential services. The continued reliance on petty marketers testified to the large amount of work these people do, and suggested it would not be easy to pass this on to other workers under present conditions.

Still, there was a more immediate way in which marketers were threatened by government actions. While the Lima papers were unveiling a campaign against the abuses of large

wholesalers and the proliferation of intermediaries, reports also
revealed government efforts to apply greater control to one
particular group of retailers, the street vendors, or ambulantes.
In establishing regulations that would affect this group, the
authorities were clearly responding to middle class pressure to
do something about the impoverished sellers who were swelling
the streets, particularly in Lima. New legislation, based on
studies of "the ambulante problem", was publicized, calling for
the zoning (i.e. the containment), increased surveillance, and
tighter control over the fee collection, price setting, and
hygienic standards of these vendors. One article (La Prensa,
August 6, 1977:10), titled "How to Eliminate the Factors that
Maintain and Stimulate Ambulatory Commerce," revealed the
government's intentions to close down some areas where
ambulantes sold in Lima, relocate others, and to direct
propaganda to consumers "to orient their attitude toward
ambulatory commerce...." Such conditions naturally made it
very difficult for many of the poorest vendors to carry on their
work.

  In Huaraz, similar measures were taken by the city council.
In one action, a committee was formed to oversee the commerce
of milk and sugar. This was designed to control the activities of
the "bad merchants that exist in Huaraz" (El Departamento,
August 11, 1977). In another decision, the Inspector of
Hygiene determined that 85 percent of ambulantes selling
bread in the city were doing so under unsanitary conditions. In
order to combat this situation, the council agreed that any
sellers not in possession of a health card would be issued heavy
fines. Furthermore, fines were to be given to those without
appropriate baskets and those who did not properly protect
bread from dust, and there was to be more stringent control of
price, quality, and weight.

  When we consider the difficulty that even the well-
established marketers in Huaraz had in paying their annual
fees it becomes clear how very unlikely it was that poor
ambulantes would be able to afford these fines. The action of
the council to tighten these regulations must be viewed as a
threat to ambulantes' way of making a living. Such action has
the further effect of creating divisions among marketers,[7] since
some are singled out for criticism. Indeed, some permanent
marketers shared the view of the council that ambulantes
constituted a health hazard and ought to be controlled.

THE SITUATION SINCE 1977

The government assault on sellers did not begin in 1977, nor was that year necessarily a turning point in national economic policy.[8] Osterling and Chávez (1979:196) comment on a campaign to evict sellers in Lima in 1969, and they (ibid.:198) point to the growing preoccupation of the city and national government concerning the expansion of commerce by ambulantes by 1975. However, the new austerity measures in 1977 marked the introduction of increasingly harsh conditions for workers in petty commerce and since then the situation of small marketers and street vendors in Peru has grown much worse. While increased inflation and a controlled political climate affect the majority of Peruvians, the marketers and, particularly, ambulantes have continued to be singled out for attack.

A 1978 article in the leftist journal Marka (July 27, 1978:19-20) on the declining economic and health conditions of the poor in Peru, noted that petty commerce was the activity to which most people were turning in an effort to overcome miserable lives. Consequently, this sector had expanded in an "extraordinary manner." Children were being pressed into service, as their families struggled to get by. Street vending had earlier been little known outside Lima, but at the time of the article, the streets of provincial cities were crowded with sellers, "in constant battle with municipal authorities." In Lima itself, there was another effort in 1978 to dislocate downtown vendors, with government agents backed by large business interests and the police, affecting the poorest sellers most (Osterling 1979:23).

During the second half of the 1970s decade, the Peruvian government retreated from the nationalism of the Velasco years, and returned to a policy of attracting and favoring foreign capital. Articles in Marka called attention to the influence of multinationals underlying Peru's "economic packages" of price hikes. Five multinational interests (among them Purina, Carnation, and Nestle) were shown to control the price increases of bread, noodles, milk, and oil (January 4, 1979:12-14). It was not the seller of bread on the corner that benefited from the rise in prices, the author noted, but rather the monopolies that controlled 60 percent of the bread industry in Peru. Sellers of milk suffered similar effects: half of the milk sold in Lima is "Leche Gloria," a subsidiary of Carnation, while the second largest beneficiary of increased milk prices is its competitor Perulac, a subsidiary of Nestle. With a monopoly over milk processing and distribution held by Leche Gloria, producers throughout a wide region in Peru are obliged to sell

to the corporation. When the government ended subsidies on
basic foods including milk and raised official milk prices "to
benefit producers," the producers saw only a five percent
increase in prices obtained from milk sales, while the real
beneficiaries were the processing industries--first among them
Leche Gloria, whose profits rose 30 percent (Marka September
14, 1978:11-12). One article concludes:

> Imperialism has us caught by the stomach. There is no
> question. The government is preparing to offer bigger
> profits to its enterprises by means of the announced price
> rises. And it will cast the blame for the people's hunger
> on the bread seller on the corner and the market woman
> in the street. (Marka January 4, 1979:14)

Marka's analysis of marketers as scapegoats points to the
need to trace the problem to its roots, to the national and
international linkages. While Peru's government seeks a
scapegoat for its troubles, it also finds the thousands of vendors
that crowd the capital city's streets selling everything from
apples to men's socks to be a national embarrassment.
Apparently, the public display of so much poverty threatens the
image the government would like to project to international
visitors and to its own middle class. The vendors' presence
might also, incidentally, challenge the notion that this
impoverished group is so largely responsible for the economic
crisis. Accordingly, before Belaúnde's inauguration in 1980, the
government undertook a campaign to clear central Lima of
ambulantes, so that the city would have a nice appearance for
its dignified guests (Bourque and Warren 1981:193).

Summer 1981, however, marked the most serious
government campaign to rid Lima of its street vendors (Peru
Update, June-July 1981:1-2). In April a mayor's committee
announced that all downtown vendors were to be removed in
mid-June to clearings on the outskirts of the city. This was
met by a good deal of anger and resistance by the vendors, who
knew that their marginal earnings would be further diminished
on the tiny, square-meter plots assigned to them on the city's
remote sites.[9]

The government nonetheless began its relocation program
in June, requiring huge financial expense and the presence of
the National Guard and tanks in the streets to ensure the
successful removal of sellers (Caretas June 8, 1981:23).
Removal was only possible, however, with the use of force,
numerous arrests, and a TV and radio campaign that
discouraged shoppers from buying goods in the streets. The
secretary general of the Federación Departamental de
Vendedores Ambulantes de Lima (FEDEVAL), the street
vendors' association, projected dire consequences as increased

poverty could only mean increased crime as people tried to survive (Marka June 18, 1981:22). Meanwhile, the New York Times (September 20, 1981) hailed the removal of vendors a great success, as crime was reduced in Lima's fashionable downtown area and women "are beginning to wear simple jewelry again."

Some members of the political left in Lima, including the well-known Hugo Blanco, then a senator, joined forces with the vendors and FEDEVAL and marched alongside them at the time of the relocation. The occasion brought together thousands of men, women, and children in peaceful protest, but ended in violent confrontation by the National Guard (El Comercio, June 12, 1981). Blanco, who was hospitalized after the march, commented a few days later on the situation of the vendors in an interview with Marka (June 18, 1981:21). He pointed to the contradictions of a capitalist government which has generated the "ambulante problem," and then tries to cover its responsibility by blaming the victims of its policies. Until the government comes up with real employment opportunities for the vendors, he predicted, we may expect their number to increase.

Similarly, the Peruvian writer Grompone (1981:98) traces the growth of petty commerce to the contradictory, and uneven, development of capitalism in Peru. He describes the process as one in which anterior economic forms and social relations are challenged yet sometimes persist. Only in this context may we understand the present tensions surrounding the persistence of small scale marketing in the country.

On my return visit to Peru in 1982, I had the opportunity to assess the effects of these national developments at the local level in Huaraz. Although the degree of overcrowding that I experienced in Polvos Azules, one of the areas where Lima's ambulantes were relocated in 1981, was not matched in Huaraz, I did discover a significant increase in the density of sellers there. My census of the same markets and streets where I had counted sellers in 1977 produced a total of nearly 1,600 sellers in 1982, or a 33 percent increase over five years. The heaviest concentration was in the streets, as in Lima.

While the proportion of female and male sellers had remained almost the same, there was a notable increase in the number of children marketing. Some children are always on hand to assist their parents in the market, but after interviewing a number of children it is my impression that more of them are working on their own now. Eight-year-old boys selling newspapers, ice cream, or shining shoes, and eleven-year-old girls selling drinks along major intersections at midnight are commonplace.

Another of my observations on returning to Huaraz was the apparently growing number of dependent sellers, i.e., those working for others on commission or for wages. For example, interviews with sellers of raspadillas (flavored ice snacks) revealed that as many as half a dozen might be working for a single absentee employer, himself a former street seller. Vendors of packaged candy and cigarettes produced in coastal factories worked as commission-sellers for distant firms whose products were distributed through local wholesalers. Small market restaurants hired assistants at low wages, or sometimes simply in exchange for meals. Not surprisingly, this social differentiation in petty commerce finds a disproportionate number of women and children subordinated to larger interests.[10]

Though Huaraz had at this time a leftist mayor, his party, Izquierda Unida (United Left), was outnumbered on the city council by conservative forces which undermined his government's effectiveness. This mayor issued a letter of strong protest to the national government, pointing to the policies of Minister of the Economy Manuel Ulloa as the cause of rising transportation and food costs, and calling for unified opposition to this recent economic aggression (El Diario de Marka July 12, 1982:2). Yet in Huaraz small marketers were still under scrutiny as the source of economic difficulties. A study of street vendors was conducted by the Ministry of Commerce in Huaraz in 1982, but little change in policy seems to have been introduced. One may surmise that rather than opening the way for reform, the study may have had the objective of further regulating sellers. Indeed, the municipal government was stepping up measures to control marketers. One group of ambulantes new to Huaraz, herb sellers who travelled to the city once a week, were repeatedly forced to leave their selling places; many arrived early to sell, then left by mid-morning when market officials appeared on the scene. Marketers in general were treated with impatience, if not abuse; and local newspaper reports of "bad merchants" continued as before.

Marketers did not passively accept criticism, but their worsening conditions were accompanied by weak leadership in the major market union. Five years earlier, when a conciliatory union president was willing to accept the city council's proposed increases in market fees, angry women members pushed him to stand up to the mayor on the issue. In 1982, however, the young man who had recently assumed the presidency for lack of another literate and willing candidate appeared entirely ineffective as union leader. Participation in union meetings was falling off as members recognized his us shortcomings, and as more difficult economic circumstances made union activity a heavier burden for the several hundred registered members. Consequently, when a unified response to public criticism would have seemed appropriate, they were silent.

An effort to hold biweekly producers' fairs in one of the city's retail markets met with little success around this time; while the local newspaper El Huascarán (May 1982:6) called the fairs a success, they were discontinued after just a few weeks. The small-scale marketers continued to supply the city and surrounding area with food and other basic goods.

By the mid-eighties, there were still no supermarkets to compete with marketers in Huaraz, only a few grocery stores stocking "luxury" items for the local elite. Although there were rumors of a two-story mercado modelo (model market) to be constructed downtown, marketers had no expectation that this would be carried out in the near future. And the Ancash Regional Fair, which I attended again in 1982 and 1984, attracted tourists and local people with time and money to spend on regional specialties, but few food shoppers. As before, there were almost no producers at the fair and only a few low-priced staples for sale, despite the "field to the pot" rhetoric.

The lifting of price controls from all but a few foodstuffs under the Belaúnde presidency resulted in little apparent change in market conditions. The "free market" is far from free in a setting where impoverished sellers-many of them dependent sellers--proliferate, struggling to obtain enough sales to maintain their often minuscule operations. Inflation has greatly affected all prices in Peru since 1977, but marketers' earnings have remained at a very low level. During my revisits, a number of marketers expressed to me their feeling that things were better when there were price controls (in part this may reflect their view that everything was better before and worse now), while others saw no significant difference. Government control and the domination of large business interests have simply taken new forms.

Underlying new forms of control, the nationwide assault on marketers has persisted. In Lima, ambulantes continue to march in peaceful protest against government initiatives to relocate them in undesirable and even dangerous locations. They have been met violently by the National Guard, who show little regard for women with small children (El Diario de Marka, June 11, 1982:6; June 15, 1982:5). Meanwhile the mayor organized "Committees for the Defense of Consumers," giving the public the right to demand sellers' identity cards and to oversee the setting of prices and weights and measures. What is more, high school students were to form support committees with their own responsibilities for "protecting consumer rights" (El Comercio, July 20, 1982:D12). One wonders how many sons and daughters of marketers questioned whose rights they were in fact protecting. This government strategy became more central to national policy, and for its 1983 economic program to "fight inflation", policy-makers created a "Prices and Consumer Defense Office" (Latin America Regional Reports: Andean Group, December 17, 1982:8).[11]

In 1984, with Peru in a state of emergency arising from the political hostilities between the government and the movement known as Sendero Luminoso (Shining Path), tensions throughout the country were mounting. Still, the government made efforts to quell widespread dissatisfaction about the deepening economic crisis by appealing to urban consumers through the news media. The daily newspaper El Comercio carried a regular supplement on "Food in Lima" with a back page entitled "Defense of the Consumer." Here were featured the current prices charged by sellers in a number of districts around the capital city, under the banner "Are You Paying a Fair Price?" Frequently, articles charged street vendors with aggravating the economic situation.

While the urban middle class received assurances of national concern, some poor and working class residents in Lima's pueblos jovenes were taking matters into their own hands. Comedores populares (communal kitchens) had been organized several years before in some neighborhoods (CELATS 1983), and by 1984 had grown to attract widespread attention. These kitchens were operated by groups of women who purchased and prepared food collectively in large quantities in order to provide nutritious meals to children, pregnant and breastfeeding women, and families of the unemployed. Not surprisingly, these self-help efforts were greeted enthusiastically by the press--and no doubt the government viewed the communal kitchens as easing the problems of the poor without requiring change at the national level. The resourceful women who have organized these kitchens form part of the same social class from which the majority of marketers and street vendors come, yet it is revealing to observe how different are the responses to the groups' efforts to improve their life conditions.

CONCLUSION

Peru's increasingly restrictive policy on the marketing of foodstuffs and other goods sold by small scale marketers-- though not the actual elimination of retail marketing--may be

viewed as an attempt to generate sympathy for the
government's handling of the economic crisis, or at least to turn
attention away from the source of the crisis. Keeping food
prices at a tolerable level is of critical importance to the
Peruvian government, yet this has been more and more difficult
since austerity measures were introduced. In an attempt to
appease middle class and working class consumers in the face of
soaring food prices, the government turned impoverished
marketers into scapegoats--scapegoats who suffer doubly from
rising prices, as sellers whose business is declining, and as
consumers themselves. National policy has had the effect of
dividing consumers and marketers, largely women, obscuring
even those problems they share in common. Marketers
themselves are differentially affected by recent legislation, with
the poorest women, as ambulantes, bearing the brunt of
repressive measures.

In his inaugural address in July 1985, President Alan
García championed the street vendor in Peru, promising help
for his country's poor. Since then, however, the APRA
(American Popular Revolutionary Alliance) government has
introduced further regulation of marketers and street vendors
and continued the use of citizen volunteers to aid in policing the
markets. New controls on basic food prices are resulting in
rising costs to consumers and small-scale traders still take
much of the blame. Meanwhile, Hernando de Soto of Lima's
conservative Freedom and Democracy Institute is predicting
serious consequences for the future of Peru's informal sector,
when street vendors and others in petty manufacture and
commerce may expand to include three-quarters of the
population (El Comercio April 14, 1986:A6). In contrast to
most analysts, de Soto calls for an end to state regulation so
that workers may compete legally in a "freer market." Up to
now, however, his institute has had little influence on
government policy-making (Latin America Regional Reports:
Andean Group, April 11, 1986:5-7). A lifting of harsh
regulations would ease conditions for traders, but broader
measures must ultimately be taken in the Peruvian political
economy if marketers are to see real improvement in their
work situation. It remains to be seen whether any significant
change in policy affecting impoverished marketers and street
vendors will be implemented and whether sellers themselves
will press for further change.

NOTES

1. A shorter version of this article appeared in <u>Ethnology</u> 26(2):137-149, April 1987. Field research was funded by a Grant-in-Aid awarded to William W. Stein by the Research Foundation of the State University of New York in 1977, by a travel grant from <u>Perú Mujer</u> in 1982, and by an Old Gold Summer Fellowship from the University of Iowa in 1984. I want to thank Ximena Bunster, Rita S. Gallin, Karen Tranberg Hansen, Mac Marshall, William W. Stein, and Stanley Ziewacz for their criticisms and encouragement in the development of this work. Most of all, I am grateful to marketers in Huaraz, Peru for their friendship and cooperation in my research.

2. Here, the word "independent" is used to distinguish these retailers from the one percent of workers employed by larger self-service retail establishments in Peru. See, however, Scott (1979) for a discussion of the subordination of "self-employed" workers to larger firms in Lima. I discuss the issue of disguised wage labor among marketers in Huaraz (Babb 1987).

3. For a discussion of the constraints on small-scale manufacture and commerce in third world areas, see, e.g., Schmitz (1982) and Moser (1977, 1980).

4. For a critical account of a similar effort in which these U.S. researchers were involved in Cali, Colombia, see Bromley (1981).

5. In other third world cities, government policy has tightened control over the pricing and distribution of goods. Bromley (1978) has examined the case of street sellers in Cali, Colombia, where official regulation contains and represses petty trade, and Gerry (1978) describes the situation of petty producer-sellers in Dakar, Senegal where government intervention has benefited only a few and the majority have undergone worsening conditions. Jellinek (1977) offers an account of a Jakarta street trader who must constantly evade government "trader clearing campaigns." And Oliver-Smith (1974), whose fieldwork was carried out in the Peruvian town of Yungay, not far from Huaraz, points to the importance of official regulation of marketers through fee collection and fines, as a means to generate public revenues.

6. While this man's comment regarding the desirability of low <u>food prices</u> and the foregoing view of women shoppers who felt the saving of a <u>sol</u> or two was not worth the inconvenience of the fair may appear contradictory, it is important to remember that both low prices <u>and</u> the convenience and services of the retail market are recognized as desirable.

7. Some divisions exist between permanent marketers and ambulantes anyway, due to their competition for sales and

regional differences among urban marketplace sellers and rural ambulantes. Even so, there is a certain degree of solidarity expressed between the two groups, stemming from their recognition of shared problems, and this may be undermined by the recent attacks on ambulantes.

8. Controversies over the role of marketers have arisen in other areas as well. The work of Mintz (1955) on Jamaican higglers became the focus of attention in a policy debate, reported in the pages of Kingston's Daily Gleaner in the 1950s (Mintz, personal communication). More recently, the stalls of street vendors in Kingston were cleared by bulldozers as part of a crack-down on petty traders, hailed by the Gleaner as "a welcome change" (Interpress Service, January 4, 1983). Other cases of tighter government control of marketers in response to public pressure are cited in note 5, above.

9. Osterling (n.d.) discusses the removal of ambulantes to one relocation site, Polvos Azules, as the government's weak response to the problem of rapid urban migration and high unemployment.

10. Zamalloa (1981), writing on the current situation of ambulantes in Lima, notes the large number of dependent sellers, working for wages or on consignment, and the majority of poor women sellers.

11. In an interview around this time with José Matos Mar, director of the Institute for Peruvian Studies, rising prices were attributed to the commercial sector, and Matos Mar called for further efforts to bring goods directly from producers to consumers (El Diario de Marka, June 21, 1982:13). An unfortunate result of such a position is that it does not distinguish large from small commercial interests, and fails to recognize the expansion of petty marketers as a consequence rather than a cause of the economic crisis.

REFERENCES CITED

Babb, Florence E.
1987   Marketers as Producers: The Labor Process and Proletarianization of Peruvian Marketwomen. In Perspectives in U.S. Marxist Anthropology, edited by David Hakken and Johanna Lessinger. Boulder, Colorado: Westview Press.

Bollinger, William
1980   Peru Today--The Roots of Labor Militancy. North American Congress on the Americas (NACLA) Report 14(6):2-35.

Bourque, Susan C. and Kay B. Warren
1981   Rural Women and Development Planning in Peru.
        In Women and World Change. Naomi Black and
        Ann Baker Cottrell, eds. Beverly Hills: Sage.

Bromley, Ray
1978   Organization, Regulation and Exploitation in the
        So-Called 'Urban Informal Sector': The Street
        Traders of Cali, Colombia. World Development
        6(9-10):1161-1171.
1981   From Calvary to White Elephant: A Colombian
        Case of Urban Renewal and Marketing Reform.
        Development and Change 12(1):77-120.

Bucklin, Louis P.
1972   Competition and Evolution in the Distributive
        Trades. Englewood Cliffs, New Jersey: Prentice-
        Hall, Inc.

Bunster, Ximena and Elsa M. Chaney
1985   Sellers and Servants: Working Women in Lima,
        Peru. New York: Praeger.

Centro Latinoamericano de Trabajo Social (CELATS)
1983   Manual de Organización y Funciones de los
        Comedores Populares de El Augustino. Lima:
        CELATS.

Esculies Larrabure, Oscar, Marcial Rubio Correa, and Veronica
Gonzalez del Castillo
1977   Comercialización de Alimentos: Quiénes Ganan,
        Quiénes Pagan, Quiénes Pierden. Lima: Centro de
        Estudios y Promoción del Desarrollo (DESCO).

Fitzgerald, E.V.K.
1976   The State and Economic Development: Peru Since
        1968. Cambridge: Cambridge University Press.
1979   The Political Economy of Peru 1956-78: Economic
        Development and the Restructuring of Capital.
        New York: Cambridge University Press.

Gerry, Chris
1978   Petty Production and Capitalist Production in
        Dakar: The Crisis of the Self-Employed. World
        Development 6(9-10):11471160.

Grompone, Romeo
 1981   Comercio Ambulante: Razones de una Terca
         Presencia. Quehacer 13:95-109. (Lima: DESCO)

Harrison, Kelly, Danald Henley, Harold Riley, and James
Shaffer
 1974   Improving Food Marketing Systems in Developing
         Countries: Experiences from Latin America.
         Research Report No. 6, Latin American Studies
         Center. East Lansing, Michigan: Michigan State
         University.

Hunt, Shane
 1975   Direct Foreign Investment in Peru: New Rules for
         an Old Game. In The Peruvian Experiment.
         Abraham F. Lowenthal, ed. Princeton, New
         Jersey: Princeton University Press.

Jellinek, Lea
 1977   The Life of a Jakarta Street Trader. In Third
         World Urbanization. Richard Hay, Jr. and Janet
         Abu-Lughod, eds. Chicago: Maaroufa Press, Inc.

Latin American Working Group (LAWG)
 1980   Peru: Economic Crisis and Daily Bread. Vol. 6(6).
         Toronto: LAWG.

Lele, Uma
 1971   Food Grain Marketing in India. Ithaca, New
         York: Cornell University Press.
 1975   The Design of Rural Development: Lessons from
         Africa. Baltimore: The Johns Hopkins University
         Press.

Mercado, Hilda
 1978   La Madre Trabajadora: El Caso de las
         Comerciantes Ambulantes Serie C, No. 2. Lima:
         Centro de Estudios de Población y Desarrollo.

Mintz, Sidney W.
 1955   The Jamaican Internal Marketing Pattern. Social
         and Economic Studies 4(1):95-103.

Moser, Caroline
    1977   The Dual Economy and Marginality Debate and
                the Contribution of Micro Analysis: Market
                Sellers in Bogota. Development and Change
                8:465-489.
    1980   Why the Poor Remain Poor: The Experience of
                Bogota Market Traders in the 1970s. Journal of
                Interamerican Studies and World Affairs 22(3)365-
                387.

Oliver-Smith, Anthony R.
    1974   Yungay Norte: Disaster and Social Change in the
                Peruvian Highlands. Ph.D. dissertation, Indiana
                University. Ann Arbor: University Microfilms.

Osterling, Jorge P.
    n.d.   La Reubicación de los Vendedores Ambulantes de
                Lima:¿Un Ejemplo de Articulación Politica?
                Unpublished manuscript.

Osterling, Jorge P., Jaime de Althaus, and Jorge Morelli S.
    1979   Los Vendedores Ambulantes de Ropa en el
                Cercado: Un Ejemplo del Sector Economico
                Informal en Lima Metropolitana. Debates en
                Antropología 4:23-41.

Osterling, Jorge P. and Dennis Chavez de Paz
    1979   La Organización de los Vendedores Ambulantes:
                El Caso de Lima Metropolitana. Revista de la
                Universidad Católica 6:185-202.

Petras, James and A. Eugene Havens
    1979   Peru: Economic Crises and Class Confrontation.
                Monthly Review 30(9):25-41.

Schmitz, Hubert
    1982   Growth Constraints on Small-Scale Manufacturing
                in Developing Countries: A Critical Review.
                World Development 10(6):429-450.

Scott, Alison MacEwen
    1979   Who Are the Self-Employed? In Casual Work and
                Poverty in Third World Cities. Ray Bromley and
                Chris Gerry, eds. New York: John Wiley and
                Sons.

Shoemaker, Robin
    1981   The Peasants of El Dorado: Conflict and
              Contradiction in a Peruvian Frontier Settlement.
              Ithaca, New York: Cornell University Press.

Thorp, Rosemary and Geoffrey Bertram
    1978   Peru 1890-1977: Growth and Policy in an Open
              Economy. New York: Columbia University Press.

Zamalloa, Edgar
    1981   Comercio Ambulatorio: Mito y Realidad. Debate
              8:39-42.

Newspapers and Periodicals:
    Caretas, Lima
    El Comercio, Lima
    Daily Gleaner, Kingston, Jamaica
    El Departamento, Huaraz
    El Diario de Marka, Lima
    Expreso, Lima
    El Huascaran, Huaraz
    Interpress Service
    Latin America Regional Reports: Andean Group,
     London 4/11/86: 5-7
    Marka, Lima
    New York Times, New York
    Peru Update, New York
    La Prensa, Lima

2

"Hard Work" and Informal Sector Trade in Tanzania

Donna O. Kerner
Wheaton College

INTRODUCTION

In the wake of a series of economic shocks which culminated in what has been termed "the crisis of the '80s," the Tanzanian government launched two concurrent campaigns designed to restructure the forces of distribution. The first of these campaigns, "The War Against Economic Sabotage" was initiated in April 1983 as a crackdown on large-scale black market racketeers trading in luxury imported items, foreign currency, and locally produced commodities, the last of which are subject to a strict governmental system of price controls. The second campaign, "The Human Resources Deployment Act," which began later in October of that year, set in motion a series of measures designed to reintegrate the informal sector into government-controlled channels of trade. The trajectory of this second campaign, popularly known as Nguvu Kazi (Hard Work), is the focus of this chapter.[1]

Nguvu Kazi was not initially aimed at the harassment of small-scale traders and informal sector workers. Nguvu Kazi was implemented with the simple aim of relocating the urban unemployed back to the rural sector where they could be gainfully engaged in agricultural production. In theory, at least, land is neither a commodity nor scarce in Tanzania and everyone who is motivated to do so can obtain access to a plot and be a self-employed small-scale farmer. However, as my description will show, the development of this campaign entailed the detention, registration, and attempted resettlement of thousands of urban jobless persons along with traders, vendors, workers, and housewives to rural areas dominated by government-owned plantations. This was supposed to alleviate reputed rural labor shortages during the 1983-1984 planting season. Furthermore, certain regional responses to this campaign indicate an attempt to redress urban/rural labor imbalances internal to regions and served as an impetus to recapture the labor of landless peasants where population pressure on intensively cultivated plots was particularly acute.

It is apparent that multiple definitions of productive labor were at stake here in this campaign. The phrase kila mtu afanye kazi (every person must do work) has served as a slogan of Tanzania's commitment to socialist development through an emphasis on agricultural production since 1967, with the announcement of the Arusha Declaration (Nyerere 1968). Yet the definition of work centered primarily on peasant cash crop production has precedent in Tanzania's colonial history. Boserup (1970) refers to the "Lazy African" thesis. In this colonial ideology, those who refuse to, or only lackadasically engage in, commercial agriculture should be redefined as parasitical at best and as troublesome, even criminal, at worst.

In this chapter, the rhetorical meaning of the Nguvu Kazi legislation is discussed on two levels. A description of the campaign, conducted in town and country from 1983-1984, is followed by an analysis which draws upon the account of this organized state exercise in order to illuminate the structural contradictions of the Tanzanian economy. In my conclusion I will suggest why restrictions on urban informal sector traders cannot be treated separately from an analysis of the rural crisis in production.

THE ORGANIZATION OF NGUVU KAZI

The City

The Human Resources Deployment Act, passed by the Tanzanian Parliament in October 1983, was broadly aimed at ensuring that every able-bodied citizen would be engaged in productive labor. It was a politically inspired piece of legislation, designed by party architects to bring about a number of symbolically potent ends, but its translation into policy and effective implementation was left to government officials.

Tanzania is a one-party state governed by both elected officials and appointed party leaders. Theoretically, the party is supreme. Elected officials, from the national parliament down to the village level, implement policy developed by the party's Central Executive Committee. The banks, most businesses, and labor unions are government-owned or controlled. Parastatal employees at middle-management and higher levels are considered to be both government employees and leaders responsible to the party leadership code and policies established through party branches at all centers of employment.

The immediate impact of this act was most broadly felt in the capital, Dar es Salaam, where those designated by the police, army, and national service militia as "jobless loiterers" were given notice to return to their regions of origin. In the initial or "netting" phase of the exercise, the treatment of jobless loiterers ranged from chasing and harassing, to registration, temporary detainment, and forcible removal from the city under armed guard. Those designated as unemployed were compelled to pay their own repatriation expenses or, if unable to afford the train or bus fare, they were to be provided transportation to rural areas where government-owned sisal, tea, and sugar plantations were suffering acute labor shortages.[2]

But who were these "jobless loiterers?" By the end of the second week of the campaign the government reported that 5,724 people had been rounded up in the capital and taken to interrogation centers for failure to produce identity documents or presenting documents which appeared suspicious; 889 of these were detained and 559 repatriated to their home regions. Three months into the campaign in January 1984, random arrests had netted 15,611 people (Daily News 10/23/83;1/4/84). In the initial phase, loitering, and joblessness were defined by the absence of a government issued identity card (kitambulisho) which designated both legal address and registered employment status. Unlicensed petty traders and casual laborers became obvious targets. Locating such individuals was not a demanding task for the police and militia charged with the implementation of this act. Not surprisingly, the so-called "jobless corners," where petty traders, vendors, and casual laborers congregated, were located near the central commercial district and port as well as in the immediate satellite core areas. One 1979 enumeration[3] reported some 329 groups of "unemployed" comprised of 3,800 individuals within the total city population of 769,445 (United Republic of Tanzania 1982a) operating out of the core urban center in the capital. Interrogation centers set up in Temeke, Kinodoni, and Ilala districts were aimed at these core and satellite urban targets.

Individual informal sector operators, however, were not the only targets. Early on, numerous reports began to document the closure of small restaurants and hotels and the round-up of housewives and domestic laborers (Daily News 10/23/83; 12/23/83). By November the exercise began to extend to blue and white collar urban workers who risked temporary detention if discovered "loitering" in the streets between the working hours of 7:30 a.m.-2:00 p.m. This amounted to a curfew during the working day for the entire capital. Workers on errands for their employers, housewives enroute to market, and school girls waiting for buses or hitching lifts were subjected to interrogation until their identity status could be verified by an employer, a husband, or a parent.

A two-pronged debate about the productive status of domestic labor ensued. Housewives were required to carry government marriage certificates to substantiate their status as wives and not as informal sector traders or prostitutes. Domestic workers were mandated to carry letters from their employers, although this ruling launched a series of angry letters questioning why government bureaucrats saw fit to define their housegirls and houseboys as productive workers, while denying the same rights to shoe shiners and cassava sellers.[4] Children, it seems, were subject to scrutiny because, in the words of one District Commissioner, "some people kept and exploited school-age children mainly from Dodoma and Singida regions [two particularly impoverished areas]. The children are [then] sent out to sell sweets and ground nuts for them in return for food" (Daily News 1/7/84). By the first of the year 1984, a country-wide registration process was under way. Special forms were issued to party leaders of each ten household unit or cell, who were required to fill them out after verifying the employment status of each able-bodied member. These forms were again verified by local boards and new identity cards were issued to each resident.

The campaign thus involved three simultaneous processes: netting, repatriation, and registration. Repatriation proved to be the most highly symbolic of the three processes. Very few of the citizens who were shipped to sisal and tea estates at the government's expense ever completed the journey to their final destinations. Thus the real effect of repatriation was negligible. In fact, the western conceptualization of a rural-urban dichtomy, implicit in many migration studies, glosses the continuous exchange of personnel and commodities between town and countryside in Tanzania. However, a change in status, from rural peasant or agricultural laborer (heavily dependent upon exchange relations determined by the state) to urban trader in the unregulated informal sector, represents a real shift in economic mobility. It is this movement, symbolized by the government in spatial terms (exit from the city and return to the country), which was the object of the repatriation exercise.

Some of the designated jobless were allowed to remain in urban centers if they promised to cultivate allocated plots in the city's periphery where lack of transportation and water made farming untenable. At one point in the campaign party

leaders debated whether all urban workers should be required
to farm as well. This plan was abandoned following the
widespread complaint that factory and white collar efficiency
would suffer an increased decline if workers were
simultaneously expected to be farmers. Such popular protest
belied the fact that most urban workers who could afford to
employ casual laborers, or who could depend on the labor of kin
for cultivation in urban areas were already doing so, since only
the highest-level members of the bureaucratic elite were able to
make ends meet on their official wage.

The Country

Regional[5] implementation of the Nguvu Kazi exercise
outside of the capital differed along the fault line of uneven
development. Local district councils were required to maintain
standing Nguvu Kazi committees to handle employment
registration, to manage repatriated persons, and to make
regular reports regarding the implementation of the campaign.
Regions such as Kagera in the northwest, where large
government sugar and tea plantations were located, were
strongly motivated to implement the campaign in Bukoba
urban and rural districts to meet a shortfall of 2000 seasonal
laborers necessary for the 1983-1984 planting season. Informal
sector traders in urban areas and landless laborers in rural
districts were deployed to meet production targets.
In Tanzania's northeast, the highly stratified Kilimanjaro
region, efforts were directed toward: (1) netting urban petty
traders in Moshi Town; (2) the harassment of rural market
women operating in regional market centers and suspected of
smuggling scarce commodities across the border from Kenya;
and, (3) the removal of landless peasants. Nguvu Kazi was
interpreted in at least one rural district in Kilimanjaro as a
method of resettling landless peasants to other regions (Dodoma
and Morogoro) in order to alleviate population pressure in
intensively cultivated zones. Such landless peasants, working as
seasonal laborers on large peasant farms and engaged in
informal sector trade, were shipped to less densely populated
areas where they were to be allocated government land in
resettled ujamaa (extended family, socialist) villages.
According to the District Council leader, none of these resettled
persons completed his or her journey.
Finally, regions characterized primarily by small-holder
peasant production broadly interpreted the Nguvu Kazi
exercise as a means to exhort farmers to increase cash crop
production. Former president Julius Nyerere, touring the
impoverished western-central Tabora region, reminded

government and party leaders that Nguvu Kazi "...would not necessarily increase production of cotton or tobacco if people did not work." He estimated that some four million rural residents were "unprepared" to farm at the beginning of the cultivation season (Daily News 10/22/83).[6] In town and country alike, the debate surrounding definitions of productive work conflated the categories of informal sector trade and casual labor with black market activities.

TANZANIA'S THREE SPHERES OF DISTRIBUTION

The Legal Sector

Nguvu Kazi is an evocative illustration of the efforts of the Tanzanian state to reorganize its three interdependent spheres of distribution. Legal channels of trade are highly regulated by the state. In 1983-1984 peasants were required to market their cash food crops through parastatal crop authorities. Producer prices were kept artificially low to raise foreign exchange revenue and to subsidize cheap cereal staples sold to urban consumers. Credit and extension services were available to peasants only through the crop authorities and the Tanzanian Rural Development Bank. Locally produced commodities were made available to urban workers and rural peasants through regional, district, and village government trading corporations and cooperative shops at government controlled prices. Ration cards held by each household specified the amount of each commodity that a family could purchase at one time. An additional legal distribution channel operated within parastatal corporations and factories. Each office or branch was allocated a range of commodities at regular intervals which were made available for purchase to employees at controlled prices.

The severity of Tanzania's economic crisis in the 1980s was clearly apparent in the absence of virtually all essential items (such as soap, cooking oil, sugar, kerosene, and batteries) in the government shops. When such items did arrive, long lines and grave shortages exacerbated consumer frustration. The reasons for such severe shortages are complex. Most of Tanzania's factories were operating at fifty percent below capacity due to a shortage of foreign currency necessary to finance the purchase of spare parts. Items which were produced were often sold to neighboring countries to earn foreign exchange, thus increasing internal shortages. Food crops subject to price control were regularly diverted to informal market channels where producer prices were higher than those paid through the crop authorities,

thus increasing the shortage of certain basic staples in
government markets and allocation centers. Tanzania earns
the bulk of its foreign exchange in agricultural exports. The
extent of the real decline in peasant cash crop production from
the 1960s and 1970s was hotly debated but widely recognized.[7]
Many peasants were actively exiting from export crop
production and switching to food crops for subsistence and sale
in the traditional market sector. This contributed to Tanzania's
foreign exchange deficit, which was already hampered by
adverse movements in the terms of trade.

Two results of this economic crisis were clear. First,
peasants could not be motivated to increase cash crop
production because none of the items they needed were
available at prices which were in line with farm incomes.
Secondly, production in both the rural and urban areas declined
as workers and peasants were occupied the better part of each
working day with the search for necessary commodities or
trading in such commodities.

The Black Market Sector

Recently the Tanzanian government relaxed its restrictions
on external trade. During the crisis of 1980-1984, however,
virtually no imported items were available through government
trading centers. These restrictions, coupled with the acute
shortages of locally produced commodities, laid the groundwork
for the highly profitable black market network. The extent of
Tanzania's black market (magendo) trade is too complex to
detail here,[8] except to mention that the campaign designed to
eliminate it, "The War Against Economic Sabotage," was in
every sense a real war. The police, as well as the militia were
mobilized to uncover and arrest the "enemies of socialism."
Normal legal procedures (for search and seizure, charging,
detention, and sentencing) were suspended for the better part
of a year. Former president Nyerere openly admitted that
black market bosses had what amounted to an economic
stranglehold on the country, and he declared that the aim of
the campaign was to recapture the state from the government
of the racketeers.

"The War Against Economic Sabotage" had its own
trajectory beginning with the round-up and detention of several
hundred large-scale black market entrepreneurs found hoarding
private banks of foreign and local currency, spare parts, luxury
imported items, and local commodities. In Kilimanjaro, several
major magendo entrepreneurs were women. In a short time
this exercise devolved into the detention of distribution
middlemen as well, who were often also government employees,

and small petty traders peddling small amounts of illegally
obtained goods in rural markets and urban street corners.

The "Shadow Economy"

There is a third distribution sphere in Tanzania which I call
Tanzania's "shadow economy". It is interstitial between
legally-regulated channels of trade and the black market
sphere. Unlicensed petty traders selling foodstuffs and locally
produced items, vendors of cooked foods, soft drinks and
newspapers, service operators such as cobblers, shoe shiners,
barbers, tailors, and urban casual laborers and domestic
workers--in other words, traders and service workers from
whom the state receives no revenue--comprise the informal
sector of most African economies. They are tolerated during
times of prosperity and harassed and restricted when the
economy is depressed. In Tanzania, during the economic crisis
of the first half of the 1980s, these traders and workers formed
the lowest tier of black market distributors as well. For all
intents and purposes, the informal sector had become
contaminated by illegal trade. Tomato sellers peddled
smuggled cans of Kenyan margarine, newspaper vendors
exchanged foreign currency, shoe shiners sold flowered
Ruandan shirts, and cassava vendors peddled cigarettes (which
were unavailable in shops) by the piece.

The shadow economy extended beyond the traditional
market or informal sector however. It extended to what can
only be termed an essential survival strategy adopted by
everyone from the highest level bureaucrat to the poorest
peasant and worker. Everyone who could manage to divert
some essential goods or services from legal channels would do
so. Commodities and services (e.g., areas such as
communications, medicine, education, and transportation) were
bought and sold at the inflated black market price or exchanged
for needed goods or services.

Those with access to foreign exchange (mainly bureaucrats
approved for foreign travel) purchased both imported goods for
trade and large-scale items such as pick-up trucks, commercial
freezers, chain saws, or sewing machines to operate unofficial
businesses. The opportunity for study abroad was widely
perceived as a significant opportunity to aid one's relatives in
their various projects back home. University professors
routinely operated enterprises in poultry and other farm
products, thus earning themselves the title "the banana and
chicken petty bourgeoisie."

One recent report (Gargan, quoting Maliyamkono in the
NY Times 10/14/85) estimated that many Tanzanians spend

little more than forty percent of their working day at their jobs due to their involvement in shadow economy activities. The shadow economy is sometimes illegal, sometimes legal, and sometimes only hazily so. It is this distribution realm which dominates the practical strategies of everyday life for Tanzanians and, contrary to official rhetoric, it is hard work, even though it is not overtly productive.

CONCLUSIONS

What can be said about the real impact of Nguvu Kazi on the Tanzanian economy? For a brief period of time shoe shiners and food sellers disappeared from the streets, clerks stayed at their desks, housewives carried marriage certificates, and school girls rode buses in clusters. A rapid underground trade in the new identity cards flourished, so that almost everyone was able to produce the new document, whether it was legally obtained or not. Casual laborers who were sent to estates and who actually arrived at their destinations worked a short season, and left after several weeks. District committees continued to file reports, while the Ministry of Labor wrestled with the question of which categories within the informal sector could be considered legal and beneficial to the nation. The actual material changes brought about by this campaign were few.

I would argue that legislation such as Nguvu Kazi, recurring historically at regular intervals since the British colonial era, is worth considering for what it reveals about the structural weakness of the colonial and postcolonial state's attempt to extract surplus value from the rural producer.[9] It is not a mere symbolic coincidence that legislation designed to capture the urban unemployed and underemployed should be linked to a program to convert poor peasants and petty traders into rural casual laborers. Also it is not accidental that there should be a rhetorical attempt to redefine work as "agricultural labor" and the failure to work "hard enough" to meet state cash crop production targets as a "criminal offense."

In a recent analysis of sex differentials in employment and income, Mbilinyi (1985b) raises the question of whether a rural labor shortage really existed during the economic crisis years of the 1980s. She suggests instead that the alarm raised about labor shortages represented the interests of employers (private and public plantations, the latter, a state/agribusiness combination) in reducing wages and securing an assured source of casual labor. Her data on female banana traders in the southern Rungwe area, which is also dominated by tea estates, indicate that these women enjoy greater mobility and a more secure income from petty trade than they do by working as either family laborers or as seasonal tea pluckers. Labor shortage, in Mbilinyi's view, is at least partly an expression of competition between capital's labor requirements and the requirements of petty commodity production/trade which lies "outside of" capital wage and capital non-wage labor relationships.

Finally, the repatriation process symbolically enacted in Nguvu Kazi is not discontinuous with the more wide-scale resettlement policy begun during the 1970s which moved several million farmers living in dispersed settlements into consolidated ujamaa villages. The overt goal of such resettlement was to provide basic services in transport, water, medical, and educational facilities and modern agricultural extension services more efficiently. This was supposed to improve both the quality of life and the level of agricultural production. While at one level the aim of such a massive scheme was economically rational and humanitarian, the aspect of state coercion was not lost on the peasants whose old villages were burnt behind them as they were removed to new settlements under armed guard.

This chapter has sketched some of the conditions which conspired to produce a situation in which the average peasant family could no longer meet the cost of social reproduction. These conditions provided the impetus not only for increased migration to urban areas where illegal and/or semi-legal trade was most profitable, but also for an expansion of activities in rural areas within what I have been calling the shadow economy.

In a provocative working paper on the extreme East African case of Ugandan magendo, Green (1981) makes the argument that the ascendancy of black market control over the structure of distribution has its origin in the deterioration of a legal economic order and weak state political control. He suggests a parallel in form and organization between the rise of East African magendo--"a distorted form of capitalism"--and the development of European capitalism in the fourteenth to eighteenth centuries. As in early European capitalism, magendo operates most strongly in areas such as transport, long distance trade, and finance, with food magendo dependent upon transport magendo. It has evolved its own internal hierarchy and security force. Magendo operations in some respects mirror the medieval practices of forestalling, engrossing, and regrating.[10] The exploitative nature of its methods of primitive accumulation are openly recognized and deplored. In its virtual monopoly over the forces of distribution, magendo begins to dominate the organization of production. In order to buy on the black market, producers are compelled to sell on the black market. It can be argued that some food crops (e.g., maize) are in fact produced with the intent of selling surplus on the black market.

Although both Tanzania and Uganda were negatively affected by downward shifts in their terms of trade beginning in 1973,[11] the two economies cannot be strictly compared. Tanzania has had a relatively stable regime since its independence in 1961, and, despite economic hardship, has managed to provide a range of basic services to its citizens, though these are in a deteriorating state.[12] In the eyes of the majority of its citizens the government is still considered a legitimate authority, although each wave of economic shocks threatens to undermine its control. A thwarted coup attempt in late 1982 preceded the initiation of the "War Against Economic Sabotage" and there is a tentative argument which can be made to link the two events.

The Tanzanian state is, in any case, not the Ugandan state and neither is strictly comparable to early European states. Where magendo exists, it does so at the periphery of international capitalism. It is unlikely to evolve in a way that will benefit relations of production, since its goal is accumulation by redistribution rather than the creation of wealth. The permeation of magendo into the everyday sphere of legal distribution in Tanzania appeared almost complete in 1984. The state's first response was to attack both the black market and shadow distributors. Its second response has been to conform to the structural adjustment guidelines demanded by the World Bank and IMF, which include: currency devaluation, elimination of many price controls, a rise in producer prices, the dismantling of parastatal crop authorities with the revitalization of peasant cooperatives, the encouragement of private business and investment, and relaxation of foreign exchange restrictions. Recent reports indicate that imported and local goods now flood the government shops. It remains to be seen whether the income earned from hard work will make such purchases attainable.

NOTES

1. The field research on which this chapter is based was conducted between 1982-1984 and was funded by The Graduate Center of the City University of New York under a Graduate Research Assistantship and the Andrew Silk Dissertation Fellowship. During my stay in Tanzania I was

affiliated with the Tanzanian National Scientific Research
Council and the University of Dar es Salaam as a Research
Associate in the Department of Education. I gratefully
acknowledge the support and cooperation of these institutions.
The data for this chapter were drawn from a variety of sources
and include: <u>interviews</u> with the District Council Chairman and
members of the council, Ward and Village Chairmen, ten-cell
leaders and village residents (Moshi Rural), informal sector
traders (Moshi Urban), informal sector traders and a range of
individuals temporarily detained during the campaign (Dar es
Salaam, Urban); <u>government reports</u> from Nguvu Kazi
committees, District and Village reports (Moshi Rural), and
statistics published in the government-owned newspaper, <u>The
Daily News</u>. An earlier version of this chapter was presented
as a paper at the 85th annual meeting of the American
Anthropological Association, Philadelphia, PA, 1986. My
thanks to colleagues who read and commented on this initial
draft: Elizabeth Brusco, Kristy Cook, Richard Downs, Roman
Grynberg, Christy Hammer, Marjorie Mbilinyi, June Nash,
Dan Santoro, and Larry Sawer. They are absolved of any errors
which remain.
2. A <u>Daily News</u> editorial, November 11, 1984 (quoted in
Mbilinyi 1986) provided the following comment:
> [The] shortage of casual workers in sisal estates, tea and
> sugar cane plantations, among others, is a recurring
> problem which needs to be viewed seriously by all of
> us...the problem, which is common throughout the country
> where major cash crops are grown, has greatly
> undermined the performance of the agricultural sector...It
> was reported at the week end that tea processing at
> Malangali in Njombe District is headed for big trouble
> because of acute shortage of casual workers. The
> plantation, which is owned by the Tanzania Tea Authority
> (TTA), is currently operating with only 50 workers of the
> required 300...Similarly, the Tanzania Sisal Authority
> (TSA) has time and again said that the leading problem
> facing the sisal industry is the non-availability of
> committed sisal cutters.
3. The methodological difficulties involved in enumerating the
urban un- and under-employed are discussed by the author
(Ishumi 1984) at some length. While this is a innovative study
in its use of a variety of research techniques to analyze the
sources and reason for rural-urban migration, urban survival
strategies in the capital and regional urban centers, and the
characteristics of the "urban jobless", it does not center this
analysis within a broader understanding of developments in the

Tanzanian economy which have substantially increased the
gains to be made in non-wage petty commodity trade.
4. One irate letter to the editor summarized some of the
contradictions in the operationalization of Nguvu Kazi.

"I would like to question those in authority if their
indiscriminate arrests of pedestrians and cyclists in the
streets between 10:00 am and 2:00 pm is legal and
constitutional. I wonder if someone can legally be arrested
if he holds a valid identity card simply because he is in the
streets during the work hours in Dar es Salaam, as if we
are in a curfew or state of emergency. Is this not abuse of
power and threaten (sic) people's freedom and liberty by
unnecessary harassment to workers and married women?
Why arrest married women? Does this country not
recognize the role of married women? One more
surprising thing is that people using cars and trucks
during the so-called work hours are not harassed. Why?
Can't someone loiter with his car for petty personal
business during work hours? Are we creating two classes
of citizens in this country--the oppressed and the
privileged?" (People's Forum, Daily News November 10,
1983).

The harassment of women (married and school age) has to be
deconstructed, for it is not fully articulated in this or any other
text published during the campaign. Women form a significant
component of the informal sector as food stuff and illegal liquor
traders and prostitutes. The restriction that women carry
government marriage certificates not only discriminated against
unmarried working women, but those women married under
tribal law which is recognized, though not registered, by the
state. Female domestic workers are often young girls fostered
by poor relations and clients to elite families in the urban
centers and they frequently have ambivalent relations with
their patrons/employers. The implicit "sexualization" of Nguvu
Kazi in the attack on unaccompanied women was acknowledged
by female informants who said they were raped by police or
militiamen who detained them or told that they would be
released (with no questions asked) in return for sexual favors.
5. Tanzania is politically divided into twenty regions which are
further sub-divided into districts, divisions, wards, and villages.
The government and party structure operates parallel
structures from the regional level on down, with the party
reaching down to the most minimal village unit of a set of ten
households (the cell).
6. The former president was ambiguous about what he meant
to construe in the phrase "unprepared to farm." He indicated
that such peasants did not have farms and had not been

prepared by the regional authorities for "meaningful farming."
Whether he was referring to landless peasants in population-
dense areas, or peasants who were actively retreating from
cash crop production, is unclear.
7. The real value of Tanzania's agricultural exports in 1980
was less than sixty percent of the 1977 peak (United Republic
of Tanzania 1982b).
8. Reginald Green's paper on Ugandan magendo (1981) outlines
the structural features of the black market, which in many
respects parallels the Tanzanian case. He goes to some length
to discuss the manner in which the Ugandan situation is
unique, and his estimate that Tanzanian magendo has not
achieved the same degree of coercive economic and political
power as Ugandan magendo seems correct, although probably
less so at present than it appeared in 1981.
9. See Mbilinyi's analysis of colonial agricultural policy in
Tanganyika (1985a, 91). She states that, the system of
migrant labour, related wage policies and price policies for
primary commodity products, and settlement policies regarding
Africans depended in part on the acceptance of the ideology of
the subsistence peasant's non-problematic existence on the land
under the supervision of Native Authorities.
10. The meaning of these terms is as follows: <u>forestalling</u>
(taking control of goods between the initial supplier and
market); <u>engrossing</u> (buying up the whole supply to manipulate
prices); <u>regrating</u> (selling retail at extortionate prices).
11. Green's 1981 estimate was: radical negative terms of trade
shifts from 1972-1980 are perhaps as drastic as forty percent,
meaning a loss of ten to twelve percent in real national
purchasing power (1981, 1).
12. See the International Labor Organization's report, "Basic
Needs in Danger" (1982), for a discussion of the current
economic crisis and its effect on basic services such as medical
care, education, housing, transport, and energy.

REFERENCES CITED

Boserup, E.
    1970   Woman's Role in Economic Development.New
              York: St. Martin's Press.

Daily News (Dar es Salaam)
    October 22, 1983   "All Must Work Says Nyerere"
    October 23, 1983   "Jobless Repatriated"
    November 10, 1983   "People's Forum: Why Pester
                          Innocent People?"

November 11, 1983	"Dar Set for Repatriation" "Editorial Comment"
December 23, 1983	"Do Not Molest People Kawawa Advises"
January 4, 1984	"Human Resources Deployment: Dar Organizes Meeting"
January 7, 1984	"Work Campaign: Police Swoop Nets 1623 Dar Jobless"

Gargan, E. A.
  1985   Tanzania Economics Lesson: Start with a
          Chicken. The New York Times (November 14,
          1985); quoting results of research paper presented
          at University of Dar es Salaam by Professor T.
          Maliyamkono.

Green, R.H.
  1981   Magendo in the Political Economy of Uganda:
          Pathology, Parallel System or Dominant Sub-Mode
          of Production? Discussion Paper, Institute of
          Development Studies, Sussex (Great Britain).

International Labor Organization/JASPA
  1982   Basic Needs in Danger A Basic Needs Oriented
          Development Strategy for Tanzania, Addis Ababa.

Ishumi, A. G. M.
  1984   The Urban Jobless of Eastern Africa. Uppsala:
          Scandinavian Institute of African Studies.

Mbilinyi, M.
  1985a   'City' and 'Countryside' in Colonial Tanganyika.
          Economic and Political Weekly 20:4388-96.
  1985b   Sex Differentials in Employment and Cash
          Earnings in Tanzania--Who Benefits? Working
          Paper Draft from larger work entitled, The Impact
          of the Economic Crisis on Women's Employment,
          Wages and Incomes. Dar es Salaam University
          Press (forthcoming)
  1986   Agribusiness and Casual Labor in Tanzania.
          African Ethnohistory 15:107-141.

Nyerere, J.K.
  1968   The Arusha Declaration. In J.K. Nyerere (ed.)
          Uhuru na Ujamaa: Freedom and Socialism. New
          York: Oxford University Press.

United Republic of Tanzania
    1982a   1978 Population Census, Vol.VII Basic
             Demographic and Socio-Economic Characteristics.
             Bureau of Statistics, Ministry of Planning and
             Economic Affairs,Government Printer: Dar es
             Salaam.
    1982b   The Tanzania National Agricultural Policy.
             Ministry of Agriculture, Government Printer: Dar
             es Salaam.

3

Price Control of Local Foodstuffs in Kumasi, Ghana, 1979

Gracia Clark
University of Michigan

INTRODUCTION

Price control and related commercial issues have been among the most controversial national political issues in Ghana. Debates and accusations concerning price control enforcement and the acceptable or actual role of traders have been used to justify the rise and fall of national governments. Successive military and civilian governments in Ghana since independence have faced rising prices, especially of imports and manufactures, which critics attributed to their soft or corrupt tactics in price control. Each new government then legitimised itself with an initial episode of strict enforcement, which tapered off and gave rise to new accusations. Price control thus plays a particularly prominent role here in the processes of state formation and regime stabilization.

The Armed Forces Revolutionary Council (AFRC), which brought Flight Lieutenant J. J. Rawlings to power on June 4, 1979, claimed that Lt. Col. Akuffo, who had ousted longstanding head of state Gen. Acheampong the year before, had not gone far enough in punishing those who had benefited from corruption. Akuffo had made arrests and ordered a strict enforcement episode shortly after taking office, but enforcement had already relaxed considerably. Declarations on price control were among the earliest proclamations of the AFRC, the day after the coup.

Rawlings considered at that point that corruption could be cured by removing corrupt individuals from the existing system. During its short term of office (June to October, 1979), the AFRC carried out what it called a "housecleaning exercise" directed at government officials, private formal sector enterprises and market traders. The first targets were those involved in illegal distribution of imports (see C. Robertson, 1983). Although official price control regulations did not include local foodstuffs, enforcement was extended to them several weeks later, without an immediate legal basis.

This paper describes that exercise, its extension and its effects on Kumasi food supplies, along with traders' responses.[1] For comparison, it also briefly describes their responses to the currency exchange exercise carried out under Akuffo earlier the same year and its effects. Although the AFRC repeatedly stated that the housecleaning exercise was not aimed at punishing the ordinary market trader, but only the middlemen and women, it damaged her more deeply and permanently than the currency exchange.

Detailed analysis of a specific encounter between traders and the state makes it easier to get beyond the presentation of either side as an undifferentiated unit in such encounters. Specific groups wielding some authority from the state, including police, soldiers, local and national government officials and traditional leaders, each had their own interests and patterns of action within the overall situation. Traders' responses also reveal critical subdivisions within their ranks, by commodity, gender, trading role and capital level, which determined both their motivation and capacity for specific responses.

The actions and reactions of these predominantly female, Asante traders show the necessity of analysing women not simply in relation to their household status, but in relation to their work status, as for male traders or wage workers. These women were wives and mothers, and in many cases their family financial responsibilities motivated their trading activities, but their commercial relations were largely distinct from household relations. Few worked in kin-based trading networks like those described for Accra Ga women (C. Robertson, 1984). Commercial relations were not extensions of family and marital relations, although Asante women also considered the latter extremely important. The tendency in many West African cultures for spouses and close kin to have separate budgets and even to avoid joint economic enterprises may partly explain this separation of work and household identities (C. Robertson 1983, p.483; Clark, 1984).

Trading roles identified with Asante women were historically constructed as gendered relations in themselves, as much so as the roles of wife and mother. As for family and marital roles, this continuing process of reproduction and reconstruction of trading roles involves both class-type economic differentiation and state intervention. The articulation of family with occupational relations is in fact an important aspect of differentiation for both men and women (Clark, 1988).

Attention to this process of the historical construction of both traders and the state itself sheds light on the course of events and on their impact. Gender, ethnic, commodity and trading role divisions among traders specify their history of confrontation and collusion with the state, and with specific agents of the state. All of those characteristics have been significant to state relations for traders (and also for other occupational groups, such as farmers), and continue to be significant in the present case.

HISTORY OF PRICE CONTROL

A long history of intervention in trade, including price formation, by colonial and pre-colonial rulers (explored in detail in Clark, n.d.(b)) gave these efforts at food price control wide local acceptance. Although import and export controls were most frequent, controls were repeatedly extended to local crops in times of crisis. The studies collected recently by Guyer (1987) show that concern for and intervention in urban food supply systems by both colonial and chiefly authorities, although not always effective, was by no means a rare phenomenon in Africa.

In nineteenth century Asante, the Asantehene[2] taxed and regulated trade in foodstuffs with neighboring chiefdoms. During public crises, he might control local food prices, requisition food for government needs, and embargo specific neighbors (Wilks, 1975; Brown 1972). The British colonial government similarly intervened during both World Wars to maintain adequate, low-cost food supplies for major cities, mines, barracks, and other government needs, although with limited success. In Asante, food prices were only set for Kumasi (the regional capital) and a few mining centers, and proved largely unenforceable. Import prices also were frequently ignored or officially raised (NAK3,7,13).

Ideological initiatives of the colonial power complemented price lists, arrests and requisitions. Colonial officials blamed rising food prices and falling real wages on supposedly parasitic market women, who were strongly defended by nationalist leaders, including Danquah (NAA4,5,6). While opposing food price controls, nationalist leaders pressed strongly for controlled prices of imports in a direct and rather sophisticated attack on the worsening terms of trade. One of the earliest nationalist actions, the 1938 cocoa holdup, also sprang from this awareness and resentment of oligopolistic commercial relations and worsening terms of trade.

Upon independence, the Convention People's Party government, led by Kwame Nkrumah, followed up on both colonial and nationalist agendas. It expanded controls over imports, especially the popular consumer items on the list of "essential commodities." This list included moderately priced consumer imports and local manufactures, such as evaporated milk, canned fish, toothpaste and toilet paper, as well as "African print" cloth.

Faced with high inflation and worsening terms of trade, government propagandists adopted the colonial rhetoric of blaming market women, despite Nkrumah's debt to their support in the independence struggle. Price controls and currency regulations applied only to imported and manufactured commodities, but public distribution agencies like the Ghana Food Distribution Corporation (GFDC) tried to undermine traders' control of local foodstuffs circulation as well. The notable failure of the GFDC to capture a significant percentage of the foodstuffs trade testifies to the complexity and value of the distributive tasks performed by the market traders, which public employees were unable to assume.[3]

Trading patterns for imports and local manufactures, especially those officially designated "essential commodities," adjusted during the 1960s and 70s to the reality of import and price controls. The cycle of episodes of strict enforcement (often in November) followed by periods of toleration for illegal trading had become routine by 1979. Traders with family or corrupt connections to police, customs or legal distributors had a greater advantage than before. In the seller's market created by acute shortages of these goods, such connections were more essential to enterprise viability than business acumen or effort.

The adjustment process widened existing gaps between traders defined by family background and by capital level, and made these correspond more closely to commodity divisions. Traders in essential commodities who lacked the official connections and capital resources to survive enforcement episodes had either gone bankrupt or switched to local foodstuffs and craft products by this time. Some individuals reported switching because of psychological exhaustion from the stress of raids, arrests and confiscations, as Smart reports for Hong Kong traders leaving illegal locations (J. Smart). The extension of price controls to local foodstuffs and craft products during the 1979 "housecleaning exercise" thus not only hit those traders with the least resources to survive such attacks, but hit numerous traders who had moved into local foodstuffs trading precisely to avoid such episodes.

THE AFRC "HOUSECLEANING EXERCISE"

The Initial Campaign

The AFRC began by punishing those who had offended against existing price and import controls on essential commodities. Their first target was the Makola #1 Market in Accra, renowned as the premier marketplace in the country for wholesaling imported and manufactured items, including cloth. This was looted the day of the coup, closed down, and eventually blown up by dynamite (C. Robertson, 1983). Although it was the seat of wholesaling, Makola #1 also included many retailers and traders in unregulated goods.

In Kumasi, price control enforcement also began with traders in imports and manufactures. The day after the coup, military officers in Kumasi entered the main Kumasi Central Market and sold off the stocks of traders in the provisions section at control prices. Sometimes the proceeds were given to the trader, sometimes they were kept for the "government chest." On the next day, soldiers broke open stalls in the adjacent cloth section and sold off the cloth, or confiscated it. Owners of confiscated goods could go to the barracks later, if they dared, to bargain with the soldiers about the "control" value which they would be paid. After they finished, a mob that had collected to buy cloth and watch the proceedings crossed the street to loot stalls in the main lorry park.

The same day, soldiers took over the major formal sector stores downtown, moving down each street in turn. They sold out their stocks completely, including many items not covered by existing price controls. Since there was no official price, soldiers set prices on the spot, at one-fourth to one-tenth the commercial price. Searches of the homes of prominent store managers, former officials and Lebanese yielded further stores of hoarded goods, which were confiscated and taken to the barracks. Seized stores or government outlets were used to sell confiscated goods from various sources. There was a even brief glut of soft drinks from confiscated supplies. Within two or three weeks, such supplies ran out, and the stores stood empty.

A high level of street violence in Kumasi, as well as other parts of the country, continued for several weeks after the coup. Turbulent crowds roamed the streets, carrying large sums of money, ready to run for a place in line when a store suddenly began selling something. Standing in line brought injuries, either from belts and nightsticks of the attending soldiers, or from the free-for-alls that erupted once sales began. Shortages of staple foodstuffs like plantain and cassava led to long lines in their parts of the market, which also broke down into fights.

Official and semi-official violence reached levels unknown since the days of party politics. Price control offenders were officially beaten, caned and flogged naked and unofficially shaved with broken bottles. One was shot. Rumors circulated about women who had miscarried or had babies beaten to death on their backs. Traders who had taken previous economic losses philosophically became obsessed with repeating these stories of beatings and humiliations.

The rhetoric of official attacks on traders combined accusations of abuses of their middleman position with a generous dose of sexual hostility, analysed in more detail elsewhere (C. Robertson 1983; Clark n.d.(b)). Resentment among educated, salaried workers, hard hit by rampant inflation, of the disappearing (or reversing) gap between their incomes and those of uneducated relatives (including almost all women) also fed the flames. Media statements whipping up public outrage that even a few illiterate women could become as wealthy and powerful as some educated men created a climate that illegitimised any attempt to preserve traders' economic or consultative rights.

As Robertson comments, the enthusiastic endorsement of condemnations of women traders by wide segments of the Ghanaian population was surprising, considering that most of that population had close female relatives in trade (C. Robertson, 1983). Kinship ideals that presume separate financial and personal interests between husband and wife and between other household members may have made such attitudes easier to adopt, since spouse or kin do not necessarily see a woman's success as a benefit to them. The only public defenses of market women portrayed them as impoverished, helpless mothers, rather than as respected social actors. The message was clear: women traders could be tolerated as long as they remained powerless and unsuccessful.

These enforcement activities for non-food items had a negative impact on food sales in the market. Many foodstuffs traders, along with most other Kumasi residents with any money in their pockets, abandoned their work to stand in long lines for bargains on not only canned milk and mackerel, but freezers, mattresses, televisions and electric fans. Rumors that soldiers would soon come to the produce sections of the market encouraged more traders to stay away from the market if they could afford it. Villagers nervous about the general violence and thievery stayed away from Kumasi, with their goods.

Serious food shortages developed in Kumasi and other major cities immediately after the coup, although the government took no direct action against local foodstuffs traders for the first two weeks. Large cities and institutions like hospitals suffered the most, since they depended most on centrally purchased supplies. For more than a month, it was difficult in Kumasi for a household to locate enough traditional foodstuffs for meals, regardless of price. Mothers told of coming to Kumasi Central Market and crying, because they could find nothing to buy for the family. Urban residents quickly realised that they were more dependent on the rural areas than vice versa. When possible, families sent their children and other unemployed members to stay with rural relatives until food supplies improved. Newspapers considered the price and supply of food in different towns a major news item for the entire AFRC period.

Food Price Control

The AFRC began food price control very gingerly. First, they called for voluntary restraint and repeated empty assurances of physical safety in the towns. They began to enforce price control on the day of the national elections, June 18. Most traders and customers alike had taken the day off to go to the polls. The authorities even took the trouble to send female police that first day. They sold off the small stocks of the traders present in the yam, tomato and plantain sections, allowing the traders to collect the money, and warned others to reduce their prices. Since no control prices existed for these goods, they simply reduced existing prices by half. To control lines they used the "female" method of throwing buckets of water, rather than the belts and nightsticks commonly used by male police or the guns brandished by male soldiers. No traders were assaulted or goods confiscated.

Price control brought chaos to the wholesale yards the next day. Arriving traders who had begun to unload their yams threw them back into the trucks and drove away when they heard the news. Villagers arriving in the lorry park also simply turned around and went home with their produce. Armed soldiers began to patrol the wholesale yards, supervising forced sales from the trucks, and make forays into the foodstuffs "lines". The lack of known legal prices prevented effective cooperation with the soldiers. If traders set a low price, hoping to avoid trouble, the soldiers simply halved it again.

Several traders expressed the view that soldiers were mainly interested in getting food for their own consumption, rather than enforcing low prices. Soldiers often took goods away without any compensation, telling an oil seller, for example, to come to the barracks in two weeks for her empty containers. Even when they sold the goods immediately, they made their own purchases first. With foodstuffs so scarce, this could exhaust the supplies available, even on July 12, almost a month later.

Setting official "control" prices for local foodstuffs presented immense practical problems, because of the wide variations in size, quality and condition characteristic of most popular foodstuffs. Price bargaining over individual units normally compensates for these variations. Standard prices for many foodstuffs cannot be widely publicised, understood and applied, because it remains unclear exactly what goods they apply to. When the first price lists came out, on June 23rd, they used units like kilos, not common in retail sales, and made no allowance for size, quality, distance from the producing region, or seasonal scarcity. The enforcement of uniform prices for chickens, for example, removed the premium for well-developed specimens. Soon only immature, small birds were for sale. The same happened with plantain, which was largely sold before maturity, if sold at all.

When foodstuffs stopped coming to Kumasi and other large towns, soldiers expanded their activities to major village periodic markets. Soldiers stationed nearby would visit these markets on the market day, confiscating goods in the possession of villagers or traders for sale at reduced prices or for use at the barracks. Villagers taking goods to sell at local periodic markets might find them purchased by the military at control price, although villagers did not usually suffer the physical abuse that traders did. Traders were conspicuous targets if they bought in wholesale quantities or transported goods on the roads, so they were afraid to visit the markets. The few Kumasi traders who still ventured to their usual markets at this time reported that villagers stayed away from them, so they gave up the effort.

Farmers even avoided the informal sales locations established at highway or farm trail intersections. Those who still wanted to sell would take a small quantity of goods and walk along the roadside. If soldiers questioned them, they could claim they were carrying it home from the farm for family consumption. Hitherto this strategy had only been used by suppliers of imports.

When even the village markets largely emptied of goods, soldiers and other enforcement personnel began to "hijack" trucks. Soldiers from more remote barracks, without the advantage of access to a major market, would lie in wait on the major highways leading to Kumasi and intercept passing trucks, confiscating whole truckloads of produce. Town-based

soldiers also captured trucks entering the outskirts of town.
This tactic could only be loosely linked to price control
enforcement, since the goods had not yet been offered for sale
at any specific price, nor had they been hoarded. These
truckloads were occasionally sold retail at control prices on the
spot, but more often they were taken off to a nearby barracks.
Not only freight trucks but mixed passenger/freight trucks were
taken. Even a single bag or basket of produce could be
considered evidence of intent to resell and confiscated under
threat of arrest.

Effects on Supplies and Prices

Despite the energy devoted to these drastic actions, they
did not achieve the desired effect of securing low-cost, plentiful
urban food supplies. Farmers overwhelmingly responded by
keeping their produce off the market. Traders themselves
cannot hoard food supplies, because limited space, poor facilities
and rapid spoilage prevent them from storing significant
amounts (C. Robertson, 1983, p.480; see Clark, n.d.(a), for
more detail). Enforcement efforts directed at traders thus could
not release extra food to consumers, even temporarily.

Farmers' ability to delay crop sales depended on the
perishability of their specific crops, leading to uneven food
shortages in Kumasi. Semi-perishable staples such as yams
and corn were stored on the farm as long as possible. The
AFRC came to power in June, before the yam harvest.
Farmers normally begin taking early yams from their plants in
July, to catch the high early prices. In 1979, they delayed
harvesting for months, as long as December, until they needed
to prepare the fields for replanting. Some still stored their
yams in pits on the farm for several months afterwards.
Likewise, some corn was normally sold green, as an early treat
before the new yams. In 1979, farmers left it all to mature.

Perishable vegetables like tomatoes and garden eggs could
not be harvested later. They came back on the market fairly
quickly, but in smaller quantities than normal for that season.
Cassava, though highly perishable once harvested, can be left
in the ground for long periods without deterioration. It is
planted on less desirable land than yams, so consequently
disappeared from the market entirely until all danger was past.

Ironically, food price control enforcement raised effective
food prices above their previous level due to trade moving to
clandestine locations, as well as from absolute urban shortages.
Under normal conditions, Kumasi buyers and sellers enjoy a
high level of information on supply, demand and prices paid.
Visual inspection of goods and prices offered is the most

common information source. Price uniformity results from these publicly available high information levels, and never indicates prices set unilaterally by either side. Constant price variations between transactions compensate for size and quality variations, but also for fluctuating supply and demand during the day. The narrow price range lowers the risk for transactors, a major reason buyers and sellers patronise Kumasi Central Market. The low risk levels further lower prices, since they allow sellers to reduce their risk cushions. Commodities with higher risk levels also show wider price fluctuations.

Good information flows extend to peripheral trading areas. Wholesale buyers from Kumasi Central Market wholesale yards regularly checked nearby informal locations, such as the lorry parks, for lower prices. Their knowledge of relative prices helps prevent artificially raised prices in the foodstuffs wholesale yards, since they are ready to buy elsewhere without delay. Likewise, when price control artificially lowered prices in the yards, these peripheral locations could and did rapidly expand the volume of produce they handled. Though effective, their role was short-lived because soldiers immediately expanded their activities to the well-known peripheral areas when goods vanished from the wholesale yards.

What food arrived in Kumasi after the markets emptied was sold at dawn from the backs of trucks in shifting roadside locations passed by word of mouth. When sales moved to street corners, back alleys, disused gas stations and vacant lots, prices were more variable, but averaged higher. Furtive, hurried, dispersed sales drastically reduce price information levels, because it is difficult and dangerous to compare prices from different sources. Competition between sellers was greatly reduced by shortages, since buyers knew they might not find another source of the item they needed. Prices also rose simply from the great reductions in supply, and the higher risk margin needed to induce sellers to participate. A negligible amount of foodstuffs was ever sold to the public at control price.

Hunger and Capital Position

This economic disruption widened the gap between urban residents, including traders, with some cash reserves and those with none. During the enforced idleness, traders with any capital had to use it to meet subsistence needs. Market porters and the poorer traders who sold on commission or on credit suffered great hardship immediately, because they depended on each day or week's proceeds to buy food. Most traders had so little capital in hand that they could not hold out for the length of this crisis. They either had to return to trading under dangerous, unprofitable conditions or go without food, usually both.

Coping strategies which had developed to see traders through seasonal shortages or individual crises such as illness or capital loss could not work now, due to the broad impact of this crisis. Many traders routinely adjusted to seasonal supply problems by switching to unaffected commodities or to craft work. Price control affected so many commodities that none were left to substitute. A surprising number of foodstuffs traders, including some who had previously fled cloth or provisions trading, began selling ice water, the most inoffensive (and unprofitable) item imaginable. Even they met with occasional rough treatment from soldiers. Craft alternatives like sewing or baking had also come to a standstill, due to lack of supplies and customers. Asking for emergency loans from trading partners or non-trading relatives or neighbors, a common strategy in individual catastrophes, was useless now, since they faced similar problems.

In fact, almost all economic activity ceased in Kumasi, between standing in lines, fear and lack of supplies. Possession of goods in normal working quantities for either trade or production brought punishment for hoarding. Drastic policy swings, usually retroactive, were so unpredictable that members of almost any occupation felt it might suddenly become illegal. Buying power was so affected that the demand for food was substantially reduced when controls were eventually relaxed and supplies returned.

Rural families with acute cash needs suffered along with poor urban families from the interruption in crop sales. Many farmers had committed their resources to specialised commercial food production to the extent that they depended on crop sales to finance purchase of other foods. Farm families also needed cash to cover school fees, medical expenses and other crises. These problems hit poorer farmers harder, since they had little cash or food reserves. The low-volume, high-risk conditions of trade made it difficult for farmers to find buyers in case of emergency, and lowered the prices the few remaining traders were willing to offer.

Ideological Basis

The AFRC justified its hostility to traders by emphasizing the economic advantages of direct sales from farmers to consumers. Traders supposedly forced prices up by frustrating this natural mechanism. Contrary to this model, direct sales are never very attractive to farmers, because of the farming days they lose in locating transport, selling their goods, and returning home. They were even more reluctant to make the trip to the city under these violent and unsettled conditions, nor was there much for them to buy there. Occasionally, military trucks were sent to buy farm produce or sell consumer goods in rural areas, but very little direct sales took place despite official exhortations. Lack of response to similar efforts in Peru suggests that economic realities, rather than fear of violence, are the determining factors on this issue (Babb, this volume). Ghanaian farmers found it more attractive to hold goods off the market, if at all possible, than cooperate with direct sales.

Realising the insecurity of their access to urban markets, farmers in more remote regions reverted to a more subsistence-oriented planting pattern, at least temporarily. The price control experience weakened rural confidence in the food distribution system and in commercialisation itself. It led to some return to subsistence farming, especially in remote areas already facing interruptions in commercial contact because of transport problems. After all, farmers complained, they had nothing to buy with the money they earned, since legal supplies of imports rarely reached the rural areas. The money itself might be again declared obsolete, as in the currency exchange exercise earlier in 1979. Both long and short-term effects on farmers thus lowered urban food supplies.

While armed enforcement proved capable of seriously disrupting and damaging the existing food distribution system, it proved incapable of substituting for it. Under conditions of strict enforcement, a government implicitly claims that the official or legal distribution system can supply all of the recognised needs of the population. As the AFRC period wore on with no increase in urban staple food supplies, these claims lost credibility and food price control was quietly loosened. The Asantehene's police occasionally made rounds to encourage low prices, but they approached the traders involved quietly and carried no arms or nightsticks. It was left to the later Provisional National Defence Council (PNDC) government (1982-4) to make serious attempts to set up an alternative foodstuffs distribution network linking farmers to urban and institutional buyers.

Demolitions

As the date for handover to civilian rule approached, the AFRC turned to a series of demolitions to make a lasting mark on the nation's marketplace system. A few days after the demolition of Makola #1, on September 5th, markets in

regional capitals, including Kumasi, were destroyed. Like
Makola #1, Kumasi Central Market was a regional center of
imports distribution. Unlike Makola #1, however, it was also
the city's only wholesale market for most local foodstuffs.
Rumors claimed that Kumasi City Council members only
narrowly managed to avert plans to demolish the entire
Kumasi Central Market, on this basis.

The demolition episode displayed divisions between
different parts of the state apparatus. City Council opposition
may have reflected the major contribution of market fees and
rents to the city budget. The Market Manager claimed to have
had no advance warning. Like the most drastic price control
enforcement, demolition was carried out by soldiers, who were
less likely to have local origins. Police and the Asantehene's
police had been noticeably more polite and less violent in
previous actions, and took no part in this one.

To implement this policy successfully, the AFRC took
advantage of internal divisions among traders by nationality,
commodity and spatial location. Demolitions began at dawn, in
a section that was marginal physically, organisationally and
economically to the rest of the market, an area of makeshift
stalls at the rear of the market called the "French Line." Here,
men from Northern Ghana and adjacent French-speaking
countries sold shoes and other imported clothing, and reputedly
changed currency through their commercial contacts. As for
Makola #1, complete demolition was supposedly required to
uncover buried hoards of foreign currency.

First, soldiers surrounded this section to prevent removal of
property. Soldiers with semi-automatic weapons rode the
bulldozers as they razed the flimsy wooden stalls, while others
searched and confiscated property. When the bulldozers had
finished the French Line, however, they simply kept going,
uprooting shade trees and levelling several small mosques and
adjacent trading areas. Within two days, everything outside
the old market walls had come down, about one-third of the
total contiguous area administered as Kumasi Central Market.
This comprised open areas where villagers sold their foodstuffs,
several wholesale yards, and sections selling used clothing, craft
goods and drugs. Ironically, the cloth and provisions sections,
the Kumasi equivalent to Makola #1, remained touched
because they lay inside the walls.

Although outside the original market walls, these areas
were official market locations. Traders using them were
registered individually and paid rent to the city, in addition to
their daily market fees. One factor in the amount of rent they
paid was the size and elaboration of the structures they had
erected, at their own expense but with city permission. Some

sold from portable tables, while others had roofed stalls or enclosed, locking kiosks. Capital investment was not necessarily lower for these traders than for those within the market walls. The area housed some businesses based on valuable equipment--sewing machines, corn mills or chest freezers. Some traders had even recently received permission to expand their buildings or build new kiosks.

Market traders were given only a few hours notice, depending on their exact location in the path of the bulldozers, to remove or sell off their goods and salvage their equipment. Traders hurriedly arranged to store their inventory and equipment in nearby houses, or to transport it to their homes. Proprietors of a walk-in cold store that sold frozen fish and ice blocks to traders negotiated two days' grace to move out their freezer equipment. Owners of kiosks, designed to be movable, either found someone to cart them away immediately or saw them demolished. Salvagers lingered to buy up the roofing sheets and lumber that were left.

As demolition progressed over two days, various justifications for the policy from official spokesmen appeared in local newspapers or circulated through rumors. Most statements referred to it as a street clearance campaign, supposed to provide for easy passage for pedestrians and supply trucks in the market precincts. The other expressed goals of tourist-oriented civic beautification and efficient, intensive land use seemed far-fetched, in view of the realities of Ghana's economic problems, although the same issues have some plausibility for the Indian, Hong Kong, and US cases elsewhere in this volume (Lessinger, A. Smart, and Spalter-Roth). In Kumasi, long-dormant plans for a clinic and "superhighway" on one side of the market were briefly resurrected, although cement and money were then unavailable even for construction projects already designed and half completed.

Only token efforts were made to keep demolished areas clear, showing that officials had little need to disguise the punitive nature of the clearance. Within a week, traders reoccupied the same areas they traded in before the clearance, with no further attempts to chase them away, and tax collection resumed. Traders sat in the same locations, selling the same commodities, but now they sat in the sun with their babies and their perishable vegetables instead of enjoying the meagre comfort of a roofing sheet or two.

TRADERS' RESPONSES

Price Control Negotiations

Foodstuffs traders did have publicly recognised commodity groups and leaders, called ahemma, providing an organisational structure capable of rapid response to such crises. Group leaders' central functions were dispute settlement and negotiations with external bodies, not commercial regulation. Negotiating skills carry high prestige in Asante culture, and traders demand high skill levels from their leaders (Clark, 1984).

In contrast to C. Robertson's report of passivity on the part of Accra market women (1983), the Kumasi ahemmafuo (collective plural) did respond quickly, requesting mediation from the city and regional officials and chiefs with whom they usually take up sensitive external issues. Soon these elderly and middle-aged women were complaining of an exhausting schedule of formal meetings and informal sessions initiated by themselves or others. It was startling to hear them complain in the same breath that the authorities did not want to negotiate.

Market ahemma claimed that "they don't want to talk" despite incessant summons to meetings, because these meetings did not follow norms of legitimate "talking" as they knew them. Precisely because negotiations figure so prominently in Asante chiefly and marketplace ideals, traders have well-developed procedural norms and expect general respect for them. Proper dispute settlement procedures call for the full expression of all views before making a decision, and the agreement of all parties to the final settlement. A. Robertson confirms in a rural setting the importance of conforming to accepted, familiar meeting styles and procedures in order to ensure effective and recognized participation (A. Robertson 1976).

The AFRC broke these norms in several important ways. They ignored the definition of negotiations by scheduling their "consultation" meetings after they had already made major decisions. During the meetings, opposing parties did not acknowledge points brought up by traders by agreeing or disagreeing, but simply repeated previous threats and exhortations. The authorities also failed to abide by agreements or promises made during meetings with traders.

For example, an attempt was made to establish standard size and quality grades for staple foodstuffs, to bring order to price control enforcement. The ahemmafuo brought samples of the major vegetable staples to the Ashanti Regional Offices. Under the sponsorship of the Regional Commissioner, they agreed with representatives of consumers, government buyers and the military on control prices for different sizes. In the next few days, however, soldiers in the market refused to recognize these prices or size grades and continued to set prices arbitrarily. The ahemma then counseled traders to stop buying from farmers unless they could obtain low enough prices to allow for this kind of sales.

The most elaborate meeting during this period led to the most resentment. Traders viewed both procedural and rhetorical features as insults to their leaders. Ahemma were not given a choice of time or place, but summoned to the meeting held in their own shed. The President and Secretary of the National Farmers' Association and a leader of the official farm laborer's association (all men) made no pretense of consultation or seeking mutual agreement. They harangued the traders about their stubborn refusal to lower prices, and threatened that traders would suffer for their evil ways. They completely ignored traders' counterclaims that farmers refused to sell at low prices. A particularly offensive speaker repeatedly asked "wati?" (lit. have you heard?), a phrase commonly used to instruct children or subordinates. One ohemma (sing.) complained, "They treat us like children, when we are old enough to be their mothers." During the meetings, the senior ohemma drew attention covertly to the fact that this meeting had no authority to decide anything by referring repeatedly and favorably to her ongoing negotiations with truck drivers over freight rates. In both sets of meetings, participants commonly referred to each other as "the men" and "the women."

It is revealing to compare these meetings with price negotiations held during the same later months of the AFRC government with leaders of predominantly male occupations, to set control prices for their products. In each case, representatives of suppliers of raw materials attended, and the prices of finished products and raw materials were set as a package. Producers of adinkra cloth, furniture and poultry linked their control prices to those of imported plain cloth, manufactured lumber, poultry feed and medicines. Meetings with drivers and transport owners likewise used control prices for gasoline, motor oil and spare parts to calculate legal passenger and freight rates.

Negotiations with male leaders did not produce exactly the desired results for either side, but procedures showed more respect. The resulting agreements were neither predetermined or ignored. Male leaders were not delegitimised for being group leaders, nor their followers for having specific occupational interests. These negotiated prices could not openly compensate for the necessity to buy supplemental supplies on the black market to stay in business, but the men used these meetings as a forum to press for larger allocations of foreign exchange for their imported supplies. Although the AFRC could not usually provide the level of supplies needed, they did abide by prices set at these meetings. These men were often idle from lack of legal supplies, or forced to resort to illegal supplies, but at least they were never harrassed for selling at the agreed prices.

RESPONSES TO THE CURRENCY EXCHANGE

The currency exchange exercise carried out in March, 1979, before the AFRC coup, provides another contrast. The AFRC government exerted itself to discredit market leaders and frustrate their attempts to help traders adjust to price control or circumvent it. Akuffo's government, although aiming the currency exchange partly against wealthy market traders, kept the official exchange procedures relatively straightforward and stable.

After closing all the borders, the government announced on Friday, March 9, that all existing banknotes would become valueless on March 26. The entire population had to exchange its old notes for new ones through the banks, at a rate of ten old to seven new cedis. Very large amounts would be exchanged at five new for ten old cedis, creating instant employment for thousands of poor persons who took the excess cedis of their wealthier relatives and neighbors for exchange. Although the deadline was extended another two weeks and extra facilities for exchange set up, the basic procedure remained the same. Individual capital losses varied arbitrarily, depending on the amount of capital in physical cash form that evening.

Market leaders' responses demonstrated their ability to expand their regulatory role temporarily in time of crisis, when left to manage their own adaptive processes. First they coordinated discussions of the procedures and practical implications of the exchange. This raised general information levels and formed a consensus on joint strategies for weathering the transition period. Leaders then publicised these decisions, so that individual traders would not suffer disproportionately. Kumasi traders and other urban dwellers suffered much less hardship than rural residents, who faced long journeys on scarce transport at exorbitant rates and waited for days at the few small-town banks, without new cedis for food or water.

In Kumasi Central Market, for example, commodity group relations helped traders decide how to respond. In the onion shed, onion traders met informally in the aisles Saturday morning to discuss the announcements. The ohemma collected information on procedures and rates of exchange and repeated it. One woman had brought a poster of the new money, which the ohemma showed around. The shed watchmen held their own conclave, which the ohemma visited. Some continued to do business at normal prices, as the government had instructed. As traders began to realize the old money had been effectively discounted, they stopped selling except for payment in coins. Individual retailers decided either to go home, or to adjust their prices and charge ten old cedis for seven in the original price.

The exchange announcement created havoc in commercial credit, especially in the wholesale yards, where large amounts were involved. Hysterical wholesalers sought advice from their ahemma when debtors tried to force payment in old notes. Travellers would not accept the old notes from wholesalers, since they expected farmers to reject them, but could not afford to stay in town indefinitely. In hardship cases, leaders negotiated reasonable discounts for the old notes. The cassava yard closed down when drivers doubled freight charges, only reopening as traders obtained new notes. The onion yard also closed in the second week, when traders decided to take a break to finish changing. Although the yards closed, the ahemma came to market daily to monitor conditions.

After the initial shock phase, commodity ahemma resumed a passive role. The level of commercial activity dropped to about half, since traders, drivers, suppliers and consumers all spent much of their time trying to exchange their money. Clients quarreled over who would receive the first few new notes when they began to appear. Although some appealed these cases to their ohemma, she could not settle them. Each trader had to decide which client was most valuable to her. Traders stated current sales prices either in new or old cedis, the latter prices climbing as the exchange deadline approached. Individual traders simply decided whether to accept old cedis or not, or to stay home. Some sellers extended credit rather than accept old notes. The ohemma could enforce these terms just like normal business agreements. A few traders with close bank connections continued accepting old cedis to the last day.

Wide fluctuations in food supply from day to day also raised ordinary commercial risks and tensions. Less perishable foodstuffs stopped arriving until sellers could demand new cedis, including cassava, dried fish and plantains. Crops that required frequent harvests, such as tomatoes, could not find enough buyers, especially with new cedis. Stress and hunger shortened tempers, and disputes in general multiplied.

Traders' responses were not effective in any absolute sense. They could not change the policy itself, or prevent capital losses

severe enough to reduce the scale of operation of many
individuals. Only a handful of individual traders had either
advance warning to deposit their cash, or close enough bank
connections to circumvent exchange channels. However,
traders' group actions did reduce or avoid the additional losses
associated with commercial disruption, such as those during
price control linked to suspension of normal information
channels and dispute settlement procedures.

The reliance on individual strategies for exchange meant
that this exercise, like price control, exacerbated tensions and
disadvantages based on existing social stratification. Exchange
procedures favored urban over rural residents, and those with
elite connections over the marginal poor. As in provisions and
cloth trading, corrupt individual relations proved more reliable
than rational or industrious choices. Workers for large public
or private employers could participate in special group
exchange facilities not available to the self-employed.
Individual traders with some capital suffered losses, but could
better survive the weeks of reduced activity than those
dependent on daily or weekly receipts. The violent conditions
of standing in line at banks, as for confiscated goods, favored
strong, able-bodied young men over the elderly or weak, or
mothers with babies on their backs.

CONCLUSION

Food price controls were exceptionally disruptive to
distribution, both because of their novelty and because of
official response to traders' adjustment efforts. Traders in
imports and manufactures had already made their peace with
episodic price control enforcement. Those without some
political connections protecting them from prosecution and
financial strength to survive periods of retreat had left the
business years before. The AFRC brought simply a longer,
more intense seige of the same tactics. Some individuals
suffered great physical and financial damage, and many went
out of business because of the length of their unemployment,
but the system of distribution itself did not break down.
Trading in essential commodities was completely illegal, so
open group negotiations were out of the question and former
leaders had long since retired.

Although not completely unprecedented, government
intervention in trade in local foodstuffs had never before been
either widespread or effective. Food traders had no established
strategies for dealing with it. Foodstuffs policies remained
"new" for months, due to rapid, radical shifts in the prices and

behavior subject to attack. Erratic and non-standardised enforcement compounded fluctuations and contradictions in announced offical policy. Each attempt by foodstuff traders to adjust to, compromise with, or evade price controls brought a change in enforcement tactics or policies, aimed at their new practices. The result was widespread demoralisation and hopelessness that persisted long after enforcement had ceased.

Government actions demonstrated hostility not only to leaders of illegal activities, but to market leaders as such. Foodstuffs commodity group leaders were ignored or humiliated in the negotiation processes already described. The mere existence of market groups and leaders was denounced in public announcements as evidence of traders' conspiracy to ruin the economy. The Asante chiefly hierarchy was recruited to attack their prestige by announcing they were not entitled to use the title ohemma, but could only be considered headmen. Market ahemma joked about their supposed sex change operations, but deeply resented the public insult by a hierarchy that had hitherto recognised them as leading members of the community on public occasions.

Comparison of the two policy crises points to the importance of market leaders in minimising both individual and group damage from hostile policies, even without formal recognition. Market leaders coordinated or facilitated traders' individual responses to the currency exchange, rather than directing a group or collective response. This indirect role, when not actively frustrated, proved more effective than attempts at direct negotiations which found no sincere response.

More contradiction between ideology and practice emerged in the AFRC's relations with ordinary traders. The AFRC continually published statements claiming it was not against the small-scale trader or producer, even advising Makola traders to go into food selling, but actions and policies both belied this distinction. Not only did enforcement efforts concentrate on the more vulnerable, poorer traders, but other policy statements revealed an intent to eliminate food trading as such.

As in other economic sectors, the poorest traders bore the brunt of both direct military action and its economic side effects. Only a few foodstuffs traders were wealthy enough to consider buying protection or stopping altogether until the situation stabilised. Most lived on their daily or weekly income, and had to try some kind of economic activity. Those without capital to lose lost weight, paying in their health and strength.

Traders' loss of capital, through consumption or confiscation, had a devastating effect on commercial efficiency

at both high and relatively low levels. Individuals able to buy
in the minimum wholesale quantity found themselves buying in
smaller quantities from intermediaries. Buyers who had filled
a truck themselves in the supply areas now shared with others,
waited for passenger transport, or fell to retailing. Considering
the importance of Ghanaian markets in food distribution, these
capital and efficiency losses were a serious blow to the national
economy.

Paradoxically, the price control episode, supposedly not
aimed at ordinary market traders, was much more devastating
to them than the currency exchange, which included traders
among its target groups. This fact suggests a very weakly
hidden agenda within the AFRC, of destroying the marketplace
system as a power center in the economy resistant to
government control (see also C. Robertson, 1983). This
interpretation of underlying motives is consistent with
historical trends in government commercial and regulatory
policies affecting markets from the colonial period onwards. As
further confirmation, this agenda was later openly avowed in
the early days of the PNDC government (1982), which included
many of the same high level leaders, including Rawlings
himself.

NOTES

1. These events were observed during a reserach project
funded by the Overseas Development Administration (UK) in
Kumasi from 1978-80. Of course, the opinions expressed here
are those of the author, not the ODA. Mona Etienne, Estellie
Smith, Karen Hansen, Jane Guyer, Marjorie Mbilinyi and
Lillian Trager made valuable comments on earlier versions of
the paper, not all of which I was able to incorporate.
2. The Asantehene is the ruler of the Asante confederacy, the
largest political unit in present-day Ghana before British
conquest in 1901. He retains substantial political, moral and
ritual power throughout Asante, but especially in Kumasi, the
capital. He supports a considerable staff and household,
drawing on state financial support and legal status as well as
indigenous properties and payments.
3. Traders' productive contributions are discussed in greater
detail by Claire Robertson (1983) and Florence Babb (1987).

REFERENCES

Babb, Florence
1987   Marketers as Producers: The Labor Process and
        Proletarianization of Peruvian Market Women. In
        David Hakken and Johanna Lessinger, eds.
        Perspectives in US Marxist Anthropology.
        Boulder: Westview Press.

Brown, James W.
1972   Kumasi 1898-1923: Urban Africa During the
        Early Colonial Period. PhD thesis, Dept. History,
        University of Wisconsin, Madison, WI.

Clark, Gracia C.
1984   The Position of Asante Women Traders in Kumasi
        Central Market, Ghana. PhD thesis, Dept. Social
        Anthropology, University of Cambridge, UK.
1988   Money, Sex and Cooking: Manipulation of the
        Paid/Unpaid Boundary by Asante Market Women.
        In B. Orlove and H. Rutz, eds. The Social
        Economy of Consumption: Anthropological
        Approaches. Monographs in Economic
        Anthropology, No.6 Society for Economic
        Anthropology and University Press of America,
        Lanham, MD.
n.d.(a) Food Traders and Food Security, forthcoming in R.
        E. Downs, D. O. Kerner and S. P. Reyna, eds.
        The Political Economy of African Famine: The
        Class and Gender Basis of Hunger. London:
        Gordon and Breach.
n.d.(b) The Political Economy of Price Control for
        Ghanaian Market Traders, forthcoming in E.
        Winans, ed. New Perspectives on African Political
        Economy. Seattle: University of Washington
        Press.

Guyer, Jane
1987   Feeding African Cities. London: International
        African Institute and Manchester University
        Press.

NAA (Ghana National Archives, Accra)
NAA4   No. 0866 ST17, Complaints against profiteering by
        trading firms. Anonymous letter to the Governor,
        23/9/41.

NAA5   No. 0866 ST17, President of the Joint Provincial
          Councils to the Secretary for Native Affairs,
          20/11/41.
NAA6   No. 0028 SF8, Irregularities in Import Control.
          motion by Hon. Dr. J. B. Danquah, 26/3/47.

NAK (Ghana National Archives, Kumasi)
   NAK3   No. 1136, Foodstuffs and Meat Regulation, item
             63. Director of Agriculture to Chief Agricultural
             Officer, Kumasi, 2/9/41.
   NAK7   No. 1315, item 44. Minutes of a Meeting of the
             Obuasi Sanitary Board Held on 18th July, 1941.
   NAK13   No. 124, item 18. Report for the Period 1st
             April 1935--31st March 1936. Ashanti Division,
             Department of Agriculture, 27/4/36.

Robertson, A. F.
   1976   Rules, strategies and the development committee.
             Community Development Journal 11:185.

Robertson, Claire
   1983   The Death of Makola and Other Tragedies.
             Canadian Journal of African Studies 17:469.
   1984   Sharing the Same Bowl. Bloomington: Indiana
             University Press.

Wilks, Ivor
   1975   Asante in the Nineteenth Century. Cambridge:
             Cambridge University Press.

4

Why the Women Went to War: Women and Wealth in Ondo Town, Southwestern Nigeria

Elizabeth A. Eames
Bates College

In the early eighties I undertook nearly three years of field research into the extraordinary economic and domestic roles of ordinary women in southwestern Nigeria. What follows is an exploration of how the legitimate political voice of these ordinary townswomen was, during 1985, mobilized for "war" against a state perceived as illegitimate.

I document here the townswomen's own critique of contemporary Nigerian society and of the functioning of its formal state structure. Nigeria's overwhelming dependence on a declining world market in petroleum has, over the course of this decade, revealed to all and sundry its internal inconsistencies and placed further constraints on an already overburdened economy. The ensuing foreign exchange crisis and import restrictions have affected the life and livelihoods of all citizens, members of the formal and informal economies alike. Moreover, government decision-makers, faced with unexpected shortfalls, must invent new ways to increase revenues. This case study will help us understand the impact such fiscal decisions have at the local level. It is a lesson in how to "read" the response of the masses.

I also demonstrate how "ripe" for political mobilization around women's interests are extant women's organizations. This case confirms recent speculations concerning the place of women's voluntary organizations in the struggle for a more equitable distribution of resources. Indeed, they may prove to be the proper vehicle whereby the apparently disenfranchised will gain (or re-gain) a resounding political voice. The vocabulary of political struggle during the Ondo Women's War involved symbolic forms of protest. Will it be possible to shift the terms of the discourse?

BACKGROUND

Guided by an optimistic western feminism, I had chosen to live and work with Yoruba women--renowned for their economic independence and their almost total association with the public arena of the marketplace. Sentences such as the following from Sidney Mintz had been impossible to resist:

> Probably no people on earth has institutionalized women's rights to engage in trading activity so fully as have the Yoruba. Yoruba women not only have a wholly acknowledged right to trade and to use their capital as they see fit, but they also dominate the internal market system. Yoruba wives are expected to make a very substantial contribution to the upkeep of the family. (1971:260)

These expectations were essentially confirmed during my years on the scene. Yoruba farmers are generally male, traders female. Not only are all traders women, but most women are traders: 97% of the women I surveyed traded, two thirds of them at official town markets.

Specifically, I lived and worked in Ondo Town, a hinterland city currently home to perhaps a quarter-of-a-million. Ondo is an ancient city-state whose political history has been overshadowed and markedly influenced by such famous empires as Benin, Ife, and Oyo (see, for example, Forde and Kaberry 1967). I chose Ondo, however, to confirm my suspicion that a certain constellation of circumstances had enhanced the position of its women: Ondo was founded by a woman, whose female and male descendants still reign; Ondo rules of descent and inheritance are significantly more bilateral than those of other major Yoruba sub-groups; historically, trade was relatively more important than military conquest to Ondo's dominance over surrounding peoples. I suggest that all of these factors are implicated in the foundation and the maintenance of Ondo's solidly dual-sex political system (Okonjo 1976), the functioning of which I explore below.

During my first field trip, I had focused most of my attention on the economic responsibilities of ordinary women. But in an effort to document the annual women chiefs' festival (for the god of wealth), I was funded for a brief return in 1985. As I witnessed the unexpected events recounted here--the Ondo Market Women's War--I came to realize the significance of political linkages between ordinary women's lives, their voluntary market associations, and the hierarchy of women chiefs. These events forced me to re-cast my previous work in the light of Ondo women's political roles.

I took a second look at the riddle posed by the position of Olobun, woman king, owner-of-markets, priestess-of-profit. Up to that point, I had unwittingly absorbed the official (male) view that the Olobun position was merely a ritual title, the holder of which was so hemmed in by taboos and prohibitions that she could have no importance in the political realm. I had failed to contemplate her significance for the structure as a whole.

In light of my analysis of the women's war, I can state with confidence, that the position of Olobun is of crucial symbolic significance, and serves as the ritual/ symbolic/ ideological capstone legitimizing (yet circumscribing) women's place in the arena of political power. Along with the usual characterization of Yoruba politics as a redistributive/ big-man system, I would argue that there is a legitimate place for the big-woman in Ondo Yoruba society, a prescribed route for her to follow, and a clear mechanism for the redistribution of her resources via bartering wealth into honor. Moreover, it is the highly revered, dangerous and mysterious title of Woman King, surrounded by so many prohibitions and taboos, that makes possible a this-world power struggle over access to the--seemingly lesser-- position of opoji, or woman chief (these distinctions are clarified in appended Tables). I must emphasize for the reader unfamiliar with West Africa that these organizations were formerly governmental in nature. Rather than an index of women's informal power they were the locus of wholly legitimate authority. Please note, moreover, that I use the term "woman king" advisedly--she is neither the wife of a king (they are called olori), nor is she a ruler by default, that is for lack of a male heir. Her epithet, Oba Obinrin, means woman king.

An instance of women's public political role and mobilization for action is documented here in an attempt to rectify their chronic invisibility in public historical and political records. But the women's war also raises other issues: How are "traditional" symbols used to communicate "modern" messages? More specifically, messages critical of the functioning of a formal state structure. By going to war, the women's organizations publicly demonstrated their power and thereby asserted their legitimacy in the peoples' eyes, even in the face of non-recognition by the central government. Herein lies, perhaps, political anthropology's contribution to recent political science discussions of the so-called "soft state" in Africa.

Let me begin by describing the Women's War in Ondo in 1985. I will then compare the gender symbolism employed during this demonstration of female solidarity with that of the

famous Aba Women's War of 1929, wherein sixty Igbo and
Ibibio women lost their lives at the hands of colonial troops
(Perham 1937). The role of these women's institutionalized
protests within the traditional state structure will lead us
directly into a discussion of their role within modern state
structures.

THE ONDO WOMEN'S WAR (IJA OBINRIN ONDO)

On November 11, 1985, the streets of Ondo Town,
southwestern Nigeria, were transformed into a sea of bobbing
headties. I had been in the kitchen area with Mama Bayo and
a handful of children, gossiping as usual while she washed
vegetables and I picked through rice. As the ordinary rumble
of street noise rose to a crescendo, my companion grasped its
significance and darted outside, exclaiming in Yoruba, "it's
women's war, no market today!"

It turned out that she was only slightly off the mark--the
war lasted ten days. Ten days of escalating civil disorder,
economic disruption, ritual invocation, curses and counter-
curses. To the common folks of Ondo it spelled turmoil, and
even hunger. I must admit, however, that for a foreign
feminist doing fieldwork it was a thrilling sight indeed!

What government policies and practices had led up to this
strike? In an effort to tap into revenues circulating in the so-
called informal sector, Ondo state had four days earlier
instituted a substantial levy on all women[1]--and only women--
based on the essentially accurate assumption that all Yoruba
women sell something. The military governor's office had not
dealt directly with the town council of women chiefs, the opoji,
but had notified the king about the state's decision.

The relationship between Nigeria's federal and state
government, its civil service, and its "natural rulers" is
complicated and tense. In stark contrast to military governors,
who rule by "might" over essentially arbitrary geographical
units, divine kings and high chiefs maintain their special
legitimacy through their sacred relationship to the land. Kings
are consulted by office-holders, their blessing is courted by
office-seekers, and their salaries are paid by the state. They
have political and judicial jurisdiction in civil (though no longer
in criminal) matters occurring within their borders.

Ondo Town's dual-sex political institutions have always
been invisible to those in charge of Nigeria's state apparatus,
hence no direct lines of communication existed between the
governor and the women chiefs. So, the Osemawe (king) of
Ondo informed the opoji. They, in turn, convened a meeting of

the heads of each market trading association at the Rex
Cinema house[2] where they drafted letters to various
community leaders and officials.

When their letters of protest were ignored, they began the
process of mobilizing for a fight by informing a certain set of
three surrounding villages that they had a grievance. As these
villages are responsible for the burial of a deceased king's body
parts, this seems to be a way of warning them that they soon
may have a dead king on their hands. Indeed, if such a war
escalates and remains unresolved, the kingmakers should
persuade a king to commit suicide.

What followed was structured and orchestrated. At first,
the women simply closed down the market as if a king had died
and marched in ranks according to what they sold, parading
their protest in song. The next day, they paraded en masse to
inform each male chief and the Chief of Police of their woes.

Their terms soon escalated. They carried symbolically
potent objects (akoko leaves and brooms), violated the recesses
of the palace, removed their wrappers and cursed the king.
While no local women opened their stalls during the war, male
traders from the North who continued to sell potatoes and
beans in the marketplace reported to the townswomen that the
Ondo king had been spotted peforming a ritual "turning of the
curse" back on the market itself. At this, the women
threatened their ultimate weapon. This supernatural sanction,
to be explained in detail below, was known as "making a
market at Iparuku" and it would certainly mean the king's
demise. On that day--the 9th day of the ija obinrin--the matter
was settled: only those women who owned their own cement
buildings were to pay the tax. The following day, the women
chiefs performed a ritual cleansing of the market and the king
made a costly sacrifice to counteract the curse born of his
townswomen's ill-will.

Of the narrative so-far presented, the salient image to keep
in mind is the highly condensed and multivocal symbolic action
of making a market at Iparuku. This non-descript but ritually
potent spot is where the prospective king is transformed into a
divine being by partaking of a cannibal stew made of the heart
of his predecessor, cooked and served to him by the Olobun, the
woman king, head of the women chiefs, and, literally
translated, "owner of the region's markets".

The West African colonial record documents other such
women's wars of resistance in nearby Eastern Nigeria and
Western Cameroon. Recent feminist scholarship has, not
surprisingly, salvaged these incidents from the heap of colonial
history, and re-analyzed the accounts to illustrate colonial
attitudes as well as indigenous practices. In their discussions of

the Aba Women's War of 1929 and the Anlu Rebellion of 1958, Van Allen (1972; 1976), Ifeka-Moller (1975) and Ardener (1975) have each argued that the gender symbolism employed associated women above all with fecundity, fertility and the "wild". Ifeka-Moller, especially, argues that in the Igbo and Ibibio cases, where women were associated with subsistence farming, their trading wealth was seen as illegitimate and threatening. Ifeka-Moller explicates the chain of cultural associations thusly: as women moved into trade from farming, their womanhood was threatened because their fertility was threatened because their link with the land was dissolving.

Although at first glance the Ondo women seem to be employing similar symbolic language--leaves, threat of nakedness, insult, etc.--I hope to demonstrate the primary and wholly legitimate association expressed was woman as office-holder and wielder of wealth. In short, Woman-As-Trader was primary, and fecundity was secondary.[3] For instance, the akoko leaves held in their hands were symbolic of legitimate political voice, invoked in this case against a king who was perceived as betraying his legitimate role. Akoko leaves are associated with title-houses, title-taking ceremonies and with the foundation of the kingdom out of chaos. Leaves communicating the message of wildness would have been palm fronds, and these leaves are indeed used during rites of passage and rites of rebellion and the chaotic half of the annual festival of cosmic ordering (dedicated to Ogun).

Clearly, then, Ija Obinrin is neither an uncontrolled riotous outpouring of rage nor a rite of rebellion providing catharsis for the masses while leaving the political order essentially intact. I did witness these two alternatives during fieldwork: Ondo's 1983 post-election riots included looting, arson and lynching. The widespread civil strife of this period culminated in General Buhari's New Year's Eve coup. Secondly, a textbook example of a "rite of rebellion" takes place every September in Ondo. During the Opepee festival, the masses spend all night roaming the town, hurling insulting songs at king and chiefs. But the women's war was something else: By going to war, the women were exercising their rights as political subjects, expressing their political voice through the proper channels--the woman king, her council of women chiefs, and the heads of their market associations. Only when this went unheeded did the protest shift into high gear--all the while remaining within the customary political boundaries of insult, obscenity, and curse.

It has oft been stated that among the Yoruba-speaking people, all status was achieved, and all personal power was based on maintaining a large loyal following. As with all other positions of prominence in this wealth-in-people system

(Bledsoe 1980), so too with the king. Though divine, he was
not an absolute ruler, but merely the premier member of the
council known as the kingmakers because they chose the king
from among the candidates lobbying for the seat. But one
might add, they could be king-breakers. To them was given the
power and the right to order a king to commit suicide or, if
necessary, to actually administer poison to the ruler. Ondo's
kinglist includes information on forty-two past rulers, and
according to my calculation, twelve (or almost 30%) were
recorded as having been dethroned in this way. The practice
has apparently persisted for almost three centuries. Even the
regional strife of the late nineteenth century entailed only a
slight rate increase. Within living memory, three kings have
been deposed, in 1901, 1925, and 1942. Among them is
included the father of the present king.
    The first and paradigmatic case of deposing a king was
Bajumu, the tenth king of Ondo, who supposedly ruled from
1702-1711. It is crucial to note that he stands accused in the
chronicle of way-laying market women and seizing their goods
(Bada of Saki 1940). His only other recorded offense was
waging an unjust war with an unnamed neighboring town. He
was warned by his people, it is said, but turned a deaf ear to
their cries. It would seem from this sketchy history that
Bajumu offended the ordinary citizens, both female and male,
by disrupting their lives and their livelihoods. As Bajumu
marauded wayfarers and incited military hostilities in pursuit
of booty for his own coffers, he would have disrupted both
women's trade and men's agricultural routine and labor supply.
    All this becomes relevant when one realizes that in 1985,
Nigeria's military rulers stood accused and condemned of
similar offenses in the eyes of its citizens. Nigeria's national
economy had suffered tremendous blows in the last few years,
as the result of a worsening export market, but also as a result
of years of inefficiency and graft. Prices of local produce had
doubled that year, and I recorded a ten-fold price increase for
imported essential commodities. The Nigerian government's
tactics employed against traders closely resemble Tanzania's
Nguvu Kazi as described by Donna Kerner elsewhere in this
volume. The government wreaked havoc when brutally
interfering with market women--they banned the sale of a wide
range of imports, confiscated contraband or hoarded goods
right out of market stalls, enforced sale at unrealistic controlled
prices, and even razed roadside markets during their misguided
"War Against Indiscipline" (known locally as WAI, pronounced
"WHY?").
    On top of these hardships, Ondo's cocoa farmers suffered a
terrible blow in 1985. Their entire crop and a sizable portion of

their mature trees were lost, due to the state-run cocoa marketing cooperatives' failure to distribute insecticide. This was viewed as almost willful incompetence since the year's supply had reportedly been in Lagos port awaiting distribution for the preceeding six months.

Austerity was biting everyone, but most especially the average male cocoa farmer and the average woman food or provisions seller. The new tax decree followed an increase in school fees for supposedly free education, increased hospital charges for ostensibly free health care, a newly announced mandatory contribution to the "Ondo State Development Fund", as well as the perpetual income taxes, which are costly to dodge and costlier to pay.

Moreover--and this was the crowning blow--it was rumored that the king had reported to the Governor that Ondo women were an untapped source of income, his evidence being that they built buildings of their own. Ondo wives are well aware that their men are acutely sensitive on the subject of women building houses. In the wider Nigerian society where women are not primarily associated with revenue from trade, this building of houses by Ondo women is taken as proof-positive that Ondo women make "uppity" wives.

All this led up to Monday, November 11, 1985, when the Ondo women's war began. Ranks and ranks, tens of thousands of women, and only women, marched from the market to the palace to the police station chanting and singing, registering their protest and demanding satisfaction, proceeding in turn to each prominent male chief's residence, reporting their difficulty. They carried certain commonplace objects with ritual potency-- two pieces of broomstick and a certain kind of leaf. Both are used by the woman king during the installation of a new king, and their use in this instance implied that a new installation ceremony would soon be necessary.

Their songs escalated from mere manifestos of tax resistance, to insult ("Out of thirty/Itiade scored zero"), to obscenity ("He takes tax/Like he takes our private parts"), to songs reserved for times of war ("There is trouble/If you see grass burning"), to implicit threats against the king's life (singing songs mourning a dead chief), to explicit threats on the king's life ("Itiade turns into a goat/We kill and eat him"). A further selection of verses is provided in an appendix to this paper.

They stormed the palace, violating the section forbidden to all women. They demonstrated their grief and their extreme emotional turmoil in the culturally prescribed way of parading in their slip but without their outer wrapper. Not only is nakedness or a disheveled appearance associated with deep mourning or the last stages of mental breakdown, but it is in this context also potent behavior: the most powerful curse of all is that of a naked woman. By parading in their slips alone, they were implying such a curse, explained to me as displaying in front of the king his own "mother's secrets".

While superficially non-violent (though highly energetic and boisterous), the protestors' words and actions served to register a vote of no confidence in the king, thereby threatening not only the king's tenure in office, but his very life. In a very real sense his life was at stake--the curses would have set in motion the process called euphemistically "making the king sleep". It is unclear if actual poison is in King Itiade's future. But supernaturally potent actions were taken which he had to counteract at great expense, much to the delight of the women I knew.

THE STRUCTURAL CENTRALITY OF OLOBUN

Unfortunately for its womenfolk, Ondo is no longer a city-state, but a city in the state of Ondo, southwestern Nigeria. The highly formalized dual-sex political structure has been dealt a series of severe blows, beginning with the colonialists' unwillingness to deal with women. To a series of foreign ethnographers they remained invisible. Even more distressing, Yoruba chroniclers of their own culture and history have perpetuated the dominant male ideology--casting a mere passing glance in the direction of Ondo's woman king and her cabinet of women chiefs, allotting at most a paragraph of text to Ondo's unique political configuration (Adeyemi 1935, Ogunshakin 1976, Ojo 1976). Olupona (1983) is the first to pay any attention to the institution, but it remains tangential to his analysis. For all these reasons and probably many more, recorded political history of Ondo ignores women's voice.

The paradox of the position of the woman king can be seen by comparing Tables 4:1 and 4:2, which indicate that the structure of her cabinet parallels the male hierarchy. In some ways it stands as an independent rival political structure, and in other ways it is made clearly subordinate to the male king.

The title is hereditary through the female descendants of the female founder of the town. The post is highly ritualized, dangerous, mysterious and revered. Her single most important function is to cook and serve a stew made of the dead king's heart during the installation of the new king. This seems to be the origin of the title's danger and mystery. You will recall that the most potent threat used during the women's

war was to make a market at Iparuku. Iparuku is the very
place this ritual transformation occurs.

She has no clout, this old woman without temporal/secular
power, yet carries tremendous ritual significance. Her
legitimization and validation function is very real, since her
duties include ceremonial installations of title holders and the
opening of new markets. She might also be called something
on the order of the "high priestess of profit".

Hence, the Olobun embodies Woman as Mother, Trader,
Domestic Laborer, and, yes, even Witch:

Mother	ritual 'mother' of the king; elder; to be taken care of by her symbolic son
Trader	controls the founding of markets and the god of prosperity/profit
Domestic Laborer	taboos surrounding her person emphasize household cleanliness and efficiency (e.g., she must not set foot on an unswept floor, she must not eat yesterday's stew, etc., etc.)
Witch	dealer in supernatural; giver and taker of life; cooking that cannibalistic feast for a new king further associates women with cannibal witches, wherein the source of power is "eating" human flesh, in this case, literally.

Only the Olobun and her cabinet of opoji may propitiate
Aje, that is, Profit. It is this cabinet of women chiefs who have
real political, judicial and economic roles to perform--settling
quarrels, voicing women's interests in the king's council,
leveling market tolls, etc. It is among the women chiefs of her
council that we find the struggle for power, where amassing
wealth can lead through generosity to gaining a following and
contesting a title. In this re-distributive economy, where
women have independent incomes and networks, here is the
way for a woman to barter her opportunity to make a fortune
in the marketplace into honor and status. This is to everyone's
advantage, since title-holders spread wealth around, yet titles
also bring with them new sources of income.

In the past, the bases of these women's power included such
things as: successful trade, a large number of dependents,
membership in voluntary societies, inheritance, land, craft

specialization, slaves, pawns, medicine, etc. Any and all of these could lead to social reputation.

Of course, in this century, Ondo's political integration has been torn asunder by such things as re-aligned trade routes, new products, new need for as well as new sources of cash, enforced peace, abolition of slavery and tolls, and the disruption of tributary and judicial payments. At the same time, a new status system based on personal fortune or western education has altered the social bases of the political system. By shoring up the faltering political structure they considered crucial to indirect rule, the British irrevocably altered its form.

Only the senior male [eghae] chiefs' judicial role has been enhanced by the colonial and post-colonial governments. No longer are their positions subject to the vagaries of ordinary citizens' shifting loyalties, but find their foundation in an external source of power.

The female chiefs have suffered in very much the same way as have the male chiefs below the eghae level. Bereft of any officially recognized judicial function, deprived of the government salary due chiefs, and with real political decisions made elsewhere than the king's council, the women chiefs' power has been on the wane.

But in November 1985, they fought back. And the government did have to modify their policy. Shrewdly, they singled out cement stalls and left alone those with tables in the open air.

One question with which we are left, then, is how can extant women's organizations be marshalled for decision-making at the national level? I hope that the preceeding analysis will highlight their potential for mobilization. The case of the Ija Obinrin Ondo does support March and Taqqu's conclusion in Women's Informal Associations in Developing Countries: Catalysts for Change? that rotating credit associations provide the most solid foundation upon which to build equitable planned change (1986: fig.1 and passim). But the sad truth is that not one of Nigeria's myriad lively newspapers picked up this story, and the government's divide-and-rule tactic served its purpose all too well.

NOTES

1. Except those paying income tax directly out of government salary.
2. The irony of this appellation must have escaped them.
3. The cultural association of children with wealth makes this separation between trade and motherhood less clear-cut.

92

TABLE 4:1
MAJOR CATEGORIES IN ONDO'S TITLE SYSTEM

In some ways, the female chiefs are subordinate to the king and
his council, and the Olobun is in this framework classed as a
hereditary priest with no executive functions.

Ugha Kekere, or small council, includes:

Osemawe	1 King
Eghae	5 Councillors

Ugha Nla, the large council, includes
the small council plus:

Ekule	7 Deputies
Elegbe	15 Warriors
Opoji	18 Female Chiefs
	[excluding Olobun
	for reasons made
	clear below]

The Alaghoro, hereditary priestly titles, represent independent
sources of ritual power and are excluded from executive
councils. Olobun fits here because:
In her capacity as Priestess of Aje, Olobun is one of three
leaders of autochthonous groups (the others: Ekiri of Ifore,
Oloja of Idoko). In her capacity as reigning descendant of
Pupupu, the founding ancestress, Olobun is one of three
powerful strangers from Ife (the others: Sora, Akunnara).

TABLE 4:2
PARALLELS BETWEEN ONDO'S MALE & FEMALE
HIERARCHIES

In the alternate framework, the structure of the woman king's
cabinet parallels that of the male chiefs:

KING

*Osemawe	*Olobun

CABINET

Lisa	Lisa Lobun
*Jomu	Jomu Lobun
Odunwo	Orangun
Sasere	Sasere Lobun
Adaja	Adafin Adaja

DEPUTIES

Odofin	Odofin Lobun
Logbosere	Ogede
Otu Palace chiefs under Logbosere	5 lesser titles under Ogede
Odofindi	Wajayo
Sagwe	Supou
Arogbo	Sean Lobun
Sara	Sama Lobun
*Lotu Omoba	Awoye Lobun

WARRIORS

Fifteen male warrior quarter chiefs under Ayadi	[nothing corresponds among the women]

PRIESTS

Ritual specialists as listed above, Table 4:1	Some of Olobun's attributes would place her here

[* hereditary title]

APPENDIX

THE SONGS OF IJA OBINRIN 1985
(TRANSLATED, AND IN ASCENDING ORDER OF PUBLIC
SANCTION):

OF TAX RESISTANCE:

Our king with such big ears,
Go tell [Governor] Akhigbe we will not pay head-paper [ie, tax]
OR:
King Itiade,
Bring us the tax your mother brought them!

OF INSULT:

Out of thirty, Itiade scored zero!
OR:
He stole timber, but he is not a thief, oh no!
He stole timber, but he is not a thief, oh no!
Our King, Itiade, he stole timber,
But he is not a thief.
[his timber lorries had been caught inside the federal reserves]
OR:
[Governor] Akhigbe's mother
Has never taken up books,
So too Akhigbe's father

OBSCENE:

He takes tax like he takes our private parts.
[i.e., he rapes us with his tax]

RESERVED FOR TIMES OF WAR:

There is trouble
If you see grass burning!

OF MOURNING (Threat is implicit):

It is today we know if he gave birth or not
[a song reserved for funerals]

OR:
So, this is how it is,
This is how it is for you, Itiade
Sorry, Adieu!
[song for mourning a dead chief]

CURSING (Threat is explicit):

Itiade must go
Our king with big ears,
Pack your load out of the town!
OR:
We kill and eat him
We kill and eat him
Itiade turns into a goat
We kill and eat him
OR:
He will not see the coming year
[ironic reversal of a common greeting]
OR:
Our king Itiade, his crown,
He will see it sprouting mushrooms
[i.e., it will rot]
OR:
Our king Itiade
Took the kingship and broke it
OR:
We have no king, we have no chiefs,
Except the Jomu alone remains,
The others
Are empty.
[The much beloved Jomu was the chief who eventually
arranged the settlement]

REFERENCES

Adeyemi, Reverend
1935?   History and Culture of the Ondo. Unpublished
          Master's Thesis. (on deposit at Harvard's Tozzer
          Library)

Ardener, Shirley
1975   Sexual Insult and Female Militancy. In Perceiving
          Women. New York: John Wiley & Sons.

Bada of Shaki
1940   Iwe Itan Ondo. Ondo: Igbehin Adun Press.

Bledsoe, Caroline
1980   Women and Marriage in Kpelle Society. Stanford:
          Stanford University Press.

Forde, Daryll and P. M. Kaberry, eds.
1967   West African Kingdoms in the Nineteenth
          Century. London: Oxford.

Ifeka-Moller, Caroline
1975   Female Militancy and Colonial Revolt: The
          Women's War of 1929, Eastern Nigeria. In
          Shirley Ardener, ed. Perceiving Women. New
          York: John Wiley & Sons.

March, Kathryn S. and Rachelle L. Taqqu
1986   Women's Informal Associations in Developing
          Countries: Catalysts for Change? Boulder:
          Westview.

Mintz, Sidney
1971   Men, Women and Trade. Comparative Studies in
          Society and History 13: 247-268.

Ogunshakin, Patrick
1976   Ondo: The People, Their Customs and Traditions.
          Lagos: Inway Publishers.

Ojo, Jerome O.
1976   Yoruba Customs from Ondo. Vienna: Institut fur
          Volkerkunde der Universitat Wien.

Okonjo, Kamene
    1976   The Dual-Sex Political System in Operation: Igbo
            Women and Community Politics in Midwestern
            Nigeria. In Hafkin and Bay, eds. Women in
            Africa. Stanford: Stanford University Press.

Olupona, J. O. Kehinde
    1983   A Phenomenological/Anthropological Analysis of
            the Religion of the Ondo-Yoruba of Nigeria.
            Unpublished Ph.D. Dissertation, Department of
            Religion, Boston University.

Perham, Margery
    1937   The Aba Market Women's Riot in Nigeria, 1929.
            In Native Administration in Nigeria. London.
            (reprinted in Cartey and Kilson, eds. The Africa
            Reader: Colonial Africa. New York: Vintage).

Van Allen, Judith
    1972   Sitting on a Man: Colonialism and the Lost
            Political Institutions of Igbo Women. Canadian
            Journal of African Studies 6:2.
    1976   "Aba Riots" or "Igbo Women's War?" Ideology,
            Stratification and the Invisibility of Women" In
            Hafkin and Bay, eds. Women in Africa. Stanford:
            Stanford University Press.

NOTES/IDEAS:

① Contrast Peru/LAm lit on inf sector
  w/ HongKong/Asia lit
    * Both sources of substl lit...

② Peru: What interrelashp (betw ambu & ___?___)
   is mjr factor in determg operatnl & orgztnl charctcs
   of strdg?
   (ex: HongK → hawkers/state interrela)

③ Discuss: various operatnl & orgztnl strats adopted by
   ambu in attempt cope successfly w/ ongoing... and
   to "mntn ecnmc wellbeing" (?)"

   → Orgztnl dynmcs of strdg can only be underst d in context
     of mkt forces/ecnmc, pol, cultl, socl forces
       → dynmc interactns
         & ambu responses to --- (crises/policies/
         chging sit/status)

④ Methodology:
   → idcn zones & density (# ambu/100 meters) in ea city
   → "My resh incl interviws w/ ----
     & observing (on a dly basis) operatn ambu in various
     zones of city
   * & wkg in conjux w/ (3) ambu at 3 resh sites
              myself

⑤ Whatever the estd of ambu, they are ubio

5

How to Survive in Illegal Street Hawking in Hong Kong

Josephine Smart[1]
York University

INTRODUCTION

Street hawking operations in most parts of the world, especially those in developing countries, are commonly described as marginal activities requiring little capital or skill and generating low income (Bairoch 1973; Fapohunda et al. 1978; Hart 1973; International Labour Office 1972; Joshi et al. 1976; McGee 1973; McGee and Yeung 1977). The marginality of street hawking and other informal activities is often used to explain the various organizational and operational characteristics of such economic activities. For instance, the limited expansion in scale of operation is usually attributed to insufficient capital accumulation as a result of the low income generated. In the particular case of Hong Kong where significant capital accumulation can be achieved in street hawking, it is necessary to examine the persistence of small scale operations outside the framework of marginality.

In recent years, there is a growing concern about the nature of the interrelationships between non-capitalist production units and the wider capitalist system. Arising from studies in Latin America are suggestions that the persistence of petty commodity producers is due to their subordination to capitalist enterprises which control their level of return to labour, their access to market for the commodities they produce and their access to capital (Scott 1979; Birkbeck 1978; Bromley 1978). In the case of Hong Kong, while there is little evidence to suggest that street hawkers are "dominated" by capitalist enterprises or that they are restricted from economic expansion because of such domination, I find that the interrelationship between the hawkers and the state is a major factor in determining the operational and organizational characteristics of street hawking. It is the objective of this paper to discuss the various operational and organizational strategies adopted by illegal hawkers in an attempt to cope successfully with the ongoing government intervention in street hawking and to maintain their economic well-being. It becomes clear that the organizational dynamics in street hawking in Hong Kong cannot be understood in the context of market forces alone, but it must also be seen in the context of the dynamic interactions between state policies and the hawkers' responses to such interventions.

This paper arose from a larger study of street hawking in Hong Kong involving a four-month period of research in May-August 1982 and an eighteen-month period from October 1983 to April 1985[2]. I concentrated my research effort on a prosperous hawking agglomeration in the Kwun Tong district which has since been turned into a Hawker Permitted Place in December 1984. This particular hawking agglomeration consisted of over 300 illegal hawkers working in a 100-meter section of Shui Wo Street. Nearby was a government regulated bazaar which officially housed over 200 licenced vendors, many of whom were known to work illegally on the street instead of working at their designated stall space in the bazaar. The bazaar was torn down in 1985 to make way for the construction of a permanent market complex. My research included interviews with hawkers, government officials and other actors; observing the operation of street hawking in various marketplaces on a daily basis, and working as a street hawker myself for five weeks at the research site.

STREET HAWKING IN HONG KONG

The British Crown Colony of Hong Kong is a 400 square mile (1067 square kilometre) area situated at the mouth of the Pearl River in Southern China. The Colony is made up of Hong Kong Island, the Kowloon Peninsula, the New Territories and 235 islands. Much of the developed areas on Hong Kong Island and in Kowloon are land reclaimed from the ocean front (Lands Department 1984:7). At the end of 1986, there were 5.6 million residents in Hong Kong, making it one of the most densely populated cities in the world with an average density of over 20,000 persons per square kilometre in the metropolitan areas (Hong Kong 1987:291).

The colonial history of Hong Kong is deeply embedded in the opium trade in China. The Nanjing Treaty of August 1942, arising from the first Opium War, marked the transfer of Hong Kong into British sovereignty. In the subsequent Treaty of Peking in 1860, Kowloon was ceded to Britain. The area adjacent to the Chinese mainland north of Boundary Street in

Kowloon and 235 islands (collectively known as the New
Territories) were leased to Britain in 1898 for 99 years.
   The long history of street hawking in Hong Kong is attested
to by the inclusion of street hawking as an occupational
category in the census as early as 1872. At that time, Hong
Kong had a population of 121,985 with a total of 2431
hawkers. In the following years, the population of Hong Kong
climbed steadily and so did the number of street hawkers. By
1931, the number of hawkers rose to 16,285, while the
population reached 849,751 (McGee 1973:35). In fifty years,
the percentage of the population in street hawking jumped from
0.2% in 1872 to nearly 2% in 1931. During the Japanese
occupation of Hong Kong (1941-1945), many people fled the
Colony and returned to their home villages in China. As a
result there was a sharp decline in street hawking activities, in
response partly to the drop in population and partly to the
shortage of foodstuffs and other commodities.
   After the occupation, Chinese migrants flooded the Colony.
Some of them were returning residents who left before the war
but many were Chinese who left China to seek a place with
greater political and economic stability. The uncontrolled influx
of both legal and illegal immigrants from China between
1945-1980 caused an increase in population from 1.8 million
in 1947 to 4.4 million in 1976, putting immense strain upon
housing and other public facilities in the urban areas of Hong
Kong (Sit 1981:3-4). Government officials were alarmed by
the sharp increase in street hawking activities in the post-war
years and its "disorderly effect on the city streets" (McGee
1973:42). In 1947, the number of hawkers was estimated to be
anywhere from 40,000 to 70,000.
   The situation in Hong Kong immediately after 1945 bore a
strong resemblance to many contemporary developing countries
where people, many of whom are uprooted from their land
base, migrate to the cities seeking wage employment
opportunities. These migrants frequently end up resorting to
self-employment in order to get by. Though there is no
analysis of the factors contributing to the rise in street hawking
activities in Hong Kong in the post-war period, it is fairly
reasonable to suggest that economic underdevelopment and
uncontrolled population growth were the major causes. In the
next few decades, however, Hong Kong underwent rapid
economic development to become a major manufacturing,
financial and trading centre (Rabushka 1979). The average
growth rate of Gross Domestic Product (GDP) was 8.9% for the
period 1961-1976 and 12.5% for the period 1976-1979 (Lin et
al. 1980:4; Lee and Jao 1982:8). By 1969, the per capita Gross
National Product (GNP) in Hong Kong was second to Japan in

Asia (England and Rear 1975:24). The impressive economic development brought significant increases in employment opportunities. In the manufacturing sector alone, close to 1 million workers were hired in 1984 (Hong Kong 1985:106). The unemployment rate for 1986 was 2.2% when most industrialized countries such as Britain, United States and Canada were suffering much higher unemployment in the same period. Hong Kong had one of the highest labor participation rates in the world, even surpassing that of Japan (International Labor Office 1984).

In the 1981 Census, 63,000 people were identified as hawkers, of whom close to 40,000 were unlicenced illegal hawkers. There is a great deal of controversy concerning the magnitude of illegal hawking. The latest government estimates were typically conservative, suggesting that there were 16,000-17,000 illegal hawkers in 1984 (Urban Council Markets & Street Traders Select Committee 1985:14). Other sources (Sing Pao, 17 April 1984) give a higher estimate of 50,000-70,000. Whatever the real number of street hawkers is, they are ubiquitous in the urban areas of Hong Kong.

Street hawkers, known as siu faan[3] in the Cantonese dialect, are best described as self-employed petty retailers involved in the distribution of a wide range of locally produced and imported goods and produce. In 1983, street hawking contributed an estimated $1 billion to the economy, representing roughly 11% of the value of the retail trade (Urban Council Markets & Street Traders Select Committee 1985:15). Street hawkers are an important link in the international network of commodity distribution.

In any discussion of street hawkers in Hong Kong, it is necessary to distinguish between legal and illegal hawkers. This distinction is based primarily on their licence status (licenced/without a licence) as well as their spatial characteristics (working in government regulated trading areas/working in public space). This distinction is particularly important in understanding the ongoing conflict between the government and the street hawkers. On the one hand, there is an increasing tendency among street hawkers to operate from the same location in a permanent or semi-permanent manner, thus creating many congestion and obstruction problems in the urban milieu. On the other hand, the government tries to preserve the motorists' and pedestrians' exclusive right to the use of public space by raiding the existing hawking agglomerations regularly, and causing frequent disruptions in hawking activities. The legal or licenced hawkers are not the target of government actions since they work in government regulated trading areas. It is the illegal hawkers who occupy

public space without government sanction that are the targets
of daily harassment.

This distinction between legal and illegal hawking is a
legalistic construct imposed by the government, one which is
not necessarily accepted by the street hawkers themselves.
Illegal hawkers do not consider themselves to be doing anything
illegal or criminal. As far as they are concerned they are
legitimate small businessmen earning an honest living by
serving the public. However, they must cope with the various
forms of government intervention in order to maintain their
economic activities.

It is difficult, if not impossible, to generalize about the
street hawkers because they are a highly heterogeneous group.
But if one must make such generalizations, one can say that
street hawkers (legal and illegal) are predominantly male,
married, non-Hong Kong born residents with little formal
education. Most licenced hawkers are over 40 years of age,
characterised by many years of participation in street hawking.
Illegal hawkers, however, are mostly younger men and women
in their 20s and 30s whose hawking experience ranges from a
few years to most of a lifetime. Many of these able-bodied,
young hawkers had some wage employment experience before
they became street hawkers. Their wage employment often
served as a source of capital accumulation to furnish the initial
investment requirement in their street hawking venture.

A striking point about street hawkers in contemporary
Hong Kong is that they are rarely "forced" into
self-employment by permanent unemployment. Instead,
people's decision to enter street hawking is usually based on
careful evaluations of the demands and rewards in street
hawking vis-a-vis wage employment. Street hawking is
neither "marginal" in terms of income potentials nor readily
accessible to everyone since much social and economic resources
are required to maintain a viable hawking operation and to
cope successfully with regular state harassment at the same
time. Street hawking attracts mostly young Chinese
immigrants who are dissatisfied with the limited advancement
opportunities in wage employment as a result of their social
dislocation, limited formal education and knowledge of English,
and limited access to social and economic resources in Hong
Kong. They perceive the higher income potential and greater
personal autonomy in illegal street hawking as the means to
improve their social and economic standing in Hong Kong
(Smart 1987). Despite the long working hours, the labour
intensiveness, and risks of arrest by government agents, many
Chinese immigrants are attracted to illegal hawking for its
potential for social and economic mobility. The strong

resistance to proletarianization among street hawkers in Hong Kong and elsewhere (see Rogerson and Deavon 1982; Lessinger 1985; Trager 1985) raises many questions about the widespread assumptions that street hawking is a transitional undertaking for the unemployed and that it will diminish once sufficient wage employment is available.

STATE INTERVENTION IN STREET HAWKING

From the beginning, the colonial government of Hong Kong had always subscribed to a policy of repression and eradication in regard to street hawking. This oppressive attitude towards street hawking in Hong Kong has a strong parallel in the long history of state intervention in street trades in Britain, from where all senior government officials were recruited. Many of the policies on street hawking in Hong Kong appeared to be ideas borrowed from the urban policies of Britain. The relocation of street traders into permanent markets and the restrictions on licence issuance were two cases that clearly had precedents in early 20th century London (see Benedetta 1936:177-179).

The earliest record of state intervention was contained in an ordinance, passed shortly after the establishment of the colonial government in 1841, which made a person liable to a fine of five pounds if he should

"...expose anything for sale in or upon, or so to hang over any carriageway or footway, or on the outside of any house or shop, or who shall set up or continue any pole, blind, awning, line or any other projection from any window, parapet, or other part of any house, shop or other building, so as to cause any annoyance or obstruction in any thoroughfare." (Hong Kong Sanitary Board, Laws relating to Public Health and Sanitations in Hong Kong, No. 14, 1845, cited in McGee 1873:32).

Street hawkers were prohibited from operating along the waterfront main street and in the vicinity of government buildings, including the Governor's residence.

In a 1936 Report by the chairman of the newly created Urban Council, Mr. R. R. Todd argued that "all hawkers (should be) cleared off the streets and hawking as a trade (should be) abolished" (cited in McGee 1973:38). He pointed out that, on the one hand, street hawking had certain positive contributions in providing a convenient service to the public, in keeping down the cost of living for the poorer classes and in providing a source of social welfare for the old and weak (McGee 1973:37-38). On the other hand, however, street hawking was the cause of obstruction, threats to public health, temptation "to the Asiatic Police as a source of squeeze", and unfair competition to formal retail outlets (McGee 1973:38-39). In Todd's opinion, the negative aspects of street hawking far outweighed its positive contributions. This extreme argument against street hawking has moderated over time among Todd's successors, but the central philosophy that street hawkers and their trading activities are not welcome in the urban milieu persists even today. With increasing urbanization and industrialization, there is a deepening conflict between street hawkers and government in their perception of the proper use of public space, and their struggle over the use right of public space has intensified correspondingly. The present policies on street hawking reflect a shift in philosophy towards a reluctant recognition that street hawking may be here to stay. Instead of attempting to eradicate street hawking, the government has now made a commitment to gain greater control over the operation of street hawking.

Licencing is probably the most longstanding means by which the government gains control over street hawking by imposing rules and regulations upon hawkers concerning their location of work, commodity type, hours of operation, scale of operation and labor utilization. The exact date of the first licencing of street hawkers in Hong Kong is unknown. A record showed that 1082 and 1146 street hawkers took out a "ticket" in the first two quarters of 1873 at the cost of 50 cents per quarter (Nacken 1968:129). The licencing of itinerant hawkers was probably first instituted in the early phase of colonialism. "Stall licences" were introduced later in 1921.

Until June 1970, the government followed a policy of liberal licencing in which anybody who applied for a hawker licence would probably obtain one. Of particular interest to this paper is the increasing criminalization of street hawking after a decision to stop the issuing of itinerant hawker licences in 1970. This process of criminalization is expressed in two forms. First, by making it nearly impossible to obtain a hawking licence, the government in effect forces all unlicenced hawkers to work illegally regardless of their intentions about legalizing their operations. Second, the government has been intensifying its prosecution of illegal hawkers over the years by increasing the number of enforcement agents and the number of raids and arrests. Since 1970 only new fixed-pitch hawker licences are issued, mostly to illegal hawkers who are relocated into government regulated trading areas (Smart 1986). Fixed-pitch hawkers are assigned specific spatial positions in government bazaars or hawker permitted places. Due to the increasing restrictions on licence issuance since 1970,

unlicenced hawkers from earlier times and most newcomers
into the street trade since 1970 find it nearly impossible to
obtain a hawker licence. These "pirates of the street markets",
as they were known in early 20th Century London (Benedetta
1936:179), can be said to be victims of state intervention.
What they consider to be a legitimate and honest livelihood in
street trade has become "illegal" by bureaucratic definition.
The criminalization of their economic activity is an imposition
from without which most illegal hawkers do not agree with.

The criminalization of street hawking affects the hawkers
in two major ways. First, it gives rise to a need for informal
regulations in the allocation of scarce resources -- such as
spatial positions, supply of electricity and water, storage space -
- and dispute settlement among hawkers over any issues that
lie outside the formal legal system. The institution of these
informal regulations, such as normative pressures and triad
(secret society)[5] interventions, affects the social dynamics
within any marketplace. The widespread triad intervention in
street hawking especially deserves attention given its strong
control over access to spatial positions and access to capital,
and its role in dispute settlement among hawkers (see Smart
1983). Secondly, the criminalization of street hawking gives
legitimacy to the state's increasing effort to displace street
hawkers from their chosen location of work. Hawkers are
attracted to busy intersections and other locations of promising
business potential, thus creating many congestion and
environmental problems incompatible with the city
administrators' perception of proper urban land use. As a
result, daily raid-and-arrest operations are carried out by
three government agencies -- Urban Services Department,
Police, and Housing Authority -- in an attempt to restrict the
hawkers' access to public space. In order to remain working in
profitable locations, illegal hawkers must adopt various
operational and organizational strategies to evade state
harassment.

Any visitor to Hong Kong who happens to be caught in the
middle of a raid of illegal hawkers by a General Duties Team
(Urban Services Department) or Nuisance Squad (Police) will
be shocked by the paramilitary flavour of the operation. One
or two government trucks approach a hawking agglomeration
and deposit 10-20 uniformed personnel who swiftly and
silently block off the major exits to the area. The street
hawkers' attempt to disappear before the law closes in is
performed with an accentuated ferocity that conjures images of
the chaos and confusion expected in the event of an earthquake
or bomb shelling. The running hawkers cry out to warn others
of jau gwai, roughly translated as "running from the ghost". It

expresses quite succinctly the dramatic phenomenon of running
and chasing by enforcement agents and illegal hawkers during
a raid. Hawkers' wheelcarts fly down the streets in all
directions oblivious of the safety of innocent pedestrians and
fleeing hawkers alike. Overloaded handcarts spill their
contents and litter the street with oranges and apples, boiling
soup and oil, fish balls, cooking and eating utensils, and dead or
live fish.

In a matter of minutes, all hawkers disappear from the
scene, save for those unfortunate enough to be caught. Speed,
agility, strength and luck are the necessary prerequisites for a
successful escape from the preying enforcement agents. There
are many niches of refuge in the vicinity of a hawking
agglomeration which are utilized by the fleeing hawkers for the
temporary storage of their hawking paraphernalia until the
storm blows over. The arrested hawkers, sometimes together
with their hawking paraphernalia, are taken to the nearest
police station for charging procedures. Most raid-and-arrest
operations last less than half an hour.

As soon as the enforcement agents leave the scene, life
returns to normal within a matter of minutes. The streets are
once again filled with the lively exchanges between hawkers
and shoppers--bargaining, joking, gossiping, and loud
proclamation of the real or imagined superior quality of the
goods.

The element of surprise is crucial to the success of any
raid-and-arrest operation. Enforcement agents revise their
attack strategies regularly to ensure the greatest efficiency.
They try to approach the hawking agglomeration from different
directions, park their transportation vehicles several blocks
away so that their approach to the target site is less noticeable
and use concealed walkways such as subway underground
walkways whenever possible.

Street hawkers are interrupted many times a day by real
and false alarms of jau gwai. The street hawkers joke among
themselves that no one with a weak heart can ever survive in
illegal street hawking. They are probably right. The frequent
and regular government harassment makes illegal hawkers
highly nervous. It also creates a feeling of comradeship among
fellow hawkers due to their shared hardship. The General
Duties Team (Urban Services Department) alone arrested over
1000 illegal hawkers in Kwun Tong every month in 1985.

The enforcement actions not only cause frequent
interruptions in street hawking and restrict the hawkers' access
to public space, they also serve as a medium to extract
resources from the street hawkers. Each arrested hawker pays
a fine of HK$100-500 depending on the nature of their

hawking offenses[4]. In addition, they lose much precious
working time at the Police Station during the charging
procedures and again at the court hearing the next day. When
goods and hawking paraphernalia are confiscated, the economic
cost of an arrest goes up significantly. In one case, a jewellery
vendor lost over $10,000 in a single arrest. In 1984, some of
the goods confiscated from hawkers included 16,000 kg of fruit,
85,000 kg of vegetable, 12,000 kg of fish, 11,000 kg of eggs,
and 4,000 bundles of fresh flowers (South China Morning Post,
6 May 1985:7). Over 200 hawking handcarts or trolleys were
confiscated every month in 1985 in the Kwun Tong district.

HAWKERS' RESPONSES TO SPATIAL
INTERVENTION BY THE STATE

All hawkers are affected by the prevailing policies on street
hawking. The limits on access to spatial positions imposed by
state intervention elicit strong responses from street hawkers
due to the primary importance of spatial positions as a means
of production in street hawking. Part of a hawker's economic
well-being hinges on the location of his/her position within a
given hawking agglomeration. A hawker occupying a spot near
the greatest flow of shopper traffic is likely to do well, whereas
someone situated at the periphery will have to work much
harder for longer hours to match the same economic success.
Similarly, a hawker occupying a spot giving easy access to an
escape route in the event of a raid will be most unwilling to
give it up. In addition, most hawkers prefer to work near
where they live for reasons of convenience and better resource
management, which provide strong incentives to keep their
existing spatial positions despite state harassment.

Illegal hawkers, lacking legal sanction for their use of public
space for trading activities, are particularly vulnerable to the
government's attempt to restrict their access to desirable
locations. Given below is a list of strategies commonly utilized
by street hawkers to maintain their access to public space for
hawking purposes. Since each strategy has certain social and
economic costs, it follows that hawkers with more resources at
their disposal are more successful in protecting their economic
interests against state intervention.

Voluntary Relocation

Tired of the high stress of jau gwai in the frequently raided
locations, some hawkers would move to less popular locations
where state intervention is less intense. Their rationale is that

while they may do less business at the new location and suffer
a certain degree of decline in income level, the accumulated
savings from fewer arrests will more than make up for the
income differential in the long run. While the economic factor
appears to dominate the decision, I suspect that there are some
psychological factors in play as well. Some people are fighters
willing to take risks, and some are not, and some of those
hawkers who relocate voluntarily probably belong to the latter.

Changing Working Hours

There are many variations under this theme. The common
goal is to avoid state harassment by restricting one's working
hours to periods of safe trading when the threat of enforcement
action is minimum.
(a) Operate between raids - once a raid is carried out at a
given hawking agglomeration, it usually takes some time, as
much as half a day, before the next raid comes. The period
between raids is an open season for street trading activities.
For instance, the first raiding of the Shui Wo Street market
area normally takes place between 8:30 am and 9 am. Many
garment hawkers take a break between 8:45 am and 9:30 am
or thereabout to avoid the threat of enforcement actions.
Garments are heavy and it is difficult to run with a fully loaded
hawking handcart. One woman garment vendor used to wait
until the morning raid was over before she opened for business.
As long as the enforcement agents kept to their regular
schedule, she could work uninterrupted between 9:30 am and
noon. She would get upset whenever they showed up late
because it cut into her working hours and business turnover.
(b) Another common strategy is to shorten or alter the
working hours in order to avoid the period of active
enforcement actions, like that adopted by a husband-and-wife
team who sell coffee and tea and made-to-order sandwiches.
Normally they worked between 6 am and 10 am. In the cooked
food business turnover often exceeds several hundred dollars an
hour. Much against the wife's argument, the husband decided
to close the operation before 9 am after a succession of arrests.
The husband would rather take a cut in income than face the
higher possibility of arrest after 9 am.
A similar case involves a middle-aged male fruit hawker
who works in the evening between 7 pm-10 pm. Once in a
while, he will get arrested by enforcement agents, but the
situation is relatively peaceful in comparison to daytime
hawking at the same location. He used to work during the day
at the same location before the frequency of enforcement
actions increased to a point where he spent more time on jau

gwai than doing business. Being a resident in the public
housing estate nearby, he was unwilling to change his location
of operation. In response to his need to protect his economic
well-being, he changed his operation time to the evening. In
doing so, his income was affected somewhat, but he considers
that as a fair trade-off for remaining in street hawking at the
same location.

Information Sharing

Most street hawkers cannot readily change their working
hours to accommodate the schedule of enforcement actions.
This inflexibility is dictated largely by their commodity type,
target income, and the customers' shopping habits. For
instance, most hawkers of perishable goods -- such as meat,
vegetables, fruits and cooked food -- work in the daytime
because most housewives shop in the mornings and afternoons.
They cope with state harassment by "outrunning" the
enforcement agents aided by information about the agents'
movements and whereabouts. With such information they can
go into hiding before the enforcement agents arrive at their
location of work. In a few known cases, such as the Pei Ho
Street agglomeration in Sham Shui Po, some kind of organized
information network seems to be at work to warn hawkers of
the movement of enforcement agents. It is rumored that triad
controlled observers are positioned at roof tops, major
intersections and even outside the local police station or
General Duties Team depot to spy upon the movement of
enforcement personnel. Information may be relayed to the
hawkers by phone or walkie talkie. It is an extremely efficient
operation. Despite frequent changes in attack strategies,
enforcement agents often find the target location deserted upon
their arrival even though it was alive with hawking activities
only minutes before.

As yet, very little is known about the extent of triad
involvement in providing information services for street
hawkers, the cost of such service, the term of payment by
street hawkers, its effects upon their income level, and other
aspects of hawking operation as well as the affected hawkers'
possible involvement in triad-related crimes. In Shui Wo
Street, there is no evidence of triad involvement in any kind of
organized warning system for street hawkers. Sometimes
individual efforts are made to track the movement of
enforcement agents. Only hawking units with spare manpower
can engage in such information gathering exercises by posting a
family member near the site of operation or even sending
someone to the nearby General Duties Team depot to watch

their movements. Whatever it may be, this kind of individual effort lacks effectiveness due to limited manpower and the difficulty of detecting the movements of enforcement agents until they are within the immediate vicinity of the site of operation.

Information sharing among fellow hawkers about the movement of enforcement agents is a norm deeply rooted in their shared hardship vis-a-vis state intervention. It is not certain that all hawkers are indeed equally committed to this normative expectation of information sharing, but it would be difficult for a hawker to keep that information secret because his/her action of leaving the site of operation would betray such knowledge quite plainly. Jau gwai is very much a chain reaction. When one hawker runs, the others will follow.

Mobility Factor

The chance of being arrested is inversely proportional to the degree of mobility in a hawking unit. The faster you can disappear from the scene of a raid, the less likely it is that you will be apprehended. In general, those hawkers who work on major streets and busy junctions are characterized by the ability to move away from their site of operation quickly. Some achieve this high degree of mobility by restricting their scale of operation and commodity type. Some hawking units consist of nothing more than a ground sheet with drawstrings which can be bundled up at times of danger. This is known among the hawkers as a "ground operation". Due to the limited carrying capacity of this highly mobile operation, the amount of goods carried at any one time is limited and thus the scale of operation is correspondingly small.

There are many other highly mobile small scale operations facilitated by specially designed trays, briefcases, and display units which can be collapsed or put away at a short notice. Many of these contraptions are individual innovations. Others are readily available at shops which specialize in the production of hawking paraphernalia.

The wheeled handcart (wooden or metal) or trolley is the most commonly used equipment among street hawkers. It offers a high degree of mobility and a greater carrying capacity. It is especially valuable to cooked food hawkers who often carry gas tanks, big pots of liquid and food, eating utensils, and water. Most fresh fruit hawkers and garment hawkers also use wheeled handcarts. A well-built handcart of superior quality can cost over HK$1000. Many hawkers build their own with plywood at a relatively low cost of several hundred dollars.

Access to Safe Refuge

Many hawkers are friends or relatives of owners of shops near their location of work. A few cases are known where the street hawking unit in front of a shop is actually an extension of the shop operation, and the hawker in question is a member of the shopowner's family. Hawkers who have access to the use of a formal retail shop as a safe refuge for themselves and their hawking paraphernalia during a raid can afford to work at locations under intense enforcement actions. Such access is always mediated by social and kinship ties maintained through a long standing relationship of reciprocity between hawkers and shopowners.

As long as a hawker is strategically positioned near an easy escape route such as a back alley or building entrance, he/she can usually evade arrest. In recent years, there has been an increasing number of street hawkers who operate from a van or truck. The vehicle is a mini shop as well as a means of transportation. At the arrival of enforcement agents, a hawker simply closes the car doors and stays put until the storm blows over, or drives away to another location. This kind of van-operation is very effective in evading state harassment in hawker control. It is also extremely capital intensive, confirming my observation that street hawking in Hong Kong is not necessarily a low capital endeavour as it is commonly believed to be.

DISCUSSION

In Hong Kong, state intervention has an immense impact upon the development and operation of street hawking. The spatial behaviour and operational characteristics of street hawkers cannot be fully understood outside the context of their response to state intervention. In turn, the nature of state intervention in street hawking cannot be fully appreciated until one has a thorough understanding of the state's response to the changing organizational dynamics of street hawking in Hong Kong.

The state's ongoing attempt to restrict hawkers' access to public space for trading activities has the effect of crystallizing certain characteristics of street hawking, the most obvious being the small scale of operation and the high degree of mobility. Hawkers cannot afford to operate on a large scale because that will impede their mobility, which in turn will affect their chances of avoiding arrest during one of the daily raids. In illegal hawking, it is not feasible to expand beyond a

certain point when the economic gain from a larger operation
falls below the cost of fines and penalties due to higher
incidence of arrest. It is a sound economic strategy to keep
one's operation small while accumulated capital is channeled
into other lines of investment -- such as property acquisition,
children's education, investment in gold and stocks -- which
yield better returns. In some cases, expansion is achieved by
setting up subsidiary units, each to be operated by one or two
family members or by hired workers in rare cases. It is clear
that even when capital is available, it is not always feasible to
expand a hawking operation beyond an optimal size given the
constraints imposed by labor availability and state intervention.
    The analysis also indicates that many other organizational
characteristics of individual hawking operations -- commodity
type, working hours, spatial location, and labour utilization --
are closely interrelated with the hawkers' response to spatial
intervention by the state. Street hawking is neither a simple
nor easy endeavour. The successful management of an illegal
hawking operation in Hong Kong not only requires the
conventional wisdom of business management, but also the
ingenuity and necessary resources to evade state harassment.
Illegal hawkers must be innovative as well as resourceful in
order to run a profitable business in spite of ongoing state
harassment.

NOTES

1. Josephine Smart is a Research Associate at the Joint Centre
for Asia Pacific Studies (University of Toronto & York
University) and the Department of Anthropology at York
University.
2. This research was made possible by an Ontario Graduate
Scholarship (1983-1984), a Social Sciences & Humanities
Research Council of Canada Doctoral Fellowship (1984-1985)
and a grant-in-aid from the Centre of International Studies at
University of Toronto (1983-1985).
3. Cantonese words used in the text are underlined. They are
romanized according to Sidney Lau's A Practical
Cantonese-English Dictionary (1977), but without the tonal
markers.
4. Triads are territorial-based criminal organizations which
operate in many activities including drug trafficking,
prostitution, gambling, loan-sharking, extortions and others.
Triads are also known as secret societies. They were founded
in the 17th century in China under nationalistic aspirations
against the Ching Dynasty. Later the element of nationalism

diminished and was replaced by increasing criminal inclinations
(Comer 1959; Mak 1981). In a 1984 Police report, the total
triad membership in Hong Kong was estimated to be between
70,000 and 12,000 strong (South China Morning Post,
27 November 1984:1).
5. All monetary figures are given in Hong Kong dollars,
abbreviated '$'. The exchange rate in 1985 was HK$7.8 to
every US$1.

REFERENCES CITED

Bairoch, Paul
    1973   Urban Unemployment in Developing Countries.
            Geneva: International Labour Office

Benedetta, Mary
    1936   The Street Markets of London. New York:
            Benjamin Bloom Inc.

Birkbeck, Chris
    1978   Self Employed Proletarians in the Informal
            Factory: the Case of Cali's Garbage Dump Pickers.
            World Development 6:1173-1185

Bromley, Ray
    1978   Introduction - The urban informal sector: why is it
            worth discussing? World Development
            6:1033-1039

Bromley, Ray & Chris Gerry (eds.)
    1979   Casual Work and Poverty in Third World Cities.
            Toronto: John Wiley & Sons

England, Joe and John Rear
    1975   Chinese Labour Under British Rule. Hong Kong:
            Oxford University Press

Fapohunda, L., J. Olanrewaju and H. Lubell
    1978   Lagos - Urban Development and Employment.
            Geneva: International Labour Office

Hart, Keith
    1973   Informal Income Opportunities and Urban
            Employment in Ghana. Journal of Modern
            African Studies 11(1):61-89

Hong Kong Government
    1985   Hong Kong 1985. Hong Kong: Government
              Printer
    1987   Hong Kong 1987. Hong Kong: Government
              Printer

International Labour Office (ILO)
    1972   Employment, Incomes and Equality: A Strategy
              for Increasing Prodcutive Employment in Kenya.
              Geneva: ILO
    1984   1984 Year Book of Labour Statistics. Geneva: ILO

Joshi, Heather, H. Lubell and J. Moley
    1976   Abidjan. Geneva: ILO

Lands Department
    1983   Town Planning in Hong Kong. Hong Kong:
              Government Printer

Lee, S. Y. and Y. C. Jao
    1982   Financial Structures and Monetary Policiies in
              Southeast Asia. London: MacMillan Press

Lessinger, Johanna
    1985   Nobody Here to Yell at Me: Political Activism
              among Petty Retail Traders in an Indian City. In
              Plattner (ed.) 1985:309-331

Lin, Tsong-biau, Victor Sit and Ying-ping Ho
    1980   Manufactured Exports and Employment in Hong
              Kong. Hong Kong: Chinese University Press

McGee, T. G.
    1973   Hawkers in Hong Kong. Hong Kong: Centre of
              Asian Studies

McGee, T. G. and Y. M. Yeung
    1977   Hawkers in Southeast Asian Citieis. Ottawa:
              IDRC

Nacken, J.
    1968   Chinese Street-Cries in Hong Kong. Journal of
              the Hong Kong Branch of the Royal Asiatic Society
              8:128-134

Plattner, Stuart (ed.)
    1985   Markets and Marketing. Monograph in Economic
              Anthropology, No. 4. Lanham: University Press of
              America

Rabushka, Alvin
    1979   Hong Kong. Chicago: University of Chicago Press

Rogerson, C. M. and K.S.O. Beavon
    1982   Getting by in the Informal Sector of Soweto.
              Journal of Economic & Social Geography
              73(4):250-265

Scott, Alison McEwan
    1979   Who are the Self-Employed? In Bromley & Gerry
              (eds.)

Sit, Victor F. S.
    1981   Post-War Population and its Spatial Dynamics.
              In Sit (ed.)

Sit, Victor F. S. (ed.)
    1981   Urban Hong Kong. Hong Kong: Summerson
              Eastern Pub.

Smart, Josephine
    1983   Dog-Kings, Triads and Hawkers: Spatial
              Monopoly among the Street Hawkers in Hong
              Kong. Canadian Journal of Development
              Studies 8(2):260-279
    1986   The Hawker Permitted Place: a Discussion of the
              Impact of State Policy on Street Hawking in Hong
              Kong. The Asian Journal of Public
              Administration, December 1986
    1987   To Hawk or Not to Hawk: A Discussion of the
              Proliferation of Street Hawking Activities in
              Contemporary Hong Kong. CUSO Journal, The
              Informal Economy, December 1987

Trager, Lillian
    1985   From Yams to Beer in a Nigerian City: Expansion
              and Change in Informal Sector Trade Activity. In
              Plattner (ed.) 1985:259-286

Urban Council Markets and Street Traders Select Committee
   1985   A Consultative Document on Hawkers and Market
          Policies. Hong Kong: Correctional Services
          Industries

6

Resistance to Relocation by Shopkeepers in a Hong Kong Squatter Area[1]

Alan Smart
York University

INTRODUCTION

In this paper, I will discuss the reaction of shopkeepers whose shops are located in squatter structures to a clearance project, that is, the demolition of their shops and homes. Squatter structures, in official usage in Hong Kong, are buildings erected on land to which the occupants do not have legal access or which do not have planning approval. Squatter clearance has a different impact upon such shopkeepers, small industrialists and others who are engaged in self-employment than it does upon those who only live in the squatter area and work elsewhere.

Studies of urban renewal of slum clearance projects have generally found a strong negative impact upon businesses in the area. In one study, 756 out of 2946 firms went out of business, and other studies have found liquidation rates as high as 40% (Anderson 1964:68-69). The problems are not equally distributed among all businesses; marginal low-income merchants are the least likely to survive the dislocation (Berry, Parsons and Platt 1968:xv). These businesses are very often dependent upon local patronage and goodwill, and loss of these resources can be critical for their economic viability (Berry, Parsons and Platt 1968:225, Rothenberg 1967:149, Batley 1982:250). A common reaction to this is to try to re-establish the business in new premises near the old location. One study found that of those businesses relocating, 75% relocated within one mile of the former location, and 40% within one quarter mile (Anderson 1964:70). These businesses usually pay twice as much rent as before, another serious problem for marginal businesses (Anderson 1964:70). Not surprisingly, there was a great deal of disaffection and resentment found among these dislocated business operators (Anderson 1964:70). One of the problems was that businesses were treated differently from families and individuals affected by the redevelopment.

Whereas it was felt that residents must have a place to live, business operators should only be compensated for the impact of the dislocation. Their prospects for survival "must ultimately depend upon the determination and initiative of the individual businessman" (Berry, Parsons and Platt 1968:219).

From October 1983 to April 1985, I studied a clearance which affected about 100 squatter structures, including nineteen shops and three workshops, in Diamond Hill squatter area in Hong Kong. The proprietors of these shops and workshops made considerable efforts to prevent or modify this clearance project. The residents who lived in affected structures but were not business proprietors did not become involved in any collective protest or resistance. This paper will try to explain why only the shopkeepers protested the clearance and why the protest ultimately failed. An examination of these issues leads inevitably into the specifics of the way in which the state intervenes to clear squatter areas and rehouse affected residents, and its differential treatment of those who live in squatter areas and those who own commercial or industrial premises there. To a large extent, the failure of the shopkeepers' protest can be traced to tactical and organizational weaknesses. However, I will argue that even if the shopkeepers had been better organized, they still could not have succeeded in changing the policies which led to their dissatisfaction, although they might have succeeded in resolving their individual problems.

HISTORICAL BACKGROUND

Squatting and Squatter Clearance in Hong Kong

Squatting has been a persistent "problem" throughout the postwar history of Hong Kong. The origins of large-scale illegal occupation of land can be traced to rapid population growth, the influx of refugees from China and the destruction of the housing stock during World War II (Wong 1976, Hopkins 1971, Pryor 1973, Drakakis-Smith 1979). Further obstacles were placed in the way of private development by a rather disorganized colonial reconstruction government which occupied a central position in the land development process (Smart 1986a). What is more important here than the origins of squatting, however, is the way in which subsequent squatting has been modified by the forms of state intervention into this illegal, but tolerated, settlement pattern.

Prior to 1954, attempts were made to prevent all new squatting and eradicate existing squatter settlements. This policy was implemented from the center outwards, so squatter settlements were gradually concentrated in the periphery of the built-up areas. In all but a few cases cleared squatters were expected to shift for themselves. For most, this meant locating in another squatter area, where they would probably rent a tiny cubicle (Annual Report of the Commissioner for Resettlement 1955:35). The year 1954 saw a shift in this pattern, when the Hong Kong Government began the Resettlement Programme. This programme facilitated clearance by resettling squatters into high-density, high-rise public housing estates (Drakakis-Smith 1979). The same period also saw the first registration of squatter structures, where existing structures were surveyed and "tolerated", though not legalized. The policy of toleration involved allowing squatters to remain in registered structures "for the time being", that is, until the land was required for development purposes. When registered squatters were cleared, they would, in most cases, receive some form of government resettlement.

These policies transformed the developmental dynamic of squatter settlements (Smart 1986b). The expectation of resettlement in the event of clearance was capitalized into the cost structure of squatting, and the likelihood of resistance to clearance became tied in with the specific policies on resettlement and compensation. One result of this dynamic is that the Hong Kong Housing Authority is now the landlord for 2.5 million people, 45% of Hong Kong's population (Hong Kong Annual Report 1984:164). Another result is that despite the clearance of at least two million squatters, there were still 480,000 squatters in 1985 (Hong Kong Standard Oct. 25 1985).

Diamond Hill Squatter Area

In 1898, Diamond Hill was a rural agricultural area with a number of tiny villages, located near Kowloon Walled City. Its relatively peripheral location delayed major development until after 1949. Much of the land was privately held, but since it was held on agricultural leases, building could not legally occur without conversion to a building site lease. For various reasons this was almost impossible during the early 1950s, despite considerable effective demand for housing. The result was that various types of structures were illegally built on agricultural land (Smart 1986a). These buildings included elegant mansions, walk-up apartments, factories, and shophouses as well as low-income squatter dwellings. The expansion of low-income squatting, and policy changes which made it apparent that the illegally constructed mansions would never be regularized, led to the out-migration of the rich and the subdivision of their mansions into rooming houses. Gradually, Diamond Hill came to look more like a conventional squatter area. Prior to this expansion, Diamond Hill had no commercial facilities at all; residents had to walk more than a mile to the market in Kowloon City. The post-war increase in population, both in Diamond Hill and newly developed industrial areas in the vicinity, increased demand for consumer products, and the influx of refugees searching for work encouraged many of them to open shops. Many of the shopkeepers discussed in this paper began their businesses during this period.

The physical location of Diamond Hill (see Figure 6.1) encouraged illegal industrial and commercial development in the area (Fung 1968:44). The largest industrial areas in Hong Kong were developed near Diamond Hill, and transport facilities are excellent, including several expressways and a subway station within the neighbourhood. There are now 800 factories in Diamond Hill which is now a community of approximately 30,000 (Wong Tai Sin District Report 1984:42). The concentration of industrial workers nearby provides a good market for merchants in Diamond Hill, particularly in providing cheap meals, and the market street is much better developed than it would be if it only serviced the local residents. Although many of the residential blocks in the neighbouring industrial area, San Po Kong, devote their first floor to retail use, the high concentration of factory workers in the flatted factories (often twenty or more stories high) has meant that there is still more demand for retail services than supply, particularly at peak periods. Illegal hawkers have taken on a major role in providing cooked food. The Diamond Hill merchants do not receive this lunchtime and quick snack business, except for clientele from those factories immediately adjacent to Diamond Hill. Rather, they compete with restaurants and street stalls providing more leisurely meals with tables and chairs for workers with longer lunchtimes, or with split shifts, or for a meal at the end of the shift. They receive many customers after midnight when the evening shift leaves work. Their attractiveness is largely based on their very competitive prices in comparison to legal restaurants where high rents are paid.

Unlike the restaurants, most of the other merchants rely upon business from the local residents. Table 6.1 lists the most common types of shops found in Diamond Hill. All of these types are those generally associated with lower-order service centers (Drakakis-Smith 1971:168) rather than higher-order centers which service larger areas. The range of shops is little different than that found in any local shopping area in Hong Kong, whether in a squatter area or in a legal retailing area,

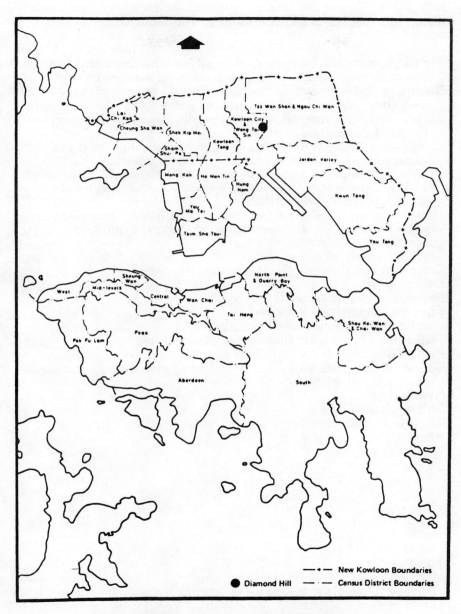

Figure 6.1 Position of Diamond Hill in Hong Kong
(Adapted from Hong Kong 1981 Census)

Table 6.1. Types of Shops Found in Diamond Hill

Mixed good store: Canned goods, soft drinks, beer and Chinese liquor, snacks and candies, soap, mosquito coils, etc.

Riceshop: Bulk rice of various grades and varieties, sometimes also charcoal, bottled propane and kerosene.

Cafe: "Western" menu: coffee, pastries, toast with condensed cream, sandwiches.

Pharmacy: Some sell "Western" drugs and other products commonly found in drugstores such as cosmetics, shampoo, patent medicines, etc. Others sell Chinese medicines. Often a store serves both functions, but with a clear physical demarcation between them.

Hardware shop: Domestic utensils, plasticware, etc.

Building materials: Plywood, cement, fixtures, nails, paint, etc.

Shoestore

Clothing store

Dry goods: Bulk cloth, bedding, notions, etc.

Barber shop

Paper and religious goods

Electrical goods and repairs

Butcher shop: Fresh and frozen meats.

Fish shop: Fresh and frozen fish and shellfish.

Fruitstall

Congee shop: Rice porridge, deep fried pastries, etc. (business primarily in morning)

Noodleshop

Chinese teahouse

Chinese restaurant

Real estate brokerage

except for the absence of banks and jewellery stores. Few
people would travel expressly to Diamond Hill to shop, whereas
many residents must go elsewhere to buy certain types of
goods. However, former residents often buy goods like fresh
vegetables and meat when they return for visits because the
prices are lower than in the relatively high rent
government-controlled markets in the housing estates.

There is a small government regulated market in Diamond
Hill. The range of goods sold is restricted to fresh fruits,
vegetables, meat and fish. Many of these commodities are
purchased in the market rather than from the permanent shops
because the commodities are usually fresher.

SOCIAL AND ECONOMIC ORGANIZATION
OF THE MARKET STREET

The basic unit of the market street is the shophouse, a
structure containing both the shopspace and the dwelling space
of the family running the shop. Commercial enterprises are
clustered on this one street, and the rest of the squatter area is
residential or mixed residential-industrial. (Although there are
a few hawkers who work in the area, the narrowness of the
street and the intensity of the traffic leave them few available
spaces within the main areas of the market street.) Almost all
shopkeepers live above or behind their shop. A number of the
shopkeepers who were affected by the clearance project were
not considered resident by the Housing Department, however.
They had had a shophouse cleared in a previous project and
already had a public housing unit. These shopkeepers in
practice, though, spent most nights sleeping in the shop, while
their children, especially older children, might stay in the public
housing unit. In all the other cases, the shopkeepers' family
lived in the shophouse.

This pattern can be easily understood in relation to the
economic organization of these shops. None of these enterprises
were large, although a few restaurants elsewhere on the
market street have as many as ten employees. In most cases,
there were no non-relatives working in the enterprise and
usually the shop was run by a husband and wife team with
children helping out when not at school or doing their
homework. In some cases, a nephew or cousin worked
full-time and lived in the shophouse. In most of these cases,
this relative held a share in the business as well.

The importance of living in the shophouse is that the
integration of living- and work-space makes possible very
long hours of operation. Many shops, particularly "mixed

goods" shops (selling canned foods, soft-drinks, packaged
snacks, etc.), stay open from 8 a.m. to 10 or 12 p.m. This is
only possible because work-time and leisure-time are
inter-woven. Lunch and dinner are eaten at the back of the
shop, and if a customer comes in, someone will pop up to serve.
When things are slow, the shopkeeper can relax and watch
television. Children can help out for an hour or two after
school. None of these things would be possible if there was a
significant spatial separation between home and workplace, and
in such circumstances maintaining such long hours of operation
would be much more onerous and disruptive to family life.

Most of these shops were marginal but stable. The
shopkeepers make a decent living, and some were even able to
send their children to university, but the average income was
usually no higher than it would be for two unskilled factory
workers. It can be seen, then, that these long hours are
essential to maintaining the viability of the retailing unit.

Business on the market street is not just a matter of
attempting to acquire a particular amount of household income.
It is also a way of life, one which is seen by many of the
shopkeepers as not being particularly lucrative but as having
substantial advantages in terms of lifestyle. They were their
own bosses and if they had to work long hours, they also had
great control over how they spent their time during their
working hours. For most of the shopkeepers, many of whom
had been working in the area for twenty or thirty years, their
shop was not just the way in which they made a living, but
rather their whole lives revolved around it. Shopkeepers in
Diamond Hill are generally not referred to by their real name,
indeed some residents who have known shopkeepers for years
do not even know their name; rather they are usually referred
to by the name of the shop. Thus, if the shop is called "Yi
Gei", then people will say that Yi Gei did something, not that
Mr. Hung or the owner of Yi Gei did it.

The architecture of shops further encourages the
all-engrossing nature of being in business. Shops do not have
doors; instead the whole frontage is a sliding door like a garage
door which is pulled up when the shop is open and leaves the
whole shop exposed to the street. Because of this, it is not
actually necessary to enter the shop in order to talk to the
shopkeeper, who typically sits near the entrance. Most people
who are familiar with the shopkeeper will say hello as they
pass or stop to exchange a few words. Those who are not in a
hurry (like anthropologists!), are often asked to come in and sit
for a while to chat between customers. This makes for a
leisurely and sociable way of doing business, and this in turn
makes it easier to bear long hours of operation. Besides

chatting with customers, there is often ample opportunity to chat with neighbouring shopkeepers.

Most shopkeepers own their stores, and if they do not, the rent is usually very reasonable. This allows them to keep prices down, particularly the restaurants which manage to attract many of their customers because of their low prices, in addition to their proximity to the factory areas.

THE CLEARANCE PROJECT

In August 1983, Housing Department officials registered all occupants of squatter structures in a small portion of Diamond Hill (see Figure 6.2). The project was undertaken in order to produce a firebreak to prevent the spread of fires, a serious problem within the squatter area, and to improve access to the area for Fire Department vehicles. The construction of firebreaks in all squatter areas expected to remain in existence for at least five more years is part of the Squatter Area Improvements Project (Housing Authority Annual Report 1982/83:87-88).

In the case of Diamond Hill, the clearance affected the north side of the market street and one residential lane in Sheung Yuen Ling and a residential area in Man Kuk New Village, which is farther up the hill. My study was restricted to the Sheung Yuen Ling clearances.

What attracted my attention to this clearance were the vehement protests made by the shopkeepers. The clearance was originally scheduled to occur by December 1983, but was eventually delayed to April 1984 because of the protests. A number of modifications were also made in the specifics of the clearance in order to meet some of the demands of the shopkeepers. Shortly after the clearance registration, a number of shopkeepers and two workshop operators who were affected started talking among themselves about the clearance and agreed upon their opposition to it. Most of the affected business operators became involved, at least to the extent of attending one or two of the meetings. The most active participants did not differ in any obvious way from the others who were sympathetic, even if they were not as actively involved. One factor was the degree of apathy or cynicism: the activists seemed to have a somewhat stronger belief that protests could achieve something. In addition, the most active seem to have had a great deal of personal interest in avoiding a clearance, although many of the others did as well. One, for

128

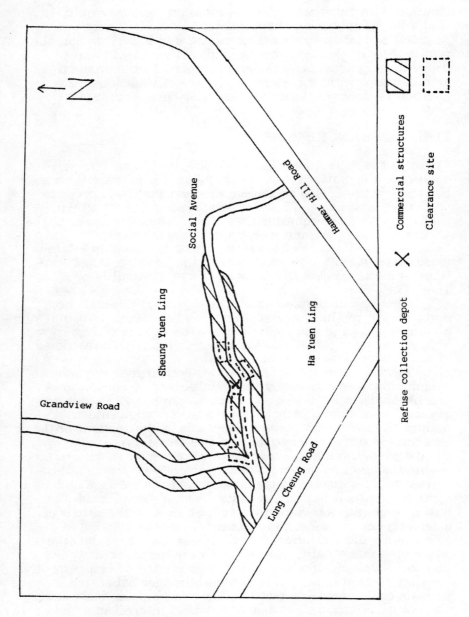

Figure 6.2 Location of the clearance in Diamond Hill

example, had just bought a second shop next door with intentions of expanding. Another shopkeeper's family had lived in the Diamond Hill area for at least one hundred years and he felt a particularly strong personal attachment to the area. There does not seem to have been any clear differences between those who were most active and the others in terms of the size of their operation, types of commodities sold, or social and educational backgrounds. Interestingly, all but one of the most active business operators planned to re-establish their businesses in the same area.

The shopkeepers approached a number of local leaders for support, These local leaders approached the District Office with their complaints, which assisted the shopkeepers in setting up meetings with some officials from the Housing Department.

These shopkeepers stressed, at the initial meetings and on many subsequent occasions, the economic costs of clearance. They also did not think that it was fair that they were to be relocated now to build a firebreak when the whole area was going to be cleared within a few years according to government plans. They argued at first that the whole clearance should be cancelled. This most radical demand was apparently dropped after the first meeting with the officials, but the desire for complete cancellation was still expressed privately until the clearance actually occurred. A District Office official told me that at this first meeting, the shopkeepers were convinced of the necessity for the clearance. It seems rather to have been the case that the shopkeepers were convinced that they would be unable to achieve this most basic of their demands, and they were intimidated by the officials and their technical presentation of the reasons for the "necessity" of clearance although they weren't convinced by this. The shopkeepers were also persuaded by their political supporters to make more "reasonable" demands which would be more likely to receive support.

The shopkeepers also questioned why the firebreak had to be positioned where it was and not, for example, in Ha Yuen Leng (farther south) or further east on Diamond Road where primarily residential structures would have been affected. All that the Housing Department officials would say was that this location was what their advisor had recommended, and they refused to explain the reasoning behind it. It will be necessary to examine the plans and the implementation of the project in some detail to demonstrate that these technical explanations do not actually account for what occurred.

One of the major justifications given for the building of the firebreak along the main road of Diamond Hill was that it would allow Fire Department vehicles to enter the area more easily in case of a fire, as well as the larger open space reducing the risk of a fire spreading uncontrollably. However, an examination of Figure 6.2 will show that the road-widening only involved an interior stretch of the road. Major bottlenecks would persist at either end of the widened section. In fact, the worst bottleneck of all, at the junction of Grandview Road and Social Avenue, would remain unaltered. This part of the road (barely ten feet wide at the junction) was always terribly congested at peak times, both before and after the project's completion. Just to <u>walk</u> the fifty feet from Lung Cheung Road to the junction could take ten minutes of squeezing past the almost immobile goods trucks and stepping through the front part of the shops on this stretch of the road. Either there was never an intention to truly improve access and this was just a spurious argument to convince the shopkeepers of the project's necessity, or something occurred during the pre-planning to change their intentions. The completed project further illustrates this. Rather than the cleared space being used as a wider road, traffic control fences allowed access for pedestrians but not vehicles. That is, it became only a firebreak and did not serve to improve access of Fire Department vehicles, although to improve such access would have greatly facilitated the capability for firefighting in the area.

If the clearance was only to serve as a firebreak, there seems to be no technical reason that it had to be at this specific location. Squatter Area Improvements Division policy is to divide squatter areas into blocks of about 8000 inhabitants, using firebreaks within which the fire would hopefully be contained. This project did not succeed in doing so, and to build it at another position would seem to have been just as effective. A survey indicated that the majority of those who lived in a squatter structure but did not have a shop or workshop there were quite happy to be relocated into public housing, and there was little protest from these residents other than for individual reasons of eligibility and so on. The shopkeepers, however, were another matter. Almost all preferred to remain if given a choice and many put in considerable efforts to cancel or modify the project. Therefore, a clearance at a purely residential site would have benefitted more people who desired public housing, inconvenienced fewer people, and resulted in less or no protest against it.

The shopkeepers also noted that choice of what structures were to be cleared seemed arbitrary. Figure 6.2 shows that the site is not regular. In addition, most of the affected structures had been there at least fifteen years, whereas on the south side of Social Avenue, many of the structures had been rebuilt ten years before after a fire and encroached upon what had previously been the surface of the road. The shopkeepers argued that these newer structures should be cleared first and also suggested that these newer structures constituted more of a fire hazard. In private, these shopkeepers informed me that one of the most powerful local politicans had himself illegally built those structures and sold some and rented out others. He continues to collect rent and would obviously prefer not to lose this source of income. The shopkeepers suggest that this politician convinced the government to build on the north side of Social Avenue, and failed to effectively help them, despite a pretense, because of his own personal interests.

In an interview with an official in the Squatter Area Improvements Division, I was given another interpretation of the decision to clear the north side of the street and not the south side. The newer structures on the south side of the street are on Crown Land, but this stretch of Crown Land is only ten feet wide and immediately behind it is private land. On the north side, however, there were about twenty feet of Crown Land. This official argued that since this ten foot strip was not wide enough for the plans, if it was taken it would still be necessary to clear the north side as well. It was better, therefore, to disrupt only one side of the market street.

The shopkeepers were unsuccessful in either having the clearance cancelled or in having the site for the firebreak moved elsewhere so that it would not affect them. They did, however, manage to get the clearance postponed for five months until April 1984. One of the pretexts for the delay was that the clearance should be postponed until at least after Chinese New Year so that they could be allowed to sell off their stocks. Other than the practical economic reasons for this, there is a Chinese belief that it is unlucky to move or close a business before New Year. The shopkeepers had as much of a social and emotional tie to their shops as a practical one, and it would have added to their psychological trauma to lose both their homes and their livelihoods just before Chinese New Year.

The shopkeepers' protest and negotiation shifted at this time to a much less radical demand which accepted the inevitability of the clearance, but which would allow many of the most active shopkeepers to reduce the economic disruption caused by the clearance. The shops of several shopkeepers extended past the land upon which the government was planning to construct the firebreak, but the whole of any structure affected was planned to be cleared. They requested that they be allowed to retain occupation of any space not required for the fifteen foot road extension. The shopkeepers believed that they could maintain some kind of business in the space that they would retain, which in some cases would still be fifteen or twenty feet deep. The Housing Department officials responded that this had never been done in the past, and they didn't wish to set a precedent. This situation aroused considerable moral indignation on the part of some of the shopkeepers. One of them explained it to me in the following manner: He was very annoyed that although the government didn't need all of his premises, they were not willing to let him continue to use the unaffected portions, resulting in him having to close up his business. He made an analogy to the situation. He said it was like the government having a banquet at his expense, and he was willing to let them eat as much as they wanted, but they wouldn't even let him have the leftovers. Although he continued to be active in the protests, he professed pessimism about the chance of success.

Regardless of such pessimism, political lobbying continued, including writing letters in Chinese and English to the highest officials in the Housing Department and the Housing Authority. As far as I know, there was never any publicly acknowledged decision to allow the shopkeepers to keep the extra space, but by February or March, a number of the most active shopkeepers had been personally informed that they would be allowed to keep the extra space. I believe that this was done during the assessment of the compensation to be paid for the commercial and industrial space (which is treated differently than residential space). This served to personalize or individuate the negotiation process: the change was thus presented not as a concession in response to collective response, but as a re-evaluation of individual cases. After this, the shopkeeper's protests gradually died out, and by the time of the actual clearance, there was no sign that there had ever been any opposition to the construction of a firebreak on the north side of the street.

The coalition of shopkeepers ultimately fell apart once the government conceded on some minor issues: the delay which allowed the shopkeepers time to sell off their stocks and make personal arrangements, and allowing a number of the politically active the continued use of their space which was not needed for the firebreak. These were very minor concessions, yet they were apparently successful in defusing this protest, because they went some of the way towards reducing the economic costs experienced by some of those who were most opposed to the clearance. Certain characteristics of those protesting and their organizational efforts also contributed to the failures. These shopkeepers used traditional forms of political lobbying in their protest, and were clearly uneasy in adopting a confrontational stance towards government officials. Traditional forms of politeness alone contributed to reducing their effectiveness in negotiation because they tended to avoid openly contradicting the officials who met with them when these officials concluded that "something was impossible". In doing so, they gave the appearance of agreeing on points that they had had no intention of conceding. Furthermore, they made no attempts to find allies among the domestic residents affected by the clearance or among various pressure groups which might have helped. Some thought that all of the domestic residents were happy with the clearance, but although others realized that some were unhappy with the clearance, there was no effort to locate such people and cooperate with them in a protest. This made it impossible for them to effectively contest the clearance itself, since the government could present it as being in the interest of the community and opposed only by a few self-interested merchants.

Shops are treated differently than domestic structures in squatter clearances. Domestic residents are given rehousing as compensation (unless they own the land, in which case they also receive compensation based on the resumption procedure). The type of rehousing (permanent or temporary rehousing) depends upon their household characteristics. Shopkeepers are also subject to these procedures if resident, but their shopspace (i.e. the portion of their dwelling used for business as opposed to that used for residential purposes) is compensated through a separate procedure. Those shopkeepers who reside elsewhere receive compensation for commercial space only. Commercial shops receive "ex-gratia" compensation at the rate of HK$120 per sq. ft. for the first hundred sq. ft. and $48 per sq. ft. after than,. with no ceiling. Workshops receive HK$12,000 for the first 50 to 200 sq. ft. and HK$60 a sq. ft. thereafter, with no compensation if the area is less than 50 sq. ft. (Diamond Hill Development Study 1983:para. 12.13).

A fascinating outcome of the clearance was reinvestment in a position near the old shop in a majority of cases. Of 19 operating shops which were cleared, I discovered that nine had reopened conventional shops in the area, while two did less conventional business hawking on the street, and one was planning to reopen until he was killed in an accident. I discovered no instances where a shopkeeper set up a shop in another area, although there were several shopkeepers with whom I lost touch. In some cases, the compromise which allowed them to retain the extra space was sufficient to allow them to maintain operations, although in less space. In other cases, the shopkeepers bought up shops on the south side of the market street. There was a marked increase in the price of commercial space at this time: several shops with little more than 100 sq. ft. sold for HK$100,000 each.

The reasons for re-establishing their businesses in the market street rather than setting up shop elsewhere were the cheap rents, the importance of custom and goodwill, and social attachment to the area. One of the activist families had a particularly good reason for wanting to stay in Diamond Hill. They sold various sacrificial items and other more mundane paper products. The husband was a master of elaborate custom-made paper objects for various ceremonies, primarily funerals and memorial services. Most of this business was directed to him by a nunnery in Diamond Hill which carried out many such ceremonies. If they had set up business in another location, they would have lost access to this trade and replacing it would be very difficult without the appropriate connections.

Renting shops in public housing estates and other conventional commercial areas was seen as being prohibitively expensive, and was not considered to be a viable alternative to re-establishment in the squatter area. These shopkeepers didn't set up businesses in other squatter areas because they would lose access to the regular customers which they had built up over years. In addition, their social networks gave them easier access to commercially viable properties in Diamond Hill than in any other squatter area.

Finally, a major part of the motivation in re-establishing businesses in the market street seems to have been social. One case should serve to illustrate this. Mr. and Mrs. Hung were extremely upset about moving to a public housing estate two miles away. Despite being in their late sixties, they both found ways to return to the market on a daily basis. Mrs. Hung illegally set up a tiny stall, about two feet by six feet, selling incense as she had before. It is unlikely that she went back into business primarily for economic reasons. Her business was so marginal that it may not have paid for her daily busfare. What was more important was that it allowed her to remain a part of the social life of the market street, a social life apart from which she had little identity. Mr. Hung's younger brother's son had a small grocery shop on the other end of the market street, and he went there every day to help out, although there was usually very little that he could do that the nephew couldn't handle. In any case, he felt useful and was happy to remain in contact with all of his old friends.

The re-establishment caused certain problems, given the importance of integration of workplace and home, as argued above. In some cases, this led to an effective splitting of the household or to exhausting commuting time on top of long hours of work. In one family, the wife complained that managing home and work was much harder now as she had to make several trips each day between the two locations. The husband often slept on a bench in the tiny shop and saw little of his children.

In another case, the husband wished to resume business, but his grown children, who worked in professional and clerical occupations, opposed the plan. They argued that their parents didn't need the income. They also feared, I suspect, that they would come under pressure to resume helping with the shop, which had previously stayed open at least 15 hours a day.

A common solution to the problem of home-work separation was not only to set up a new business, but also to take up residence there. A family which ran a small plastics workshop bought a new shop near their old location. The husband and wife spent almost all of their time and most nights at the workshop, but the children stayed at the new public housing unit, only occasionally coming to visit and help out in production. This situation led to the effective splitting of the household.

CONCLUSION

In order to understand the way in which residents of Diamond Hill reacted to the clearance, it is necessary to take into consideration the relationship between them and the community, the specific features of squatter clearance policy, and the economic organization of small retailing enterprises.

At least some portion of the resistance to the clearance project by the shopkeepers seems to have been based upon social and emotional attachment to Diamond Hill. This attachment is not just to Diamond Hill as a residential community but also to doing business in the market street, not just as a livelihood, but also as a way of life. This is particularly clear in those cases where there was no financial need to resume business operations, and no significant economic benefit from doing so.

The economics of marginal retail businesses in Hong Kong mean that if a decision is made to resume operations, it is almost essential for the shopkeepers to live in the shop. The costs of home-workplace separation are often sufficient to render the business nonviable. Thus, a decision to resume the business will usually lead to a reproduction of the shophouse pattern, a pattern which is also conducive to making business a rather pleasant way of life rather than just an activity engaged in solely for reasons of profit.

Although it is important, it is not possible to explain the reaction of the shopkeepers solely by reference to their attachment to business as a way of life. It is not only the shopkeepers who have social and emotional ties to the community. In a survey of 156 households in Diamond Hill, nearly 13% preferred staying in their home to resettlement in any of a range of public housing estates. However, no significant resistance to clearance by domestic residents developed in this case, suggesting that emotional ties are not sufficient in themselves to generate protest. Although there has been such resistance in other clearances, these protests can be traced to different resettlement policies which had previously prevailed (Smart 1986c: Chapter 8.). In a 1968 survey, 75% of the owners of commercial establishments in Diamond Hill favoured resettlement, while only 60% of domestic residents favoured it (Fung 1968:35). This is a complete reversal of the present situation in which generally domestic residents favour clearance and shopkeepers oppose it. This change is presumably not due to changes in the nature of shopkeepers but should rather be traced to policy changes in the intervening years. In 1968 cleared shopkeepers were given a shop in a public housing estate at a very reasonable rent. Now, however, cleared shopkeepers have no special rights to commercial space in public housing estates and must bid on the open market if they want to open a shop. At present, commercial rents are extremely high.

Although the failure of the shopkeeper's protest can be traced to tactical and organizational factors, there are also fundamental structural reasons which constrain the possibilities of success of any such protest. Although they could, if well organized enough, possibly postpone or get a particular project shifted to another location it would be almost impossible for them to achieve the change of the basic policies (no relocation in a public housing estate shopspace at a "reasonable" rent) which are likely to encourage shopkeepers to oppose squatter clearance projects.

Policy on commercial rents is a crucial aspect of the current budgeting of the Housing Authority. In 1983-84, there was a deficit from domestic properties of HK$189 million (Housing Authority 1985:5), while there was a surplus from non-domestic properties of HK$359.5 million. 79% of the revenue from non-domestic properties is from shops (Housing Authority Annual Report 1983/84:118). Thus, high rents from commercial properties are a major factor in making possible the avoidance of huge deficits in the current accounts. (It should be noted that high rents for shops must eventually be paid for by public housing tenants in the form of higher prices for commodities.) Given the more limited nature of public support for merchants than for wage-earning squatters, the chances that even well-organized squatter shopkeepers could have these policies changed are rather minimal.

The tenacity with which the shopkeepers protested the clearance and tried to resume their businesses in the same area was not simply a result of their social and emotional attachment to their community and business as a way of life. It also resulted from changes in clearance policy which make it much more detrimental to their interests, and from high market rents for commercial premises which make it nearly impossible for them to re-establish their business in conventional commercial areas.

NOTES

1. The research upon which this article is based was made possible by a Research Fellowship provided by Emergency Planning Canada from 1983-1986, and by the kind cooperation of the residents of Diamond Hill.

REFERENCES CITED

Anderson, M.
1964   The Federal Bulldozer.

Batley, R.
1982   Urban Renewal and Expulsion in Sao Paulo. In A. Gilbert (ed.) Urbanization in Contemporary Latin America. Pp. 231-261. John Wiley and Sons: Chichester.

Berry, B.J.L., S. J. Parsons and R. H. Platt
1968   The Impact of Urban Renewal on Small Business. Chicago: Centre for Urban Studies.

Commissioner for Resettlement
1955   Annual Report.

Diamond Hill Development Study
1983   Consultant's Report

Drakakis-Smith, D. W.
1971   The Hinterlands of Towns in the New Territories. In D. J. Dwyer (ed.) Asian Urbanization pp.167-181. Hong Kong: Hong Kong University Press.

1979   High Society: Housing Provision in Hong Kong.
          Hong Kong: Centre of Asian Studies.

Fung, B.C.K.
1968   Diamond Hill Area: A Geographical Study of a
          Squatter Area. An Unpublished B.A. dissertation,
          Dept. of Geography, University of Hong Kong.

Housing Authority
1983   Annual Report 1982/83.

Hong Kong Government
1984   Annual Report.

Hopkins, K.
1971   Housing the Poor. In K. Hopkins (ed.) Hong Kong:
          The Industrial Colony. Pp.271-335 Hong Kong:
          Oxford University Press.

Pryor, E. G.
1973   Housing in Hong Kong. Hong Kong: Oxford
          University Press.

Rothenberg, J.
1967   Economic Evaluation of Urban Renewal.
          Washington: Brookings Institute.

Smart, A.
1986a   The Development of Diamond Hill from Village to
          Squatter area: A Perspective on Public Housing.
          Asian Journal of Public Administration
          8(1):43-63.
1986b   Invisible Real Estate: Investigations into the
          Squatter Property Market. International Journal
          of Urban and Regional Research 10(1):29-45.
1986c   The Political Economy of Squatter Clearance in
          Hong Kong. Unpublished Ph.D. dissertation,
          Dept. of Anthropology, University of Toronto.

Wong, A.W.F.
1976   Implementation of the Resettlement Programme.
          In G. U. Iglesias (ed.) Implementation. Pp. 268-
          308 Manila: EROPA.

Wong Tai Sin District Board
1984   District Report 1984

7

Trader vs. Developer: The Market Relocation Issue in an Indian City

Johanna Lessinger
Columbia University

INTRODUCTION

To read the anthropological literature on India is to gain the impression that the country lacks the linked regional marketing systems, the urban market places and the occupational groups of traders which loom large in studies of West Africa, Latin America, the Caribbean and Southeast Asia. Despite India's huge peasant population and vast cities, such markets and such traders are mentioned only in passing in Indianist literature; they are rarely the primary focus of study. This peculiar neglect seems to be a byproduct of the intensely idealist bent of most of those who study India--a bent leading to an emphasis on the study of village communities, caste organization and symbolic systems, rather than on urban areas, on occupational groups or on economic and political relations.

One of the purposes of this paper, then, is to reassert the economic and social centrality of such markets in India, particularly in the towns and cities where markets are major public amenities for all classes. From the point of view of the urban economy, petty trading in established market places is an unusually stable source of work within the informal sector, employing many of the urban poor. This paper, however, approaches the problem from a different angle, pointing to the fact that markets in India are frequently contested terrain.

Thus Indian markets need study because they are crucial institutions in any examination of urban growth processes and urban political systems, because they are the locus of political organizing and political struggle. Manuel Castells has argued that cities are in part shaped by the grassroots struggles for neighborhood control in which their inhabitants engage (1983). This seems particularly applicable in the case of petty traders in the large south Indian city of Madras, whose unsung and unrecorded history of creating markets and of defending their selling spots against would-be developers has helped to shape the physical and social face of the city.

Using case material drawn from field work in the central fresh produce wholesale market and in eleven retail produce markets in Madras,[1] this paper outlines a situation of prolonged unrest and conflict. During the British colonial period Madras emerged from its status as a collection of traders' warehouses and fishing villages to become a major port, and the region's administrative and political center. Today, although facing competition from Bangalore and from the new port at Vizagapatnam, Madras remains one of the largest Indian cities, outstripped only by Bombay, Delhi and Calcutta. For at least twenty years traders in most major market places of this bustling city, capital of the state of Tamilnadu, have found themselves in opposition to city authorities and to sectors of the city's bourgeoisie over real estate development which threatens to displace and destroy markets. Over the past ten years this conflict has intensified under the pressures of Madras' capitalist urban development. Indian leftists now speak of "two Indias," one Western-oriented, technocratic, and involved in a modern world capitalist order and one impoverished, "traditional" and incorporated primarily into local capitalist relations. These market-based conflicts are one of the arenas in which the two Indias come face to face. Petty retailers (essentially part of the city's working class[2]) and unWesternized, petty bourgeois wholesalers are pitted against a property-owning elite with vastly greater resources and political clout.

In Madras natural population increase, a steady influx of rural migrants, a growing tendency among the bourgeoisie to invest in urban real estate rather than agricultural land and the recent massive injection of remittance capital from abroad have increased the competition for urban working and living space. The efforts of the state government under the late Chief Minister M.G. Ramachandran to increase the city and state industrial base and to boost the tourist industry have also had their effect. Today new shops, office buildings, blocks of expensive apartments and enormous new hotels are going up everywhere. Traffic congestion is more extreme than it ever was. It is very much in the interests of the bourgeoisie to push existing market places out of their central locations. In part these markets are often dirty, smelly and a source of major traffic jams. More critically, however, the sites they occupy can be put to other, more profitable, uses. In the dispersal or relocation of markets, traders risk being deprived of their very livelihood, since the work they do is highly dependent on location--the same kind of central location amidst the flow of commerce, pedestrian traffic and transportation routes which makes the real estate valuable in the first place. It is no suprise that traders have countered attempts to remove them with vehement resistance and political organizing.

My contention, therefore, is that market relocation (like slum clearance), and the resulting opposition, are integral to the process of India's urban capitalist development itself. In Madras clashes between traders and officialdom do not stem from objections to the kind of people traders are, nor from official attempts to regulate food prices and distribution. Retail produce traders, visibly poor themselves, cannot be seriously regarded as major profiteers. Nor are these market-based conflicts caused by official attempts to clean up or reorganize the city; instead a "neat and clean" rhetoric, stressing the dirt, disorder and traffic disruption of markets, is an ideology invoked to justify and to win middle-class support for market clearance attempts. This "neat and clean" view of the world is increasingly espoused by the city's Westernized professional middle class, which, under the influence of foreign travel and overseas immigration now often makes explicit comparisons between Western European cities and Indian cities. This view is obviously not shared by Madras' poor. Rather, they see the public street as a legitimate extension of their own cramped and unsanitary housing and work places. They firmly believe that their right to earn a living on the public thoroughfare takes precedence over aesthetic considerations, even over bourgeois conceptions of private property ownership. These opposed visions of cities and city markets highlight the class nature of much market conflict, but they are not its root cause.

When examined in detail, these conflicts can be seen for what they are: deep-seated struggles over the control and use of urban space--space which is now a commodity growing steadily scarcer and more valuable every year. In this process the state, acting through the police, the courts and the city administration, tends to side with property owners and with would-be developers who want to appropriate the often sizeable patches of real estate on which existing markets are located. Owners of private markets would like to use those same sites for housing or offices.

Likewise, the sites of municipal markets and illegal street markets offer interesting possibilities for bold, unscrupulous entrepreneurs with the right connections to acquire and develop public land or land whose ownership is unclear or disputed. As in many Western cities, the dividing line in Madras between public and private land has not always been firmly drawn: the politically powerful seem always to have had access to some public land, either for their own use or for distribution to their clients as house sites. Thus the transformation of public land into private property is an ongoing process. In that process, traders are frequently simply posing a counter-claim. They insist that they have prior rights to market property because they have used it for a long time.

Over the years traders, usually with the backing of political parties or particular politicians, have often been able to hold their own. They have been able to keep particular markets from being dispersed or relocated to obscure, out-of-the-way sites. They have even gotten some once-illegal markets legalized. Market landlords have been forced--temporarily--to leave their trader tenants alone. Given the power disparities, these have been significant victories, but they have rarely been permanent. City authorities and politicians, mindful of their property-owning constituents, are unwilling or unable to legalize all markets, to establish permanent tenancy protection for all marketers. Perhaps some of this inability is actually reluctance, stemming from the fact that there is political advantage (as well as political headache) to be had from a permanent state of market instability and precarious legality. Fragmentary evidence from other Indian towns and cities suggests that similar conflicts over the location of markets are being replicated elsewhere in the country. Sarin (1979), for instance, describes political controversy over the location of petty trading and attempts at forcible relocation in the north Indian city of Chandigarh. In 1986 the Madras press reported that the towns of Srirangam and Tiruchi in provincial Tamilnadu had both relocated their once-central markets to out-of-the-way locations. Traders had promptly abandoned their new markets and the authorities plaintively wondered why (Indian Express 1986). Although the newspaper account emphasizes the empty official market places and neglects to say where actual trading is now carried on, it is likely that each market has reformed more or less spontaneously, somewhere near its original location, soon to present these municipalities with further difficulties. Who, one wonders, is now building on the real estate vacated when these markets were relocated?

These market disputes have very clear parallels with the forcible slum clearance which has facilitated the construction of luxury housing blocks and hotels in Bombay and Delhi as both cities experience development booms even more vigorous than that in Madras. Given the balance of political power in most Indian city administrations, and the absence of definitive political resolutions to the underlying conflicts of interest, market relocation disputes, like the disputes over slum clearance, are likely to remain a permanent feature of Indian urban growth for some time. Indeed, anecdotal evidence from many other places in the world suggest that the process is typical of cities everywhere at certain stages of their development.

In Madras these confrontations have, over the years, run the gamut from pitched battles between traders and the police to long-drawn-out court cases between private market owners and trader tenants. Traders, despite their less powerful class positions, have certain public relations weapons at hand in such conflicts which make outright repression politically risky. They have the advantage of market organizations, which can lead their members in demonstrations, petition drives and bloc voting for the parties and candidates which offer protection and support to embattled markets. In the 1960s, when some of these confrontations were violent, the fear of civil disorder obviously pressured city authorities to resolve, or at least defuse, these situations.

Traders enjoy a further advantage in the realm of purely symbolic political discourse. Tamilnadu is a state in which all three major political parties--the All-India Anna Dravida Munnetra Kazhagham (AIADMK), the Dravida Munnetra Kazhagham (DMK) and the Congress Party--have been dominated by the rhetoric of populism for some 30 years (Hardgrave 1965; Barnett 1976). Retail traders in particular can play upon their role as one of the most highly visible sectors of the urban working poor. Traders constantly dramatize this role through the flags, political portraits and party colors with which many markets adorn themselves. When a market is under attack traders can invoke their collective public persona as representatives of "the people," humble working people trying to hold onto their only means of making a meager, respectable living. When the crusade to move a market hinges on the cleanliness argument (with its added overtones of ritual impurity in a pollution-conscious society), traders agree fervently that the market is dirty, and proceed to demand that it be improved. "We are poor, but we are decent," a Zam Bazaar leader snapped as he recapitulated the arguments he had employed in trying to get the city health department to move against the woman market owner. She had cut off the water supply and removed the cleaning crew in the market in retaliation for traders' refusal to pay higher rents.

Trader resistance to relocation is also possible because there is widespread public recognition that markets provide an important urban service, offering convenient locations, low overhead costs and competitive structure to keep inexpensive food available to consumers.[3] In addition, produce retailers, operating from temporary stalls or from mats on the ground, are usually welcome to bazaar shop owners. Shopkeepers see the fruit and vegetable marketers not as competitors or as nuisances who lower the tone of a neighborhood, but as valuable adjuncts whose presence makes commercial areas busier, "hotter" and thus more attractive to consumers. This tolerance is possible because bazaar shopkeepers, paying relatively high rent for permanent stores, rarely deal in vegetables and fruit; they are delighted to leave the sale of these risky, perishable, low-profit items to others. This reservoir of public support for retail markets means that they are less easily dislocated and scattered than many slum communities which have been similarly uprooted in the large cities of north India.

MADRAS' MARKETS

In Madras, produce retail trading represents a relatively stable informal sector occupation which unskilled men and women, recent rural immigrants and long-time city dwellers alike, can enter fairly easily. Little initial cash capital is needed and trade can profitably utilize the labor of all family members as well as the social capital embodied in kinship and regional networks. In 1971-73, some two-thirds of the 250-odd retailers interviewed were rural migrants, former small tenant farmers, agricultural workers or artisans who had left their villages because farming no longer yielded them an adequate living. Members of more prosperous rural agricultural families find comparable advantages in the urban wholesale trade. They or their families have capital to invest in an urban commerce in agricultural products; their influential social networks encompass the potential suppliers in their districts. At both the wholesale and retail levels traders express a keen awareness that trade offers otherwise-unavailable work opportunities in a city where un- and underemployment are rife at virtually every level (Lessinger 1985, 1986).

One of the particular appeals of market trading in Madras is the fact that rapid urban growth has helped to make the occupation at present a relatively open one. It is not controlled by any particular caste or ethnic group. As the city continues to grow through rural in-migration, it needs more markets and more traders to serve a population which has swelled from almost 1.5 million in 1951 to around 2.5 million in 1981 and an estimated 5 million in 1986. Much of the growth has been created by shifts in the regional economy. A transition to capital-intensive forms of agriculture continues to drive small farmers and landless laborers out of the villages and into the

city looking for work. Urban entrepreneurs have filled the
city's outskirts and mushrooming suburbs with small factories,
although first-generation migrants of the kind who enter petty
trading rarely have the skills or contacts needed to get factory
work. In addition Tamil refugees from Sri Lanka have flooded
into the city since 1983. Those who are poor simply add to the
congestion. The wealthy among them have considerable capital
to invest.

Sheer increase in the city population and a steady
expansion of the city limits has created a demand for new
markets and more traders. Thus a heterogeneous, multicaste
group of workers is drawn into two linked occupations which
still offer room for newcomers (Lessinger 1976). What unites
traders of particular market places are on-the-spot cooperation
and a common class position. What traders have not yet
developed is a political unity which might bind several markets
together to oppose neighborhood redevelopment.

The Central Wholesale Market

The city's central wholesale market, called Kottuwal
Chavadi, is located in a warren of small eighteenth century
streets in George Town, the city's oldest section. At the area's
core is a 900-stall market place of small sheds with platforms
in front of them, which fills the equivalent of a large city block.
This market was originally constructed by the Shri Kanyaka
Parameswari temple as a retail market for public use, probably
in the eighteenth century. It has been extended repeatedly,
most recently sometime between the 1920s and the 1940s. The
temple houses the caste deity of a group of Chettiar merchants;
the temple was their special preserve. Today some remain in
the area's jewelry and wholesale businesses. None engage in
selling in the produce wholesale market. The profit levels are
too low for a group which is now wealthy and influential. Some
Chettiars retain real estate in the area, however.

Over the years the original retail market gradually took on
more and more wholesale functions, and is now entirely
dominated by wholesale dealers who advance money to
cultivators in return for rights to an entire crop. These small,
family-operated firms generally work on commission, remitting
the sale price to farmers after the produce has been resold to
retailers. In the city the Kottuwal Chavadi wholesalers act as
the major source of supply for fresh produce. Retail traders
from all over the city travel to the market almost daily to buy
sacks and baskets of goods. These are transported to local
markets for resale to consumers, and to commercial and
institutional kitchens. Those traders who, by virtue of

inheritance, bribery or subleases, have shops within the old temple market, still pay relatively low rents for the space they occupy. These low rents, which nevertheless brought the devasthanam (temple trustees) a healthy Rs. 100,000 a month in 1972, continue to trouble the temple managers. Much of the conflict within this section of Kottuwal Chavadi over the past twenty years comes from devasthanam attempts to extract higher rents from the wholesalers.

The growth in the city's wholesale business, paralleling the city's own growth, has caused Kottuwal Chavadi's activities to spill out of the old market place to engulf surrounding streets. Many of the one-, two- and three-storied buildings on Badrian, Malayaperumal, Anna Pillai and Audiyappa Naicker Streets house wholesalers' combined shop-warehouses. These were once private residences; a few merchants still live in them but most are given over to the commission agents' commercial transactions and storage. Many of those with rental space inside the temple market also lease additional warehouse space in surrounding streets, a fact which helps bind the whole area into a single economic unit. Political issues in this area of the wholesale district usually involve questions of street blockage and police harassment.

In the early 1970s Kottuwal Chavadi adjoined a flourishing general purpose outdoor retail area known as China Bazaar, where one could buy everything from plastic soap dishes to smuggled watches and transistor radios. By 1986 China Bazaar had grown vastly. Moore Market, once a competing bazaar building some distance away, had burned down some years earlier and had never been replaced. Those who once worked in Moore Market have relocated to the Kottuwal ChavadiChina Bazaar area. Living amidst this densely-packed commercial concentration are large numbers of the city's street dwellers, who sleep on shop porches and steps at night and find casual portering work there during the day. The area also harbors liquor shops and a good deal of prostitution, so that its nighttime reputation is unsavory.

Despite its deteriorated physical state, Kottuwal Chavadi has survived thanks to its central location, at the junction of several major roads, near the law courts and the harbor, near several major bus terminuses, train stations and suburban rail lines. The transport links in particular are crucial to the market's functioning and existence, since produce comes in from the countryside by bus, by train, and increasingly by truck and leaves again, in the hands of retailers, by bus, truck and cycle rickshaw. The same locational advantages have attracted other businesses and wholesale concentrations as well. Interspersed with the produce wholesalers' shops in the streets around the temple market are wholesale areas devoted to papermaking, printing, the sale of fertilizers, jewelry and metal utensils, the offices of shipping agents and truckers.

This kind of physical concentration among wholesale trades remains essential to the way local commerce works. All merchants dealing in a particular product need to be in close proximity to their competitors, if only to judge the flow of supply and demand and to make contact with new suppliers. In fact there is a great deal of cooperation between competitors, ranging from mutual loans to price fixing. For retailers who buy from the commission agents the concentration is also essential, since they can obtain all the various vegetables or fruits they need for a well-stocked retail stall in one shopping expedition. Moving between adjacent wholesale shops they have some chance to lower prices by playing off one wholesaler against another.

Since the late 1960s, city officials, sometimes in cooperation with the Sri Kanyaka Parameshwari devasthanam, have advanced several schemes to relocate or rebuild Kottuwal Chavadi. Merchants have steadily resisted these efforts. In part they knew that any relocation would disrupt the elaborate system of tenancy, subtenancy and sub-subtenancy that exists within the old market, formally unrecognized by the devasthanam. Both those who have inherited stalls which they rent to others and those who hold some form of sub-tenancy stand to lose if the present socio-spatial arrangement is ended. Merchants also know that the proffered new sites, on the city periphery, cannot provide the same advantageous access to major transportation routes. In addition many of the early plans involved splitting up the single concentration of wholesalers among several wholesale centers, thus destroying a crucial aspect of the market's economic organization.[4]

However, the intense crowding of the area had, by the 1980s, gone to the point of no return. Roads that might, by courtesy, have been called paved in 1973 had become pure mud by 1986. Appalling traffic jams are daily occurrences. Many of the old streets around the original market are too narrow to admit anything larger than a bullock cart. Even in the wider streets trucks get hopelessly wedged at abrupt turns; vehicles often bog down in the area's potent mixture of mud, sewage flooding out of ancient drains, decayed vegetables and discarded leaf packing material. When that happens the neighborhood's porters are summoned to push and heave the vehicle out by brute force while other traffic backs up in surrounding streets. The wholesaler who once compared the area to "one of the circles of hell" was not simply giving way to rhetorical excess.

"Write it down in your book, lady," he admonished me. "Not even a dog would live here if he could avoid it."

The Local Retail Markets

Many of the problems of the central wholesale market are replicated, on a smaller scale, in local retail markets. Retail markets show one critical difference, however. They vary in the kind of tenancy relationships by which they came into existence. Although a good number of retail markets are either privately owned structures or are very similar municipal markets, some of the busiest of Madras' markets are technically illegal. These "squatter markets" have grown up, like squatter housing colonies, by accretion. They occupy otherwise vacant land which is either public or to which title is ambiguous. They exist by virtue of official tolerance or official neglect; some of the oldest and most entrenched have in the past 15 years won legitimacy and been transformed into municipal markets. The history of retail markets, therefore, is shaped by the kind of legal right traders have--or can win--to the space they occupy.

Madras' private markets usually date from the more spacious days of the late nineteenth and early twentieth centuries. These relatively large enclosed areas, lined with raised, roofed platforms, are the result of shrewd charitable investments on the part of temples or wealthy individuals. At the time these structures were built the small rents the retailers paid for daily use of the market seemed adequate; space was less scarce, rents were generally lower, and the builder received compensatory prestige for anchoring a market in a neighborhood.

Thannithurai Market in Mylapore was, for instance, reputedly founded by the eminent Brahmin judge of the High Court, Sir Bashiyam Aiyangar, who flourished in the 1880s and 1890s (Lethbridge 1985). According to the origin myth recounted by Thannithurai's sellers in 1971, Sir Bashiyam was moved to build an enclosed market after he found himself obliged to walk each day through a disorderly crowd of street sellers blocking the footbridge over the Buckingham Canal. The final straw came when an old NonBrahmin[5] woman seller cursed him one day as he tried to bargain with her. Sir Bashiyam is said to have, in response, bought land beside an abandoned temple tank (pool), to have built Thannithurai, and to have settled a number of hand-picked traders in it. Each was given a Rs. 10 cash inducement to relocate in return for a vow of clean living and clean speaking. The story suggests that the "neat and clean" approach to market management has a venerable history--but also that class conflict was latent in the situation even then, albeit an older form involving Brahminical demands for deference and control over the behavior and morality of lower castes.

Municipal market places, of which Madras has relatively few, are usually built on the same pattern as private markets; those in the central areas of Madras seem to date from the 1930s and 1940s, at a period when private charity apparently no longer sufficed to create new selling locales. Their relative scarcity may reflect the fact that the British colonial administration concentrated its expenditures on the more important administrative centers of Bombay, Calcutta and Delhi and never got around to giving Madras all it needed in the way of a modern civic infrastructure. The city's reluctant decision, after years of battling, to replace a squatter market with a specially constructed municipal market in Pannagal Park was the more remarkable because it was such a rare event.

Both kinds of market are increasingly under pressure to relocate so that the sites they occupy can be used for the construction of vastly more profitable rental housing or shops. In the case of privately owned markets this is a fairly straightforward process: owners try to force traders out through refusal to provide necessary services and upkeep or through demands for large rent increases reflecting the "market value" of the property. This was the strategy pursued by two successive owners of Zam Bazaar, once the premier market in the city's Triplicane neighborhood.

Theoretically immune, municipal markets are not necessarily protected from this kind of incursion by private individuals: Mandaivalli Market was, in 1986, in the process of being sold off to a developer. In maneuvering of this sort, those who want to use the market site for their own purposes may try to get the city authorities to offer traders a new site, a strategy employed toward the Mambalam Market in the mid-1970s. Unfortunately the city, chronically short of funds, is now unable to purchase expensive new land on which to relocate traders even if it were willing to do so.

Confronted with pressure to leave their markets, traders can either fight to retain their markets or move back to street selling. Part of the incentive to retain market locations comes from the fact that each market constitutes a network of important social relationships and socially recognized "ownership" rights to selling space. These ownership rights, unprotected by the formal legal system, nevertheless are bought, sold and inherited among retailers, and may constitute the only property that a poor family ever controls. One old lady, discussing her intention to leave her grandson her selling spot, remarked that she owned nothing in the world but that she could still leave the boy something: a chance to earn a living in a busy market place.

If forced out on the street, traders lose these kinds of customary ownership rights. In the process many of the social relations which make a selling spot valuable are also ruptured; although dislocated markets do re-form, not every retailer has the strength and perseverance to face regular arrest for blocking the thoroughfare or for illegally occupying private or city property. Much of street sellers' time and energy goes into bribing the police to be left alone, scurrying off when a police van is sighted, or scraping up the money to pay fines when booked. In a full-scale police raid, sellers usually lose their day's stock of goods, and may have their scales smashed and their small shelters torn down as well. Mandaivalli Market sellers arrested in 1971 were exasperated to waste an entire day sitting in the Saidapet court on the distant outskirts of the city, waiting for their cases to be heard. None had the bus fare to get home at the end of the day. Some were rescued by friends; others walked the six to eight miles back. In spite of the hazards, street selling is prevalent everywhere, and some of the busiest markets in the city are, or were until recently, illegal street markets.

The illegal street market in Madras has typically grown up in a central location near a temple, a bus or train terminus or a major intersection which already has shops. Such a market has a history of bitter official persecution. Like squatter housing colonies, squatter markets generally have an organized core of sellers who bring their mats, baskets and sunshades to the same spot every day. The market then grows by accretion, and may acquire more permanent thatched roofing if it succeeds in surviving. Street markets have certain attractions to sellers since their locations are usually superb for drawing customers and there is no rent to pay. (Sellers point out, however, that the need to offer the police regular bribes amounts to a rent.) The drawback is that all sellers are legally vulnerable to arrest since they are guilty of "encroachment" on public space or, in some cases, on private property. Attempts to build wooden selling platforms and thatched roofs to keep off rain and sun provoke organized police raids because such structures, if allowed to remain for any length of time, render the traders "tenants" with some claim to the legal protection against eviction tenants enjoy. Authorities are anxious to avoid any semblance of legitimation for illegal markets. It is the role of local political brokers and of political parties which back the traders to find some kind of legalistic formula which will regularize occupancy of these chosen selling spots.

In addition to the full-fledged illegal market, which is an independent entity with no other spatial base, many private and municipal markets also have illegal overflow crowds outside their gates. In some cases this is a genuine overflow because a busy market--like Zam Bazaar in its heyday--has no more room. Newcomers have to station themselves around the market door or along the approach road and hope to "catch" customers as they arrive. With time the "outside people" may accumulate enough capital and influence to move inside. In other cases outside selling takes place because business is declining and sellers would rather not pay daily rent in the market place, although they are happy to use it for storage space, midday naps and shelter during the monsoon. In either case the personnel of such a market are partially legal, partially illegal; whether the legal inside sellers offer support and shelter to their illegal outside colleagues during police raids or whether they covertly applaud police action depends on the political configuration of the particular market.

The Political Arena

The Madras situation, in which markets are constantly growing, changing, shifting their locations and their legal status, takes place against an evolving political background. Since the 1930s Tamilnadu has been distinguished by its succession of regional/cultural chauvinist parties with a populist bent. These have contended for influence with the national Congress, largely dominated by north Indians.

In the early 1970s the two most important parties in both Madras City and in Tamilnadu as a whole were the DMK and a local faction of the Congress Party. The DMK was populist, anti-Brahmin, espousing regional separatism and the primacy of the Tamil language. The DMK claimed to represent the poor and the oppressed. Urban workers, landless rural people, students and some intellectuals were the DMK's major supporters. Since the 1960s the DMK had controlled a majority both in the state government and in the Corporation Council which governed Madras.

By 1971-3 the DMK was rather far removed from its crusading, idealistic early days. Its leading politicians had grown blatantly corrupt. DMK Chief Minister M. Karunanidhi periodically invoked the region's resentment of the central government and local anxieties about the imposition of Hindi as a mandatory language to bolster his party's position, but inefficiency, sloth and corruption within the state and city government and within the party were widespread and widely acknowleged even among those who supported the DMK on ideological grounds.

Despite its minority status, the Congress Party never entirely lost its hold in the state and in the city, since it linked its supporters to the central government and to the national ruling Congress Party. As elsewhere in India, Congress is in Tamilnadu the party of rural landlords and rich peasants and of the urban bourgeoisie. In Tamilnadu it is additionally identified with Brahmins. However, one of its local factions, known locally as "Kamaraj Congress" or formally as Old Congress (Congress-O), had a populist appeal comparable to that of the DMK. Its late leader, K. Kamaraj Nadar, was a Tamil NonBrahmin who attained national prominence within the Congress Party, although he eventually broke with Indira Gandhi. An honest, approachable man with a Gandhian appeal, he remained a revered figure even after his death. Thus Congress-O continued to attract considerable support from the urban poor in Madras, unlike the rival "new Congress" or Indira Congress (Congress-I).

By 1973, when this writer's first period of field work was ending, the DMK faction which eventually separated to form a separate party, the AIADMK, was already emerging. The new party was led by the movie actor M.G.Ramachandran, fondly known as M.G.R. and famed for his filmed performances of incorruptible hero roles. The AIADMK, invoking the name of the early DMK leader C. N. Annadorai, sought to reassert the populist values of the DMK and announced plans to cleanse the state of its corrupt politicians. By 1973 several former DMK markets were beginning to turn to the AIADMK, rapidly reflecting the division taking place in the party organization. The progression of this sea change was observable in the pictures of party leaders which suddenly appeared on the backs of many retailers' stalls: some had pictures of Karunanidhi and Annadorai, while others carried pictures of Annadorai and M.G.R. One man showed me a picture of M.G.R. which he kept out of sight, since his market was still solidly pro-Karunanidhi.

Some time later the AIADMK won state power and M.G.R. became chief minister. One of M.G.R.'s achievements was to reach an accommodation with the Congress-ruled central government, particularly after the election of Rajiv Gandhi. As a result Tamilnadu, which had suffered central government neglect during the regional separatist phase of the DMK, finally began to benefit from some of the economic development money flowing from the center. M.G.R. continued to rule the state until his death in December, 1987. Shortly thereafter the

AIADMK split into two factions, amidst riotous scenes of
yelling and chair-throwing in the legislature.

In Madras one of the most significant political changes of
the last 15 years was the dissolution, under orders from the
central government, of the 120-member Corporation Council.
Since 1973 the city has had neither mayor nor corporation; its
commissioner is now a professional civil servant appointed by
the central government. The result has been a significant
increase in honesty and efficiency. The police, who in 1971-73
looked on markets, particularly illegal markets, as major
sources of graft revenue, were far less rapacious by 1986. At
the same time the new administration seemed anxious to
resolve market disputes by regularizing squatter markets and
turning them into legal, rentpaying municipal markets. The
present commissioner, a young but formidable woman,
indicated in a 1986 interview that it was city policy to
regularize the existing illegal markets as well as to build thirty-
six new markets. She went on to say that the city intended to
take a hard line against the formation of future illegal street
markets. A sincere proponent of the neat-and-clean ideology,
she clearly has not reckoned with the amoeba-like habits of
market places, which continue to divide, reproduce and spring
up in new locations.

At the same time the elimination of an elected Corporation
Council removed a whole layer of local politicians who had once
been crucial power brokers in markets' struggles to win political
protection and legitimacy. As members of the Corporation's
administrative committees and as loyal "partymen" they could
win favors for markets in their own or adjacent electoral
divisions, and were particularly anxious to do so for "party
markets" which publicly proclaimed their allegiances and
delivered the vote at election time. Not surprisingly, all the
markets which were experiencing difficulties over their tenancy
in 1971-73 were highly organized and allied with either the
DMK or Congress-O [6]; these groups wielded the most power
within the city government. By late 1973, however, the
ADMK (later to rename itself the AIADMK) was already
making inroads in a few DMK markets.

In return for protection the market offered the local
politician a bloc of votes at election time, and symbols of
political support at other times. Some of the larger markets
would hold celebrations at which politicians were honored.
Markets displayed party colors or symbols and would, in case of
a general strike, close or remain defiantly open in response to
the orders of their party [7]. In a few cases markets offered their
patrons more tangible rewards. The Congress-O godfather of
Pannagal Park Market succeeded in getting a former squatter

market on public park land legalized and housed in a new and fancy market building in 1973. Yet the size of the bribes he demanded to do so caused a local uproar. The traders, very grudgingly, had provided the man with a good deal of cash and a motor scooter. The sticking point, which delayed the inauguration of the market for several months, was the politician's demand that several of the already-scarce stalls in the market be allocated to his own followers, men who had no previous connection with the market. The market association refused, apparently feeling that the demand was too much of a threat to its autonomy.

There is also evidence to suggest that the Corporation Council only agreed to construct that market building because a politically powerful Congress-O construction contractor wanted (and got) the municipal contract to build it. Certainly the hope of an equally lucrative contract, as much as interparty rivalry, encouraged the DMK market association of nearby Mambalam Market to demand a building of its own in 1973. The Mambalam Market Association's ambitious schemes collapsed when the DMK was swept out of power soon after.

THE CONFLICTS OVER TIME

In Madras it is possible to see three general phases in the development of market disputes. During the last twenty years the conflicts have been increasingly politicized, and markets have been squeezed by a mounting pressure from investors to acquire and develop urban real estate.

The 1960s

Events of this period can only be reconstructed from the accounts, gathered in 1971-3, of participants. It was a period in which street markets like those near the Mylapore Kapaliishwarar temple tank and Pannagal Park in Theagaraja Nagar (known as T. Nagar) were forcibly relocated several times. Conflict with the police over the question of "encroachment" was constant and occasionally violent. The situations were resolved by the mediation of prominent local figures, motivated more strongly by a sense of civic duty than by partisan party politics.

In Mylapore vendors had originally sold near the temple's abandoned tank some blocks from the site of the present market. They were chased off repeatedly by the police. Finally this harassment, in which vendors lost their goods and their scales, culminated in the arrest of several market leaders with

Congress-O connections. A shouting crowd of vendors surrounded the police station where the men were held. The mob refused to leave until their heroes were released. Probably because the situation raised the possibility of prolonged rioting, a prominent police official finally intervened. The compromise he arranged allowed the market to re-form in its present site, along one edge of the existing temple tank. At the time, all involved assumed that the land belonged to the temple. Traders were to be immune from arrest as long as they confined their activities to the strip of land between the fence edging the tank and the curb of the road.

A similar settlement was reached in the nearby Mandaivalli Market, where the private market building was unpopular with vegetable sellers although still heavily used by fish and meat vendors. The vegetable sellers instead congregated on the street outside. After the usual round of harassment, instigated, vendors said, by "those rich people going in their cars," traders were allowed to settle on a tiny strip of pavement in front of a school. That strip was only large enough to hold a few stalls, and it was monopolized by the DMK market leader and his closest allies. Others remained subject to periodic arrest.

In Pannagal Park, in the wealthy residential suburb of T. Nagar, a market had formed on one of the streets leading up to the large public park there. It was chased off by the police, re-formed, and was chased again. In several cases the traders resisted arrest; today they recall with some glee the period of the "soda bottle wars," in which sealed bottles of soda, shaken up vigorously, made bomb-like projectiles. In one police raid several passers-by were arrested by mistake. One of these, a prominent local bookseller and Congress Party member, then took up the cause of the traders. He arranged a settlement which allowed a single line of sellers to operate along the edge of the public park. The market became a municipal one, and traders paid rent for their spaces. Conflict was renewed because the success of the market attracted a second row of sellers. There was official resistance to accepting the market's growth. Then the Corporation refused to provide electric light or a water tap, although vendors paid rent and insisted that they were entitled to the facilities other municipal markets had.

In Mambalam, the railway station market had begun to form on a piece of land of disputed ownership (was it city land or did it belong to the suburban railway authority?). There was the familiar police harassment. A Congress Party "social worker" (community organizer/activist) suggested that the traders elect officers and form an association. He also recommended that the association pledge its members to a life

of honesty and clean language. His advice was followed and for
some time the market was Congress, eventually switching its
loyalties to the DMK at the instigation of one market leader
who was a rising star in the DMK local party structure.

The privately owned Zam Bazaar in Triplicane was one of
the largest markets in the city. Traders had begun, in the
1960s, to be pressured by the market owner, a very prominent
woman member of the Congress Party, to pay higher rents.
Traders resisted an effort to change their tenancy status, from
stall tenants protected by rent control laws, to "license holders"
paying rents subject to increase. The market was in bad
repair, a factor which the market association used to demand
that the city's Health Department take over administration of
the market. Despite a protest march, a demonstration at the
Corporation office, and a campaign to collect signatures on a
petition from customers, the Health Department declined to
take on the responsibility for the market. As a result of the
unfavorable publicity, designed as much to embarrass the
Congress Party owner as to publicize traders' grievances, some
of the rent increases were rescinded and the highly unpopular
market collector was replaced.

The 1970s

By this period all the markets which had experienced
difficulties with the authorities or with market owners had
become firm "party markets." Mylapore and Pannagal Park
were Congress-O, Mandaivalli was rabidly DMK, as was
Mambalam. Zam Bazaar was DMK but, as the 1973 local
elections approached, allowed itself to be courted by other
parties, including Congress and the Communist Party of India.
Politicians were now clearly aware of the value in offering
protection and patronage to markets. Meanwhile traders'
difficult position vis-a-vis city authorities remained, and real
estate pressure on the very existence of certain markets was
becoming obvious.

In Mylapore there were still periodic police raids on those
vendors selling outside the permitted zone which sent traders
and anthropologist alike scrambling for safety. The temple
devasthanam continued to have reservations about the presence
of a market at a major tourist and pilgrimage site. In a 1973
interview a devasthanam member confided that the trustees
wanted to oust the market altogether and erect a row of shops
on the spot. In his opinion the city might be persuaded to
relocate the market, perhaps to a nearby school yard. The
Mylapore Market Association was at the time unaware of this
scheme. Around 1974 both the devasthanam and the

Corporation tried to evict the market. Some versions say the
temple wanted to build a beautifying garden alongside the
tank. Others say the real aim was still shops. The Corporation
wanted to widen the road. Protests eventually convinced the
Corporation that the market was important to the public.
Politicians from both the DMK and the Congress Party
intervened in that dispute, demanding in return market stalls
which they intended to sell to their own clients.

In Mandaivalli police raids also continued, despite the
market leader's position as a low-level DMK functionary. The
police pointed out, with some reason, that there was a perfectly
good market building across from the market which vendors did
not utilize. The rather inefficient local corporation councilor
was in 1972-3 trying to arrange that the street portion of the
market be moved back some yards into an adjoining school
yard.

Pannagal Park market had achieved its own market
building, as described earlier, thanks to Congress Party
connections. Mambalam Market Association, always a rival of
the Pannagal Park market on both political and economic
grounds, was planning a campaign through the Corporation to
get a big market building erected for its own use. The traders
had larger ambitions, however. They wanted the building to
pass into the ownership of the association, rather than
remaining a municipal market under city control.

Thannithurai Market, which passed out of the control of Sir
Bashiyam Aiyangar's family in the mid-1960s, was bought
around 1979 by a group of 20 traders in the market. Each
contributed Rs. 20,000; the woman owner lowered her selling
price to accommodate sellers who pleaded poverty. After
buying the market the owners continued to collect rents.

In Zam Bazaar, which had some 200 traders, the market
owner had begun to threaten to demolish the market and to
erect shops and offices on the site if traders refused to pay
"market value" rents. Litigation about whether the traders
were tenants or license holders dragged through the courts.
The physical state of the market remained poor; traders
particularly worried about the lack of a water tap or latrine,
and were resentful that the market collector had prevented
them from erecting a small shrine in one corner.

In the central wholesale market, meanwhile, there was also
litigation over the tenant-license holder question, because the
devasthanam felt the Kottuwal Chavadi market should bring in
rent comparable to that being paid for shops and warehouses in
adjoining streets. The devasthanam was contemplating the
construction of a new, two- or three-story market building,
which would, they reasoned, leave some of the site for other

commercial redevelopment. The temple refused, however, to undertake the venture without substantial city funding. City officials, meanwhile, were enthusiastic about a market relocation plan which would split the wholesale market into three sections, at the north, east and south edges of the city. This, planners argued, would make the market more accessible to retailers, who would simply travel to the supply depot nearest them. Wholesale merchants pointed out that they could not possibly maintain and supply three separate warehouses and that they had no intention of dividing the city trade up among themselves on a regional basis. Each wanted access to the full range of suppliers and buyers.

The 1980s

By 1986, there had been certain startling changes in the situation of individual market places. As indicated earlier, there is now generally less police harassment and policemen make fewer routine demands for bribe money. Shanta Sheila Nayar, the city's new civil servant who acts as Corporation Commissioner, is credited with legalizing the existence of several once-illegal markets. Still faithfully mirroring the evolution of state politics, most DMK markets now support the AIADMK; there is less overt hostility among markets affiliated with different parties. As a woman member of the state legislature remarked, "People tend to work with the government, not just with one local politician who protects them." Certainly the disappearance of elected Corporation councilors removed an entire group of political patrons from the scene. However, it was now evident that real estate development was about to engulf several market places. There is apparently discussion in official circles about making all private markets into municipal markets, to protect them. Many traders believe that this is already law, although they themselves remain locked in endless disputes with private landlords trying to evict them. An unexpected sidelight of these situations is that trader resistance is increasingly shifting from protest activities to litigation.

Mylapore Market is one of those which has achieved legitimacy. Traders now pay rent to the Corporation as a municipal market and police are still strict about those selling outside the prescribed area. The market is closed to newcomers. This state of relative bliss was only achieved, however, after a long law suit over whether the city or the temple owned the land. After several years of litigation the High Court eventually determined that the land did, indeed, belong to the city. The market may face future relocation. As

traders understand it part of the agreement which made them
a municipal market also pledged them to move when the city
decides to widen the street.

Mandaivalli Market's outside sellers also now pay rent to
the Corporation, although they still suffer from periodic
harassment. They acknowledge that a new police commissioner
has reduced the actual abuse they suffer. In 1985, however,
there was a new drive to clear the market which some vendors
attributed to a road-widening scheme. Traders organized a
protest march and a delegation which called on an AIADMK
politician. He in turn presented their case to M.G.R., who
decreed that the traders could stay but that their roofing had to
go. Traders spent six weeks baking in the sun before venturing
to re-erect their roofing.

Meanwhile there is elaborate maneuvering going on to gain
control of, and redevelop, the old private Mandaivalli Market
building. A group of merchants in the shops on the outside of
the market building have formed a new Mandaivalli Merchants'
Association, which includes the vegetable vendors. The stated
aim of the group is to resist the proposed sale of the market;
the group has held at least one well-publicized meeting
attended by leading politicians. Coinciding with one of those
meetings was a newspaper report, perhaps apocryphal, saying
that the Corporation was planning to take over all private
market places. This badly frightened the Mandaivalli Market
landlord, who faced both a determined association and the
possibility of government expropriation. The rich merchant
who is spearheading this effort says, with much satisfaction,
that the market owner will eventually be forced to sell his
property cheaply to the market association since nobody else
will buy. The association, in turn, will resell a portion of the
area, at a large profit, to a private developer. It is clear that
this man, the secretary of the association, intends to profit at
every turn. He himself has just constructed a large three-story
shop across the road from the market, on a portion of the school
yard once discussed as an alternative site for the market
vendors.

The traders who bought Thannithurai Market are trying to
build a cheap rooming house and restaurant along the front
edge of the market. Other traders are opposing them, since
they realize that retail use of the space will be gradually
pushed out by other commercial interests.

Zam Bazaar is still locked in bitter dispute, both with the
charitable trust that now owns it and with the city. The
dispute with the trust involves the old question of rent versus
license fees. The matter was fought out in a prolonged court
case. Traders lost and their rents increased, but apparently not

enough to satisfy the new owners. Meanwhile no money has been spent on repairs or cleaning. The dispute with the city involves the orders of Shanta Sheila Nayar who, after two personal visits, demanded that the market be demolished and a new one constructed on the site. She is reported to have sworn that if demolition did not begin within two months she would order the gate sealed, to which vendors, looking at the structure's collapsed state, replied, "Where is the gate to seal?" Traders fear, quite realistically, that if the market is torn down it will never be rebuilt as a market place. They are therefore organizing against demolition.

New Janda Market in Triplicane has been partially demolished over the heads of its sellers. The owner has repeatedly ordered the sellers to vacate the place, saying he wants to demolish the structure. Some years ago, when a cyclone allegedly tore off a portion of the market roof, the owner sent his men to tear down the "damaged" section, dislocating more than thirty sellers. Those individuals filed a court case which dragged on for years, but which they eventually won in 1981. The market's owners are legally charged with providing selling space for those who brought suit--but nothing has been done. Large numbers of sellers have moved on, and now sell in a lane behind the market, or on the street near the Parthasarati temple. Those who moved out were primarily the poorer vendors who could not afford to contribute to the legal fight against eviction.

In Kottuwal Chavadi, the temple finally won its fight to convert its merchant tenants into license holders, and stall rents rose to around Rs. 100 a month, still less than the rents paid for private shop space in the streets around the market. The city has also finally begun constructing a new wholesale market in a single location on the western edge of the city. The relocation plan met initial resistance from those with cheap stalls inside the old Kottuwal Chavadi market, but was vigorously supported by those in the surrounding streets, to whom Corporation rents would be a welcome relief. Skillful work on the part of the Madras Redevelopment Corporation, which began holding regular meetings with the wholesalers' leaders, eventually made an agreement possible. In 1986, as the new 1100-stall wholesale market neared completion, the political negotiating involved both rent levels there and a rush of demand from agricultural suppliers in other Tamilnadu towns, who hoped to acquire stalls and thus to break into the Madras wholesale trade. What the Corporation appears not to realize, however, is that most wholesalers do not actually intend to give up their Kottuwal Chavadi stalls. Most talk happily about the chance to have two "offices."

CONCLUSION

What this exhaustive discussion of Madras markets seems to suggest is that any city administration, in India or elsewhere, must devote serious attention to the protection of existing retail market places as the city expands and undergoes development or redevelopment. In many third world cities such markets remain crucial sources of food for most of the population, which cannot afford to use supermarkets even if such things exist. Markets are also crucial sources of employment for large sections of the urban poor, both male and female. To destroy them is to destroy the livelihood of thousands of people, since the offices, apartments and expensive retail shops which appear on markets' sites do not employ large numbers of very poor people. Planners need not only to construct new markets in new areas of the city but to preserve and rebuild old markets in congested old neighborhoods. To do so, however, brings the state into direct conflict with the property interests of the urban bourgeoisie. For many city governments, this proves an insoluble dilemma, usually handled through further inaction.

It is also clear from the example of Madras that the struggles of petty traders to find and keep selling spots have shaped the configuration of the city. Would Mambalam, Mylapore or the Zam Bazaar area of Triplicane have such bustling and prosperous commercial areas if petty produce vendors had not fought to establish markets there? This aspect of working-class urban history and urban politics, although hard to unravel and reconstruct after the fact, needs further examination. What would be particularly useful is some kind of crosscultural examination of markets' developmental struggles, since there is at the moment only anecdotal evidence which nevertheless suggests parallel processes of trader resistance in widely different parts of the world. Efforts to save Philadelphia's city-owned Reading Terminal Market from the developers who want to build a convention center on the spot sound very familiar in the Indian context.

Finally, it seems evident that as developers move in to swallow markets, the entire process is again forcing out the poorer traders in any one market. Mylapore Market is now closed to newcomers, which favors the wealthier, more established sellers. In Thannithurai and Mandaivalli the richer traders are themselves involved in attempts to buy, and then redevelop, market sites. Again, the less wealthy get forced out. The experiences of New Janda Market and Zam Bazaar suggest that as the form of struggle moves from the relatively egalitarian riot or protest march to litigation funded by the wealthier in the market, poorer traders return to street selling. For them the familiar cycle of new market formation, insecurity in the face of the police, and eventual political struggle are repeated. Thus the process of capitalist development has a very direct role in accentuating class differences among petty retailers. A few, who can contrive to become part owners of a market, may prosper. Others, who manage to hang on to their selling spots through expensive court battles, may do well enough. The rest go back amidst the urban poor, to begin again.

NOTES

1. Field work was done in Madras during two widely separated periods. The work of 1971-3 was done under a National Science Foundation predoctoral grant and involved interviews with 85 wholesalers in Kottuwal Chavadi and some 250 retailers in 11 local retail markets. The work of 1986 involved restudy of the original research sites.
2. Following the lead of Babb (1987) and Moser (1978), I have argued that petty retailers in India, despite their entrepreneurship, are essentially parts of the urban proletariat (Lessinger 1985).
3. Significantly, many Tamilnadu and Andhra Pradesh villages lack any place to buy fresh vegetables, although grain and pulses may be available in small general-purpose shops. One either grows one's own food, travels to a larger market town to buy it or does without.
4. Planners the world over seem unable to grasp the fact, obvious to any marketer, that all the sellers of a market must be located in close proximity to each other if the market is to function vis-a-vis either suppliers or buyers. In 1986-7 planners and entrepreneurs in New York City decided to split the city's wholesale fish market into two sections. Sales to restaurants and retail customers were to go on in Manhattan's Fulton Fish Market, as they have done for years. Sales to fish packagers were to go on in a new market across the river in Brooklyn. The plan failed disastrously, since both kinds of customer wanted to be able to look over the full range of fish available. Fishing boats refused to sell their catch at the new market. That fish which did arrive went unsold. The new market will probably close.
5. The caste hierarchy of south India involves three major categories: Brahmins (former priests and landlords);

NonBrahmins (a large group of cultivating, artisan and service castes with marked status differences within the category) and Adi Dravidas or former Untouchables. The Thannithurai incident, almost a century old, was recognized by contemporary informants as a Brahminical reproach to the old lady's act of lese majesty in cursing a Brahmin. Bashiyam's charitable act can be seen as a reassertion of high caste moral and political control, in a period when Brahmin hegemony was still unchallenged (see Gough 1981). The ascendancy of anti-Brahmin ideology in this century via the DMK party has altered the old order considerably. Brahmins are nowhere near as oppressed as they would like to believe, but they cannot exercise their control as openly or highhandedly as they once did.
6. Individuals who privately support another party will nevertheless go along with a market's expedient choice of a party to support. This is usually a DMK or AIADMK sympathizer in a Congress market, who acknowledges that a local Congress politician offers more secure patronage in the particular electoral division.
7. The general strike, or hartal, is a demonstration of party strength as well as a form of political protest. Can a party paralyze the city? Can it halt buses and trains (via the unions), take rickshaws off the streets, persuade shops and markets to close down? Can the opposition persuade its followers to go to work, open their shops and stalls? Occasionally the situation gets tense since each party may send thugs around to enforce closures or openings.

BIBLIOGRAPHY

Babb, Florence
    1987   Marketers as Producers: The Labor Process and Proletarianization of Peruvian Market Women. In Perspectives in U.S. Marxist Anthropology. David Hakken and Hanna Lessinger, eds. Pp.166-185. Boulder, Colo.: Westview Press.

Barnett, Marguerite Ross
    1976   The Politics of Cultural Nationalism in South India. Princeton: Princeton University Press.

Castells, Manuel
    1983   The City and the Grassroots: a Cross-Cultural Theory of Urban Social Movements. Berkeley: University of California Press.

Corporation of Madras
    nd   Administration Report for 1970-71 (Part I).
           Madras: Corporation Printing Press.

Gough, Kathleen
    1981   Rural Society in Southeast India. Cambridge:
           Cambridge University Press.

Hardgrave, Robert
    1965   The Dravidian Movement. Bombay: Popular
           Prakashan Press.

Indian Express (unsigned article)
    1986   A Costly Lesson. August 11, 1986, p. 14 of Indian
           Express published in Madras City.

Lessinger, Johanna
    1976   Produce Marketing in Madras City. Ph.D. thesis.
           Department of Anthropology, Brandeis University.
    1985   Nobody Here to Yell At Me: Political Activism
           Among Petty Retail Traders in an Indian City. In
           Markets and Marketing. Stuart Plattner, ed. Pp.
           309-331. Lanham, MD: University Press of
           America.
    1986   Work and Modesty: The Dilemma of Women
           Traders in South India. Feminist Studies 12
           (3):581-600.

Lethbridge, Sir Roper
    1985 (1893)   Prominent Indians of Victorian Age, A
           Biographical Dictionary. New Delhi: Archives
           Rare Reprints.

Moser, Caroline
    1978   Informal Sector or Petty Commodity Production:
           Dualism or Dependence in Urban Development?
           World Development 6 (9/10): 1041-1064.

Sarin, Madhu
    1979   Urban Planning, Petty Trading and Squatter
           Settlements in Chandigarh, India. In Casual
           Work and Poverty in Third World Cities. Ray
           Bromley and Chris Gerry, eds. Pp. 133-160.
           Chichester, England: John Wiley and Sons Ltd.

8

The Sexual Political Economy of Street Vending in Washington, D.C.

Roberta M. Spalter-Roth
The George Washington University and
The Institute for Women's Policy Research

INTRODUCTION

Street vending, the selling of goods from tables and carts on city sidewalks, is a small occupation in the United States.[1] Despite its small size, in cities across the country, there is a policy debate between those who see vending as a way of providing animation and safety in otherwise anonymous downtown area and those who see vending as a public nuisance that creating unfair competition for fixed-location businesses. While there is a growing literature on the positive aspects of vending (Project for Public Spaces, 1982; Whyte, 1980; Henig and Maxfield, 1978), officials in such cities as New York, Philadelphia and Los Angeles are clamping down on the growing number of street vendors by developing new regulations designed to reduce their numbers, curtail the kinds of merchandise that they are allowed to sell and ensure that they pay taxes (Freed, 1985; Blumenthal, 1983; Bell, 1983; Getlin, 1981; Eisner and Sutton, 1984; Freed, 1985; Mitchell, 1983). In this study of street vending in Washington, D.C. (the District of Columbia) I focus on a previously neglected aspect of the topic: the right of women to earn a living at this occupation in safety and free from sexual harassment.

In 1985, the District of Columbia (D.C.), the nation's capital city, joined those cities that have developed strict new vendor regulations. These new regulations were developed in response to the demands of the retailers, developers, and investors that the city government wanted to attract to a "revitalizing downtown." The effect of this policy was to remove two out of three vendors from the streets.

The new regulations represent the latest in a long series of efforts by the D.C. Government to mediate the conflict between the more established fixed-location businesses and the more informal unregulated economy of street vending, usually in the interests of the former. They were enacted after years of commissions, public hearings and private meetings of these conflicting interest groups.

The right of women vendors to work safely in public spaces was not a part of the policy debate. This absence is not surprising given cultural patterns of who speaks and who listens in the public policy arena (Ferguson, 1984). As Warren and Bourque state, "It's not that women are less verbal, but that women's perceptions may not reach community forums" (1985:258). Interviews with 75 women vendors from the fall of 1984 through the spring of 1986 gives voice to their perceptions of the situation. Along with presenting the views of the women vendors, I examine changes in the distribution of vending licenses before and after the implementation of the new regulations to determine if they had a particularly negative impact on women vendors.

For D.C. women vendors, selling goods on the streets means a higher income than they could earn at many pink collar jobs and freedom from close supervision, despite the fact that prior to the new regulations more than half worked for someone else. In exchange for these advantages, they are targets for several types of street harassment, including sexual harassment. By assuming that the effects of the policy would be gender neutral, despite specific regulations that especially disadvantaged women vendors, city policy did remove proportionally more women than men from the streets and made vending a more dangerous and more costly occupation for those women who remained. I conclude that while the impact of this policy on the city's political economy was not major, it did reinforce gender-based patterns of dominance in public and economic life. This is what I mean by the "sexual political economy" of street vending.[2]

The women whose views are heard in this study are more than just victims of a city policy, however. They are also strategists who devise ways to try and overcome conditions they do not create and regulations that do not reflect their interests, if not very successfully. As Karen Tranberg Hansen says in her forthcoming article,"State policy sets limits but within those limits women make their life histories" (Hansen, n.d.).

The remainder of this paper first summarizes literature on women's use of the streets in North America and Europe. Second, it tells the women vendors' story -- what they sell, why they vend, the problems they encounter and the strategies that they use to deal with these problems. Third, it describes the conflicting interests groups in the policy debate over the new regulations. Fourth, it details vendors', and especially women vendors', struggle against the new regulations. Fifth, it analyzes the impact of the new regulations and their especially negative impact on women vendors.

Women's Use of Streets

While not relevant literature appears to exist on women vendors in "first world" countries there is a growing literature on women's use of public space in urban areas (see especially Boys, 1984; Cranz, 1981; di Leonardo, 1982; Enjeu and Save,1974; Hapgood and Getzels, 1974; Ritzdorf, 1986; Salem, 1986; Stimpson et al. 1981; Wekerle et al.,1980; Wekerle with Gaddie-Thomas, 1986; Stansell, 1982). This literature has begun to explore how ideological notions of the "proper spheres" for women and for men find their way into urban public policy. As a result of middle class women's relegation to the private sphere of the household and an urban reform movement in the 19th century that tried to remove prostitutes from the streets, women who continued to use streets as a workplace did so at their own risk and were open to sexual bantering by would-be customers and harassment by police (See especially Stansell, 1982). Kerner's article in this volume indicates that a campaign in Tanzania to send unemployed urban workers back to rural areas also equated women loitering with prostitution and made loitering on the streets a crime. Women are still considered to be asking for trouble if they linger on city streets without the protection of men or unaccompanied by children.

The city is described here not as a neutral arena but rather as a power structure with a set of rules that represent the interests of dominant groups, especially men. As a result of this gender-based power structure, all males regardless of race or class are seen as having the right to harass women. These scholars see street harassment as a form of social control which establishes men's ownership of the streets and increase women's fear of using them. Women's greater fear of crime in urban areas, compared to men, has been well documented, as has their greater use of precautionary strategies such as avoidance of certain streets, parks and other public places (Riger et al, 1978; Gordon et al, 1981). Yet as Wekerle states,

Little research has been done on women's actual usage of public space and facilities, how women are given the message that they are out of place, and the kinds of changes that would make women feel both entitled to use and socially accepted in using the urban public environment (1980:192).

I hope that this study of a group of women who use city streets as a workplace should contribute to an understanding of the economic consequences of gender-based patterns of street harassment.

WOMEN VENDORS' STORY

Before the new regulations were implemented, approximately one in five vendors was a woman.[3] Thus, in the District of Columbia, unlike numbers of third-world cities street vending is not a predominantly female occupation. Nor does there appear to be a "typical" woman vendor in terms of age or marital status.

Of the women interviewed over the course of the study, 40 percent were black, 40 percent were white and the remaining 20 percent were Latina or Asian (See Table 8:1). Black women were more likely to be young and currently unmarried than the others. Black and white women in the sample were relatively well educated, with two-thirds of the white women having at least some college education and only slightly more than one in ten of the black women having less than a high school education. The majority of women we interviewed were literate, and the lack of formal education was not the reason they became vendors.

Women vendors are less likely to own their own stands than their male counterparts, as can be seen in Table 8:2, below. Those women who worked for someone else and thus were what Babb (1984) refers to as "disguised wage laborers" were most often employed by a friend who owned and supplied several stands.

Of the women interviewed for this study a much higher percentage of white women (60 percent) owned their own stands than did the total sample of black women (37 percent). The difference in ownership patterns did not appear to result either in a different consciousness of their situation or in public hostility toward one another.

What and How They Vend

Prior to the new regulations, the largest number of women vendors sold a variety of mass-produced goods. In winter they offered hats, scarfs, purses, gloves, and legwarmers, along with stoc kings, belts and jewelry. In summer the vendors switched to sunglasses, tee-shirts, Indian cotton dresses and jewelry.

TABLE 8:1: CHARACTERISTICS OF A SAMPLE OF
WOMEN VENDORS IN WASHINGTON, D.C., 1984

CHARACTERISTIC	BLACK	WHITE	OTHER
AGE IN YEARS			
20 - 29	11	9	1
30 - 39	2	5	1
40 - 49	2	3	3
50 - 59	0	3	0
MARITAL STATUS			
Currently married	0	5	4
Currently unmarried	15	15	1
EDUCATION			
Less than H.S. Grad	2	1	2
H.S. Grad	7	6	3
More than H.S.	6	13	0
PREVIOUS JOB			
Sales & Cashiers	6	5	0
Clerical	5	4	0
Other*	2	8	1
Not previously emp.	2	3	4
DAILY EARNINGS			
Less than $75.	1	2	2
$75 - 99	4	4	2
$100 - 124	5	8	1
$125 - 149	2	2	0
$150 and over	2	4	0
No info.	1	0	0
OWNERSHIP			
Self-employed	11	18	7
Works for other	19	12	8

*including waitress, nurse.

TABLE 8:2: PERCENTAGE OF D.C. VENDORS WHO
WORKED FOR SOMEONE ELSE, 1984

Sample	Percent
All licensed vendors	47.0
All licensed female vendors	51.0
Total Number	(4348)

Source: March 1984 Street Vending File, Management
Information System Division, District of Columbia Government,
Department of Licenses, Investigations and Inspections, Office
of Consumer and Regulatory Affairs.

While most vendors sell a mix of goods, some specialize in toys,
ethnic clothing, oils, and incense, art objects, leather goods,
jewelry, fruit and flowers. Because of stiff health regulations,
relatively few sell food, the staple of many third-world
vendors. They vend little that is hand-crafted, home-made,
or unique. They frequently sold fad merchandise such as Gucci
look-alike purses and faux Ralph Lauren polo shirts. At
Christmas, they sold cheaper versions of the latest toys like
Transformers and Cabbage Patch dolls. The same kinds of
goods can be purchased (although usually at a higher cost) a
few feet away at a fixed-location retail outlet.

Despite accusations by fixed-location merchants of selling
inferior goods, women vendors think of themselves as providing
a convenient and less expensive alternative consumer service.
As one woman put it, "Rich people go to Raleigh's (a local
specialty store). My customers are secretaries who can't afford
shopping at expensive department stores." Other vendors said
that customers buy from them because they like a bargain and
they like to bargain.

Most vendors begin to set up before 9:00 in the morning,
unloading their merchandise on to tables from station wagons
or small trucks, often with the help of partners or men they
hire to help them out. Those women who work for someone
else usually meet their employer at the site to help them
unload and pack up, often going to and from work by subway.
The owner's role is to obtain the merchandise, to cover its cost
and to bring it to the vending site each morning and collect it
each evening.

Eleven a.m. to 6:00 p.m. are prime vending hours with the most traffic occurring at lunch hour or from 4:00 to 6:00 p.m. as people are getting out of work. The best times to vend are during the good weather of spring and summer when tourists are at their peak in the nation's capital or just before the Christmas holiday.

<u>Why They Vend</u>

Most of the women interviewed were previously employed; about sixty percent had been employed in pink collar jobs, mainly as sales clerks and cashiers. The balance had been in jobs such as file clerks, bookkeepers, secretaries and waitresses. A small minority had been on welfare. They all made it quite clear that they were happy to leave those jobs. The reasons given for leaving were that they disliked close supervision, resented the lack of decent pay, and found the inflexibility of work hours very difficult. In contrast, women vendors liked the feeling of autonomy and the decent wages that they claim vending offers. Almost none of them regarded vending as a transitional occupation.

Whether self-employed or working for someone else, the women thought of themselves as autonomous workers. For those women who worked for others, it was the absence of the close supervision found in many women's workplaces that gives them a sense of autonomy. For example, Selena previously worked as a cashier in a supermarket and in several restaurants. She hated the shift work involved in these jobs, complaining that there was always "dead" time in between shifts that ended up costing her extra transportation money going home and returning to work. She had to buy uniforms for some of the jobs. Mostly, however, she hated "people always telling you what to do." Rhea, who had worked as a saleswoman in a department store summed it up, "It was warmer inside in the winter and cooler in the summer, but at least now no one is telling me what to do."

Others value the flexibility of working hours without sacrificing pay. According to Maureen, who supports two children, "The work is relatively easy and I can always take off days if there is some emergency and I can work shorter hours. And I can make those decisions."

The women who owned their own stands saw vending as a way to own a small business without having to invest a significant amount of start-up capital. In exchange for ownership, they worked 10 to 12 hours a day, with total responsibility for the success or failure of their ventures. In addition, they did a fair amount of travelling in order to pick up supplies from wholesale outlets in Pennsylvania, Virginia and New York. They also reported that during both holiday and tourist seasons they had to get out as early as 5:00 a.m. in order to guard their spots. Yet despite these hardships, none of these women wanted to return to their previous jobs.

While personal autonomy, flexibility of hours, and having one's own business were all important reasons for vending, a decent income was the primary reason. The women interviewed reported earning on the average of $75 to $100 a day. Those who worked for someone else were paid a flat fee and did not appear to know how much their employer made in profits. Assuming that weather conditions prevent them from working more than 40 weeks per year (this estimate was arrived at after consultation with the National Bureau of Weather Services), the average annual income of these women in 1984 would have been approximately $12,600 working four days a week and $18,000 if they worked five days a week. While they are not paid for sick leave or for vacation days, their earnings are higher than the annual income earned by cashiers, waitresses and sales clerks.[4] As Shirleen concluded, "I vend because there's money and freedom in it."

Problems and Strategies

While women vendors see very positive aspects to their jobs, part of the struggle to stay in business includes dealing with the experience of being one of the few groups of women who work the streets. Because they are on male turf, they are seen as visible targets by men on the streets, by shoplifters, by male vendors and by the police. Describing her main on-the-job problems, Verna said "cops, guys, and people trying to rip you off."

Like men, women vendors told of being harassed by the police. They complained that the police do not protect them if they are robbed or harassed, but instead operate in the interests of fixed-location businesses. In addition, they reported that the police treat them like criminals and frequently contribute to keeping customers away by constantly scrutinizing their licenses, measuring their tables, and looking for other violations. The women did not think that the police do this to them more often than to male vendors; however, they did feel in greater need of police protection and did not think that the police were either sympathetic or present when they needed help.

Unlike for men, for women the issue of sexual harassment was a recurrent theme. Women vendors were faced with hostile and threatening remarks and actions that made the

streets a demeaning work environment. The offenders were
mostly male customers, men on the streets, and sometimes
male vendors. Elaine said that "I never wear jeans or tight
clothes because men have literally come up behind me and tried
to feel my ass ... and it's not only the creeps, but real
respectable looking ones too." Jackie concurred "Men try to
hustle you all the time, both customers and other men--you
have to be cool and unfriendly."

In addition to being harassed by customers and men on the
streets, women vendors also reported being both physically and
verbally harassed by male vendors whose actions were
attempts to push the women off the streets, literally and
figuratively. Several women said that they were physically
"pushed around" by male vendors. They claim that often these
men insist that they have a right to a woman's spot, and they
will threaten or intimidate her until she moves. Susan
described how male vendors "frequently set up right on top of
you and try to crowd you back into the wall. They only do this
to women because another man would punch the shit out of
them."

Male vendors also harassed the women by comparing them
to prostitutes. Verna described the following unsolicited
opinion a male vendor offered her: "He said he would never let
his woman work on the streets. He wanted her in an office
where there is a desk between her and everyone else." Earlene
added "The men vendors are a pain in the ass; they think they
own the streets and can tell you where to go and where to set
up." One male vendor actually said to her, "If you're going to
sell on the street, why don't you sell something expensive like
your pussy and really make some money."

The women also felt that they were especially easy targets
for shoplifters. As a result they were more limited in their
choice of vending locations than men vendors, and some of
them are sure that there are certain areas of the city that they
have to avoid entirely. Rhea described a situation where
another woman vendor had merchandise stolen from her stand
in full view of other vendors . She said "Only the women
vendors tried to help her--the male vendors claimed not to see a
thing." Feeling particularly vulnerable to this kind of attack,
few women would work on the streets at night.

Survival Strategies

Women vendors learned to use a variety of survival of
individual and cooperative strategies to deal with these daily
problems of harassment. Some women made a concerted effort
to appear, "cool, distant, and unfriendly." Others learned to be

aggressive and give tit for tat. Still others modified their dress so that they never appear to be wearing anything that could be described as provocative. Some of the younger women said that they went so far as to try to make themselves look unattractive and keep as much of their bodies covered as possible. Many of these women consciously learned to be as aggressive and abrasive as their attackers. Celeste told us, "You learn very fast to be as quick and as vulgar as they are, because if you do the standard female thing of being coy and shy and try to back off gently, they take it as encouragement and it gets worse."

Another widely-used strategy is the selection of vending spots. Whenever possible they choose spots with heavy pedestrian traffic. Although the crowding made for more cut-throat competition for customers, it also resulted in feelings of greater safety and less possibility of being ripped off and harassed. As Lorraine said "If you aren't in a good location with lots of traffic it's easy to get robbed."

It is more difficult to engage in cooperative strategies because vending spots are spread out across the city and their is no necessary daily contact between women vendors. Some women did try to work in fairly close proximity to one another, and others reported moving to different parts of the city that they thought would be safer and then passing on this information to other women vendors. They also reported warning each other when they see police officers coming and most said that they would come to another woman's aid if she were in trouble.

A final strategy is for the women to give up their right to work on the streets unattended and to seek out male protection. Some women have husbands, boyfriends or hired men watch out for them. Several women said that they would not consider vending without this protection because the streets are dangerous and they get treated with more respect and less like prostitutes if they have a man with them.

The variety of strategies that women vendors use for daily survival were put to the test when the D.C. government joined officials in cities such as New York, Philadelphia and Los Angeles in clamping down on the re-emergence of vendors selling their wares on downtown streets. The promulgation of the new regulations led to the development of a new more collective form of action--a vendors' union--as well as the continuation of individual acts of resistance.

CONFLICTING GROUPS IN THE POLICY DEBATE

The latest attempt to regulate D.C. street vending took place in a downtown area which is in the process of gentrification whose small retail shops, five and dimes, and dowdy department stores with bargain basements catered to the city's largely black, working-class population. An advisory committee, composed largely of private developers, investors, retailers, city government officials and a few vendors, was established in 1984 by the D.C. Office of Business and Economic Development to issue policy guidelines and to suggest new regulations.

The developers, investors and retailers, represented by the Board of Trade, argued that vending displaced jobs from legitimate businesses, provided unfair competition and failed to pay its "fair share" of taxes. They also claimed that vendors gave the city a "bazaar-like image" by selling shoddy goods, creating dirt and crowding. They suggested that vending be greatly curtailed if not banished from gentrifying downtown streets.

City officials stated that the government was not trying to ban vending, rather they were exercising their responsibility to regulate it. The widely held opinion was that street vending was not congruent with the image that the city government wished to project to investors. Vending was seen as unattractive to investors.

The new regulations issued by the D.C. government, based on the recommendations of the Advisory Commission, did not ban all vendors from the streets as the Board of Trade desired. The rules did contain the following provisions to discourage vending: a large decrease in the number of vending licenses to be issued and a limitation on the number of vendors allowed in the most desirable downtown locations; a seven-fold increase in the cost of a license along with the payment of a $500 cash bond; an increase in the space required between vendors, and the vendors and fixed location businesses; and a limitation of the kinds of goods that could be sold. In addition, the new regulations mandated that vendors sell their goods from a wooden cart that met a precise set of design criteria, cost at least $700 to buy and was extremely heavy to move.[5]

VENDORS AND THE STRUGGLE AGAINST THE REGULATIONS

Vendors contended that the new regulations were the result of an effort by traditional businesses to stifle low-cost competition and that the city was "in cahoots" with the Board of Trade. Despite their agreement as to the source of the problem, the lack of a collective strategy among vendors was particulary evident in the early days after the regulations were issued. Due to the lack of enforcement many vendors were able to ignore the regulations with relative impunity. Most did not purchase the specially designed wooden carts, some sold goods prohibited by the regulations. Still others were in spots that were illegal under the new regulations.

Believing that individual acts of selective disobedience would not keep them on the streets, a group of 150-200 vendors banded together to found a union as part of Local 82 of the Service Employees International Union.[6] The organizers of the vendor unit, mainly black Muslim men, did make efforts to get other ethnic groups involved in the union, even appointing a Korean vendor as a representative to the "Oriental vendor community."

In addition to a law suit, the union used a variety of other tactics in order to get the regulations modified.[7] They met with the Mayor and with members of the City Council. They began displaying signs depicting the Mayor as a puppet to bigger business interests. They picketed, demonstrated, held press conferences, and had petitions signed by their customers. These tactics produced some relief for the vendors--the pre-enforcement period was extended, carts were abandoned, merchandise constraints were narrowed and the Mayor appointed yet another commission to study the problem. The $606 bond and license fee, the spacing requirements and the curtailment of downtown vending spots, however, became law.

Women Vendors' Resistance to the Regulations

During this period women vendors were frustrated, worried and angry. They had difficulty finding out what the new regulations were. They worried about keeping their spots, the new fees, and the cost of the new carts as well as the difficulty in handling them. The women also worried that their jobs would become more dangerous if too many other women vendors left the streets. In daily conversations with other vendors, the women vented their anger at the city government. Once again, they used a variety of strategies to deal with these new threats to their livelihood.

As shown in Table 8:2, women vendors were less likely to own their own stands and therefore felt less able to pay the fee. Two out of three of the women who own their own stands said that they would try to keep working as a vendor, but one-third said they could not afford the new fees. Among the women

who worked for somebody else, more than one out of two
thought that they would be forced to quit or were not sure that
they would be able to continue vending. Thus, between
one-third and one-half of the 40 women interviewed during
this period did not expect to be able to continue as vendors.
Tawana, who could not afford the $606 license and bond fee
and whose employer would not pay for her spoke for others
saying "I support my two kids on my vending income. I will go
back on welfare. This city is so stupid. Here they have people
working and off welfare, but with these new regulations lots of
jobs will be lost."

While the licensing and bond fee was considered a burden
by many of the women, the regulation requiring the heavy
wooden carts to be removed from the streets nightly brought
forth even more ire from the women. As Shirleen said "Those
carts are a real problem. They have to be taken off the streets
at night. Where can I store it? I don't have a car and I can't
get it into my apartment building." It was claimed that
women would have trouble loading and unloading the heavy
carts and that this requirement would make them less able to
survive on their own.

The women were equally worried that the new regulations
would make the streets more dangerous for them because they
would not be able to use some of their usual survival strategies.
For example, by requiring that stands be at least ten feet apart
and by decreasing the number of vendors allowed at many
locations, the new regulations make it more difficult to use the
"safety in numbers" strategy. They worried about the
dwindling numbers of vendors even if, as a result, they did
more business. Maureen reflected,

"If there are a lot fewer vendors no one can help anyone
out. On a regular Saturday there are lots of vendors so
you can take a break and have someone watch your stuff.
With fewer vendors it's harder to work. It's not good to be
too busy to watch for shoplifters. It may be less
competitive, but I don't like it."

Like men vendors, the majority of women we interviewed
did not join the union, even though they had a consciousness of
themselves as vendors in opposition to the Board of Trade.
Rose did not join because she thought that the Board of Trade
was too powerful and unionizing would not do any good. But if
the union did win any battles, she reasoned, the benefits would
spill over to her anyway whether she joined or not. Other
women said that they were not interested in paying dues or
sitting through meetings, or "paying for the privilege of being
ignored" by the men running the union. Women were
discouraged from joining by the men they worked for. As

Earlene said "The man I work for thinks that the union is
garbage and just a way to get another trade to pay dues." The
pattern of half owners and half paid workers was a drawback
to union membership and solidarity. In addition, a union
organizer suggested that the police discouraged many vendors
from joining. The lack of daily contact between vendors spread
out over the city made organizing them difficult. And last but
not least, women did not join because they didn't have the
time.

Despite these problems, some of the women did take the
step of engaging in collective political action and did join the
union. Like men vendors, the women joined because they
wanted more political clout to effectively fight the regulations
so that they could continue to work on the streets. Those
women who did join were active in the local--attending
meetings, producing posters, demonstrating, circulating
petitions, encouraging other vendors to join, and lobbying City
Council members.

Problems with harassment of women and safety were not
raised as an issue in the union campaign for economic survival.
It was felt that economic survival was more important. In
addition the structure of the union and its predominantly male
membership made it difficult to raise this issue. As Betty said
"Most of them were Muslims who thought that women should
be at home with the kids--they didn't respect women who were
out on the streets." Joan claimed that she had tried to raise
some women's issues, but that they got "washed over."
"Maybe later," she suggested, "when there are more women in
the union." This later was never to come because the union fell
apart shortly after the revised regulations went into effect.

THE IMPACT OF THE REGULATIONS

In response to the strict new regulations, women vendors,
like their male co-workers, used a number of strategies to stay
in business. The most effective of these strategies was the
formation of a union. While the union was successful in
modifying some of the regulations, it was not successful,
however, in getting rid of the licensing fees and the spacing
between vendors. With the implementation of the revised
regulations many vendors left the streets. By March 1986, as
Table 8:3 shows, there were less than 1500 licensed vendors on
the D.C. streets, down from 4,300 when this study began in
1984.

TABLE 8:3: CHANGES IN CHARACTERISTICS OF
LICENSED STREET VENDORS IN PERCENTAGES, 1984
AND 1986

CHARACTERISTIC	1984	1986
SEX OF VENDOR (with allocation of unknowns)*	100.0	100.0
Male	73.5	76.2
Female	26.5	23.8
WORKS FOR SELF OR OTHER	100.0	100.0
Self	52.5	87.7
Other	47.5	12.3
TOTAL NUMBER	(4348)	(1451)

*   Assumes that the percentage breakdown of unknowns is the
same as the population of knowns.

Source: March 1984 and March 1986 Street Vending File,
Management Information System Division, District of Columbia
Government, Department of Consumer and Regulatory Affairs,
Department of Licenses, Investigations and Inspections.

District of Columbia government officials called the results
"a success." According to one such official, "Vending had
gotten out of control. This year, the streets are less congested.
We lost more than 4,000 vendors when the bond requirements
went in." The dramatic decline of the vendors who worked for
someone else from approximately half of all vendors to less
than one in eight means that the "hidden wage workers" have
left the street at least for the present.

The regulations, though gender neutral in their wording,
did especially disadvantage women vendors. The data in Table
8:3 shows that while the regulations have had an extremely
negative impact on male vendors, the impact on women
vendors appears to be worse. The percentage of women
vendors decreased from approximately 27 percent to
approximately 24 percent of all vendors. This finding is not
surprising. Women vendors were less likely to own their own

stands and hence were less likely to be able to afford the new licenses. The earlier predictions of those women vendors that their bosses would not pay the new fees so that they could continue to work turned out to be true.

In this paper I used women vendors' words to tell of their efforts to earn a decent living on Washington, D.C. streets in an occupation which offers relative autonomy from close supervision. By adding their voice to that of the other more powerful protagonists, I hope to broaden the debate over the new regulations to include the issue of women's right to use the streets as a safe work environment.[8]

The study revealed that women who work on the streets as vendors are visible targets for harassment from male customers, vendors and police. Because urban streets are still seen as male turf, places where nice women do not linger, many men feel free to act as if the women themselves are objects for sale. Women vendors use a number of strategies to protect themselves including a strategy of "safety in numbers." Harassment is especially severe when there are few women on the streets to help protect each other. With fewer women vendors on the street, those who remain feel more need for male partners, male assistants and the police to protect them. For the women who remain, the new regulations have decreased their autonomy and increased the economic costs of harassment.

The intended purpose of the new regulations was to curtail vending in the city's gentrifying downtown area rather than to increase the costs to women vendors of street harassment. The issue of women's right to work safely on the streets did not become a policy issue because the belief that sexual harassment is a personal problem is strong; even women vendors had trouble articulating it as a policy issue. City officials assumed that the regulations were gender neutral because the language was. The result was that a somewhat greater proportion of women than men left the occupation. Although the policy did not have major consequences for the city's economy, several thousand vendors did leave the streets, perhaps to other jobs. A small group of women are less economically independent as a result of the new regulations, in a city with more than 40 percent of female-headed households in poverty. I conclude that the new regulations reinforced, if only in a small way, male domination of economic and public life at least for the present.

There is evidence that the proportion of foreign-born vendors appears to have increased with the implementation of the new regulations. About 40 percent of licensed vendors listed in the 1986 printout were foreign born. While this data was not available in 1984, eyeball street censuses indicate that the ethnic and national composition is changing. Based on a review of the 1986 printout, with the assistance of relevant native speakers, it appears that some of these groups (e.g. Koreans) appear to vend in family groups while others (Indians, Ethiopians, Iranians) appear to be almost entirely male. In addition there has been an expansion of vending into some city neighborhoods where it is less strictly regulated. The sexual political economy of the new groups and new patterns of street use is a topic for future research.

ACKNOWLEDGEMENTS

I would like to thank The George Washington University's Center for Washington Area Studies and especially Professors Howard Gillette and Jeffrey Henig for all their efforts in making this study possible. In addition, I would like to thank Mindy Shapiro for interviewing and coding, Geetanjali Chanda, Kyung Sook Lee and Roxana Moayedi for their aid in identifying the gender of foreign-born vendors. Eileen Zeitz deserves thanks for all her help with the study. Without her it would not have been completed. And I would like to thank Gracia Clark for her support and editorial suggestions.

NOTES

1. Vending is such a small occupation that it is not listed separately in the U.S. Census' detailed occupational code.
2. A somewhat longer definition of sexual political economy is: The economic consequences (in terms of the distribution and control of economic resources) of state legitimated relations of power and dominance that are gender-based with men as the dominant group. The term itself comes from Batya Weinbaum (1978: 31) who distinguishes between the term political economy of sex which she thinks assumes that the sex and gender system is separable from the political economy and her preferred term, "sexual political economy". The definition is also based on Jean Grossholtz (1983) who describes a set of power relations, legitimated by state force, that assume the dominance of males in public positions, politics, economic life and social life.
3. The gender distribution of vendors was determined by their given name. The researchers went through the printout of the 4,200 vendors listed in the District of Columbia Department of Consumer and Regulatory Affairs 1984 license master file

independently, categorizing each licensed vendor as "male" or "female" or "don't know". Comparisons were then made and disagreements were discussed. When agreement was not reached, names were put into the "don't know" category. This category includes names such as Robin and Terry. It also included a high proportion of vendors with Asian, Middle Eastern and African names. The results of this procedure were: 65 percent male, 22 percent female as the proportions of the "knowns" with 13 percent remaining in the "unknown" category. The unknowns were then divided in the same proportions as the knowns and allocated to the male and female categories. The final results (with allocation) were: 73.5 percent male and 26.5 percent female.

4. See <u>Women, Employment and Training: A Status Report on Programs and Needs in the District of Columbia</u>, compiled by the D.C. Women's Employment and Training Coalition (Washington, D.C.: Commission on the Status of Women, 1985) esp. p.46 for annual income for these occupations. The average household size of those vendors we asked was three. According to the Employment and Training Department of the U.S. Department of Labor (1984), the cost of a lower living family budget for a three person household in Washington, D.C. in 1984 was $14,912. The cost of a poverty budget in 1984 (based on 1983 income data) was $8,850. Hence, working full time as a sales worker or cashier ensures a life of poverty, while street vending allows these women and their households to move out of poverty and toward a lower or moderate living standard, if women vendors were correct about their daily income and if the annualized estimates are also correct.

5. McGee and Young (1978) have developed a paradigm for rating government action toward street vending from positive to negative. A rating of "A" is based on pro-vendor policies that include: allowing vendors to sell legally from locations they desire; encouraging vending through government loans and other inducements to enter the occupation; educating the public to use their services; and requiring large firms to distribute commodities though vendors. A rating of "D" is based on anti-vending policies that include: clearing vendors from all locations in the city; discouraging vendors by high license fees and legal punishments; offering high salaries to enforcement officers; and stressing the dangers of vending from the point of hygiene. According to this scheme the D.C. regulations, if enforced, would get about a "C" rating.

6. The story of the vendor union and women's role in it is told in greater detail in Spalter-Roth, (1988).

7. Of the ten regulations challenged by the plaintiff (Local 82 of the Service Employees International Union) in Service

Employees Local 82 v. District of Columbia et. al. (1985), which included:(1) bars to vending in a zone for which the vendor does not have a license; (2) restrictions to sidewalks; (3) bars to vending before 5 a.m. and after 10 p.m.; (4) restrictions on the type of merchandise that can be sold; (5) bans on overnight storage of equipment or merchandise; (6) compliance with cart design standards; (7) requirements to keep records of sales and receipts of purchase and expenses that must be made available for inspection by "any authorized representative of the District of Columbia government;" (8) penalty for failure to do so by immediate seizure of license; and (9) payment of a bond in the amount of $500 for D.C. residents and $1500 for non-D.C. residents. Only the last regulation was found to be without merit or precedent by the presiding judge. It should be noted that the Apartment and Office Building Association (AOBA), the Connecticut Avenue Association, the Capitol Hill Association of Merchants and Professionals and the Business and Professional Association of Georgetown joined the District of Columbia Government as friends of the court. Expressing how "livid" he was with the Mayor's decision to modify the regulations even though the city had won the court case, a spokesman for AOBA noted that the case cost them $11,000.
8. An earlier version of this study (Spalter-Roth and Zeitz, 1985) with specific policy recommendations was directed to D.C. City Council members and other relevant policy officials. It can be obtained from the Center for Washington Area Studies, The George Washington University, Washington, D.C. 20052.

REFERENCES

Babb, Florence
    1984   Women in the marketplace: Petty commerce in Peru. Review of Radical Political Economics 16(1) :45-59.

Bell, Charles O.
    1983   Avon may be calling in Slidell, but other peddlers can't. New Orleans Times Picayune, September 15, 1983.

Blumenthal, Ralph
    1983   Sanitation by food peddlers worries New York officials. New York Times, August 2.

184 Street Vending in D.C.

Boys, Jos
    1985   Women and public space. Pp. 37-54 In Matrix
            Books Group (eds.) Making Space: Women and
            the Man Made Environment. London: Pluto Press.

Cranz, Galen.
    1981   Women in urban parks. Pp. 76-92 In Catherine
            R. Stimpson, Elsa Dixler, Martha J. Nelson and
            Kathryn B. Yatrakis (eds.) Women and the
            American City. Chicago: University of Chicago
            Press.

di Leonardo, Micaela.
    1982   Political economy of street harassment. Aegis
            1(Summer):51-57.

District of Columbia, Office of Business and Economic
Development
    1984   Notice of Proposed Rulemaking. District of
            Columbia Register, November 9.

Employment and Training Administration, U.S. Department of
Labor
    1984   Job training partnership act; lower living standard
            income level. Federal Register
            49(154):31664-31665.

Eisner, Jane and William W. Sutton.
    1984   Sidewalk sales: Despite city efforts, street vendors
            remain an issue. The Philadelphia Inquirer.
            November 5.

Enjeu, Claude and Joana Save
    1974   The city: off limits to women. Liberation 19(9):9-
            13.

Ferguson, Kathy E.
    1984   The Feminist Case Against Bureaucracy.
            Philadelphia: Temple University Press.

Freed, John C.
    1985   Surge in street vendors evokes mixed reviews.
            The New York Times. July 20.

Getlin, Josh
    1982   L.A. Council puts off action on pushcarts. Los
            Angeles Times. February 26.

Gordon, Margaret T., Stephanie Riger, Robert K. LeBailly and
Linda Heath
    1981   Crime, women and the quality of urban life. Pp.
            141-157 In Catherine B. Stimpson, Elsa Dixler,
            Martha J. Nelson and Kathryn B. Yatrakis (eds.)
            Women and the American City. Chicago:
            University of Chicago Press.

Grossholtz, Jean
    1983   Battered women's shelters and the political
            economy of sexual violence. In Irene Diamond
            (ed.) Families, Politics and Public Policy. New
            York: Longman. Pp.59-69, esp. p. 60.

Hansen, Karen
    n.d.   The Black Market and Women Traders in Lusaka,
            Zambia. forthcoming in Jane Parpart and Kathy
            Staudt, eds. Women and the State in Africa.
            boulder: Lynne Rienner.

Hapgood, Karen and Judith Getzels (eds.)
    1974   Women, Planning and Change Chicago: American
            Society of Planning Officials.

Henig, Jeffery and Michael G. Maxfield.
    1978   Reducing fear of crime: Strategies for
            intervention. Victimology: An International
            Journal 3(3/4):297-313.

McGee, T.C. and Y.M. Young
    1977   Hawkers in Southeast Asian Cities: Planning for
            the Bazaar Economy. Ottawa: International
            Development Research Center.

Mitchell, Constance
    1983   Downtowns overflowing with vendors. U.S.A.
            Today. August 23, A1.

Project for Public Spaces, Inc.
    1982   Improving the Management of Downtown Public
            Spaces: A National Overview of Programs for
            Private Sector Downtown Organizations. New
            York.

186 Street Vending in D.C.

Riger, Stephanie, Margaret T. Gordon and Robert LeBailly.
   1978   Women's fear of crime: From blaming to
           restricting the victim. Victimology 3:274-284.

Ritzdorf, Martha.
   1986   Women in the city: Land use and zoning issues.
           Urban Resources: Special Issue on Women in the
           City 3(2):23-27.

Salem, Greta
   1986   Gender equity in the urban environment. Urban
           Resources: Special Issue on Women in the City
           3(2):3-8.

Spalter-Roth, Roberta M.
   1988   Vending on the streets: City policy, gentrification
           and patriarchy. pp.272-294. in Ann Bookman
           and Sandra Morgen (eds.) Women and the Politics
           of Empowerment. Philadelphia: Temple
           University Press.

Spalter-Roth, Roberta M. and Eileen Zeitz
   1985   Street Vending in Washington, D.C.: Reassessing
           the Regulation of a "Public Nuisance.
           Washington,D.C.: The Center for Washington
           Area Studies, The George Washington University,
           September, 1985.

Stansell, Christene
   1982   Women, children and the uses of the streets: class
           and gender conflicts in New York City,
           1850-1860. Feminist Studies 8: 309-335.

Stimpson, Catherine B., Elsa Dixler, Martha J. Nelson and
Kathryn B. Yatrakis (eds.)
   1981   Women and the American City. Chicago: The
           University of Chicago Press.

Warren, Barbara Kay and Susan C. Bourque
   1985   Gender, power and communication: Women's
           responses to political muting in the Andes. Pp.
           255-286. In Susan C. Bourque and Donna
           Robinson Divine (eds.) Women Making Change.
           Philadelphia: Temple University Press.

Werkerle, Gerda R.
  1981   Women in the urban environment. Pp. 185-211.
          In Catherine B. Stimpson, Elsa Dixler, Martha J.
          Nelson and Kathryn B. Yatrakis (eds.) Women
          and the American City. Chicago: University of
          Chicago Press.

Wekerle, Gerda R., Rebecca Peterson and David Morely (eds.)
  1980   New Space for Women. Boulder: Westview Press.

Wekerle, Gerda R. with Lisa Gaddie-Thomas.
  1986   Space and women's safety. Urban Resources:
          Special Issue on Women in the City 3(2):28.

Weinbaum, Batya
  1978   The Curious Courtship of Women's Liberation and
          Socialism. Boston: South End Press.

Whyte, William H.
  1980   The Social Life of Small Urban Spaces.
          Washington, D.C.: The Conservation Fund.

9

Overview:
The Informal Economy and the State

M. Estellie Smith
SUNY-Oswego

INTRODUCTION

The papers in this volume address various aspects of what,
on the one hand, most marxists prefer to link to that sector
which they label "petty (or simple) commodity production" (cf.
H. Friedmann 1978, 1980) but what, for many others,[1] reflects
a varied range of economic activities that in format and degree
indicate the extent to which such enterprises elude the
monitoring and usually extractive intrusions of the state.
Indeed, so many and, for some, intuitively different types of
operations are included that there appears to be a growing
attempt to redefine the category. Thus, there is a plethora of
alternative terms--to mention only a few: "irregular,"
"shadow," "alternative," "excluded," "black," "unregulated,"
"underground," "unscheduled," "clandestine," "subterranean,"
"second," "on the left" (rather peculiarly, I think, a phrase
located in Eastern European socialist countries) and, the term
that seems to be gaining the widest currency, "informal." This
issue will be returned to below.
Traders are a particularly problematic component of the
informal economy. For one thing, are they "penny capitalists"
(see Tax 1953) or are they embedded in the process of simple
commodity production? For another thing, and despite the
suggestion in the title of this volume, Traders versus the State,
do those in the informal economy--traders or producers--
necessarily stand in an antagonistic relation with the state? I
think not. State personnel may simply not take note of certain
activities that may be part of a lifestyle that the more
educated, affluent and/or urbanized know nothing about (e.g.
systems of barter between rural producers who gather wood,
hunt and fish, gather wild foods, or plant small gardens with
confined surpluses). Secondly, they may be known but treated
as too trivial to track--as is often the case for the urban poor
who make a living "recycling" products from the urban trash

cans. Thirdly, they may be known and deemed significant but, at least for the time, ignored because monitoring costs would be far in excess of any utility the state might reap. Lastly, they may even be given tacit encouragement to flourish because, as several of the papers in this collection indicate, the state may in fact depend on this sector to provide necessary goods and services (as well bolstering the economy through the multiplier effect of monies circulated). In such cases, the activities take on, at the least, a quasi-legitimacy, and labels such as "unregulated," "unscheduled," "second," or "excluded"--all emphasizing the extent to which the goods and services produced in this sector are (a) ignored in the system of national accounting and (b) required to satisfy popular rather than official regulatory criteria re, say, standards of quality or price. This form of what many would see as benign neglect is more common than one might suppose, particularly in polities where the organization of the state is weak, where it is undergoing transformation and lacks an adequate infrastructure, trained personnel, techniques, facilities or funds for monitoring, or where state personnel themselves derive benefit from the opportunities it supplies (through such forms of corruption as blackmail, bribery, or their own ability to participate and thus supplement their real or perceived "meager governmental income"). Several of the papers in this collection touch on these state weaknesses.

It should be stressed that those engaged in informal sector activities can be (a) primary producers solely, (b) producer-traders, selling goods and/or services that they themselves produce, or (c) they may function solely as intermediaries between producer and consumer--transporting, processing, and/or trading, traders, acting as brokers or intermediaries between producer and consumer. As several of the papers in this volume have shown, those who function in the third category, as intermediaries, are much more likely to be targeted as, at best, unnecessary and, at worse, undesireable. On the margin and literally as well as figuratively "in the middle," not uncommonly, they become scapegoats for all and sundry, blamed for economic woes as well as society's ills by state functionary, primary producer, and consumer alike, often getting little sympathy from any save their fellow merchants, traders, therefore, may, at any given time, be viewed by others as adversaries, critical linchpins, and/or convenient demons to be exorcised.

This said, however, the papers collected in this volume focus in varying degrees on the conflict between, on the one side, those who, for whatever reason, must or prefer to function in the informal sector and, on the other side, the state functionaries who try to eliminate or "regularize" the activities. In order to understand the basis of this conflict it is necessary to look at the larger field of the informal economy as a whole. First, what are some of the characteristics of a significant number of those who make up this sociocultural segment? In the studies presented here (though this is not true in all settings): (1) they are often women and, whatever their sex or age, they are frequently at the economic bottom of society; (2) they are not uncommonly the newly arrived, e.g., refugees and displaced, landless rural migrants--somehow marginal in the context in which they find themselves; (3) they are hard workers, many often working at several jobs simultaneously not just because they have to but because they wish to "get ahead," not infrequently hoping to regularize their position and leave the risks, uncertainties, and real physical dangers that too often punctuate existence in the shadow world they inhabit; (4) they are resilient and sometimes downright "tough," challenging those in authority who make repeated efforts to rid society of such types; (5) they are (as, e.g. Babb discusses in her paper) often held responsible for a myriad of problems--doubly afflicted since they are the most susceptible victims of but most likely to blamed for a myriad of social maladies.

Despite these commonalities, the papers also reveal that the informal economy includes a wide and fundamentally very disparate group of activities. This may be an historical accident since such lumping is characteristic of an investigatory focus in the initiatory phases of analysis. And, as we grow more informed and sophisticated, the substance and typological rigor improves. It is clear, however, that some of the activities currently included under the general rubric of "informal" are more socioculturally "legitimate" than others. Some of this is contextual, the result of cross-cultural, intra-cultural and even temporal variability. In modern state or would-be nation-state societies, for example, what is acceptable to the poor, a denigrated ethnic or religious group--even, I think, a clandestine political activist group--is likely to be decried by those who are or believe themselves to be integrated into the mainstream of the society. Thus, in some parts of the world, rural peoples, often those designated as "tribal," survive by growing those crops that are part of a world-wide drug network; and those living in urban fringe barrios or inner-city ghettos frequently come to see various forms of criminality as the only genuinely lucrative avenues for escape from poverty-- especially as that may be defined in a society with an emphasis on conspicuous consumption among the affluent. Further, there is the powerful argument that laws and regulations identifying "criminality" are attempts by the ruling class to suppress activities that challenge their control.

From one perspective, the categories of "formal" and "informal" can be viewed as fuzzy sets, the lines between them being blurred in the real world. Granted, large scale drug movements, theft with the implied threat of violence, organized prostitution rings, and extortion are viewed by even the majority of their practitioners as criminal. But it is also true that, for example, legal action against some who traffic in drugs is viewed more as persecution than prosecution ("she only passed out some joints at a party"); petty pilferage is often treated as a joke ("I always steal hotel towels") or justified as "ripping off" an exploiter who "deserves it," "won't miss it," "can afford it"; what might be called "independent prostitution," is glamorized and urged to be classified as, at worst, a "victimless crime"; and even major crimes such as bank robbery (cf. the folk hero, Billy the Kid), hijacking (the heroics surrounding the act of stealing a vehicle in order to make "a dash for freedom" from east to west), "diversion" of governmental materiale (Corporal Radar of the TV series M*A*S*H is admired for his ability to cut through red tape via bartering and bribery) or kidnapping for ransom (from Robin Hood to the present seen as a way of obtaining funds for as well as a technique of attacks on a repressive political system)-- can be romanticized and legitimized. Yet, these particular actions are usually classed as a special informal subset better labeled as "black," "underground," or "subterranean." There are also the far more commonplace, in some ways even "socially acceptable" acts of "moonlighting," individual or corporate tax evasion involving downright fiddling of account books, undeclared "gifts" obtained for "cooperating" or "helping someone out," and including hidden barter exchange of goods and services. The latter can range from, say, a commercial fisherman agreeing to supply some of his daily catch to a grocer in return for food to supply the crew on their fishing venture, to a contractor's remodeling of a physician's office in exchange for medical services, to arrangements such as those that can take place at the highest level of government--e.g., the concealed transfer of monies and military goods with the quid pro quo of more favorable relations between two states.

THE "DISCOVERY" OF THE INFORMAL ECONOMY

Recognition of some class of activities identifiable as the informal economy is very recent. Anthropologist Keith Hart seems to have been the first to employ the term, using it in a

paper initially prepared in 1971 ("Informal income
opportunities and urban employment in Ghana," 1973).
Economists, political scientists and a range of governmental
technical experts began to take note of such phenomena in the
mid to late 1970s. What was it that generated this interest
then--and not sooner or later? Why does research on this sector
continue to expand and attract the attention of an ever more
diverse group of investigators? Is it, as some have argued, that
such enterprises have suddenly mushroomed, becoming more
pervasive and proportionately significant both at the macrolevel
and in everyday life? Like all sociocultural questions, the
"answer" appears to be grounded in a complex matrix. Let me
suggest that, among others, the following factors must be taken
into account.

The Urban Dilemma

Increasingly cities are recognized as structures fraught with
problems. The shift of the world's population from the pre-
World War II situation-in which the majority of earth's people
lived in rural environments--to the current projections for the
year 2000, little more than a decade away, at which time the
majority will live in an urban setting, is presenting officialdom
with critical dilemmas. They must make decisions as to what
to do with a constant influx of people (who, as Kerner [this
volume] points out, present the double dilemma of straining
the urban infrastructure and its resources while simultaneously
draining the productive hinterland of needed producers).
Potential flash points include: squatter settlements which
frequently though not invariably carry the potential for disease,
epidemics, and massive human suffering caused by
uncontrollable catastrophes such as flood, fire, or mudslides--all
going hand in hand with a potentially devastating loss of life
given population density; urban sprawl; traffic congestion as
well as transportation inadequacies; pollution; the urban milieu
as a loci for social unrest due to the variations in power
between the elite, bourgeoisie, and underclass, dramatically
juxtaposed inequities of poverty and affluence--the list goes on.
In the need to manage, the most vulnerable segments of the
population are the focus of change from the top down since,
whatever the implicit payoffs, the hidden agenda, or the covert
primary aims, such management can be validated as necessary
for the larger good and, in the long run, "beneficial" for the
disadvantaged (see, for example, the paper by Alan Smart).
Thus, the dramatic mushrooming of cities, especially but not
alone in LDCs, has led (indeed, required) urban and national
managers to address such problems as inadequate housing, an

inadequate infrastructure and insufficient numbers of trained
personnel to provide necessary services, a floating underclass of
homeless and other street people who appear to be the genesis
of crime, litter, and (not the least concern of many urban
dwellers) a deterioration in a range of characteristics that
might be generally categorized under the rubric of "urban
aesthetics." We must not, however, resort to a variant of
blaming the victim--even when that victim is one for whom
there is rarely any sympathy--the state apparatus and the
personnel who service it. Despite the compassion that can be
elicited for those targeted for administrative reform efforts, the
problems the local and national managers address are real and
attempts must be made to constrain what sometimes seems to
be the anarchy of urban growth and individual strategizing.
But remedial activities are costly, and it is difficult to cut from
existing budget lines. From where are the monies to come?
    Simultaneously, then, with determining the dimensions of
the problems, prioritizing them, and working out "solutions" as
well as effectively implementing them, local and state
functionaries see a need to seek increased revenues in order to
fund them. From this perspective (and aside from such
considerations as the state's responsibility to establish and
maintain standards of health, fair and safe work conditions as
well as fair recompense, control over weights and measures,
etc.), intruding into the informal sector can, for one thing, add
to the public coffers by increasing the number that are
monitored by and thus susceptible to extraction from the state
in fees, taxes, etc. To use the reified language of marxian
analysts, "the state works to control the market to
appropriate...[its] surplus" (Watts 1988:201) and finance its
own corporate activities;
    Another function of the state's involvement is its capacity
to eliminate competition to
        (a) the state sector and (at least theoretically) allow for
        more rational management, politically and economically,
        (b) the private sector where increased profits will (at least
        theoretically) increase government revenues--see, for
        example, Spalter-Roth's discussion [this volume] of
        Washington merchants' lost sales due to street vendors'
        discounting only steps away from their shops.

The Technological Revolution

    One cannot underestimate the impact of equipment and
techniques that greatly facilitate storing, retrieving and
manipulating data (cf. "the computer revolution," and all of its
attendant software). Not only do managers everywhere

recognize the practical utility of having such data (after all, the earliest states in the old and new worlds quickly recognized the necessity of inventing ways to gather, record, and monitor information that would allow them to regulate as well as maneuver production, distribution, and consumption), its lack may represent a symbolic and real inability of the state to control its citizens. Next, the mere possession of the technology signals modernity. Further, it has the additional advantage of posing a threat to those who would try to evade the state net. Finally, the data are required by external lending agencies who implicitly mandate that such equipment and procedures be installed. Thus, there has been a critical thrust to utilize the technology and, in truly systemic fashion, once in place, increasing use requires continuing expansion, refinement and updating of the technology--which, in turn, signals expansion of its use. And so it goes. It is an obvious and therefore trivial prediction that this component alone will lead to growing pressure to "regularize" any part of the economic system currently not rigorously tracked in the national statistics. In short, for a variety of reasons, in order to make informed and timely decisions states must be able to track what the citizenry do; they must have as adequate and complete a system of national accounting as is possible. To the extent that things go on about which the state does not know, to that extent the decision-makers are at risk. For this reason, I am defining the informal economy as any component of production, distribution or consumption which wholly or partially eludes inclusion in the information system upon which polity managers base calculations relevant to present and future public policy.

Society Against the State

It may be that, as Clastres (1977) and others (e.g. Duvignaud 1970, Poulantzas 1978) have argued, the attempt by those who control the functioning and determine the function of one sociocultural sector, the state, will always lead to the adversarial results that the papers in this volume discuss. The basic raison d'etre of the state requires that its managers must intrude into and, if you will usurp control over what they themselves define as the optimum number of components in most if not all other sociocultural sectors, however those are determined in the ordinary lives of ordinary people. The state of course, has the ultimate tool, the ability to delimit "proper" from "improper," legitimate from illegitimate (see Smith 1988). The current debate about the informal/formal economy issue highlights this process.

Early kingdoms and states monopolized and exercised proprietory rights over the most profitable activities; rights to allocate privileged access in the production and/or trade of particular, highly profitable commodities and rights to impose taxes and tolls as well as to collect fees to permit certain economic processes to proceed. They left low- or non-profit activities (as well as innovative and risky or declining and unprofitable operations) to religious organizations, private or quasi-private associations (e.g. guilds and unions, death indemnity sodalities) and private "venture capitalists." The historical appearance (sometime in the late 18th or early 19th century in Europe) of the caretaking state represents a dramatic shift in the functioning and supposed function of the state.

In the late 1970s, however, a trickle of "privatization" began which, in the 1980s, has become an avalanche of dumping business, industries and even caretaking services that, aside from non-material benefits, must be reckoned as unprofitable when costs/profits are accurately measured. As several of the papers in this volume illustrate, the preference of political and administrative state personnel is now shifting to utilizing vastly improved techniques of monitoring the economic system so as to better "skim the profits" (as a trader informant from the informal sector put it to me) while reducing the state's economic costs and the political risks generated by charges of inefficiency and incompetency in public sector operations - whether they be the postal or railway system, or education and medical care.

It seems reasonable to suggest that there is a natural relationship between the attempt to privatize and the expanded efforts to track (and, in the process, regulate, extract from, and criminalize) those activities the state classifies as belonging to the informal sector. To support an ever increasing administrative and regulatory bureaucracy (whether elected, selected, or appointed)[2] state personnel are required to have as thorough a knowledge as possible of all economic components in order that taxes, licensing fees, duties, and, of course, fines for non-compliance extract the maximum income.[3] The technological revolution that began in the 1970s has played an important role in the florescence of attention to the informal sector. The capacity to monitor will no doubt continue to grow and enhance the state's capacity to expand and intensify its surveillance of market dynamics.

All of this and more strongly suggests that we are seeing only the initial stage of the struggle between the state and those identified as belonging to the informal sector. Attention to and concern with it is bound to expand and intensify, with a particular emphasis on, first, capturing and incorporating the economic wealth and dynamics generated by those actively engaged in informal activities; secondly, by criminalizing or delegitimating such activities, not the least because of the factors just discussed. However, as state managers intensify their efforts to increase their control over and withdraw resources from an ever-widening range of activities--whether those are identified as private or public, legal, quasi-legal and tolerated, or criminalized--we will see increasing attention paid to the issues discussed here.

CONCLUSION

The papers in this volume have addressed the multifaceted issue of the state vis-a-vis those perceived as actors in the informal or simple commodity production economy. The writers, as anthropologists tend to do, have stressed the human dimension, using the perspective of those at the bottom looking up. Few of the contributors would be so arrogant as to argue that this vantage point presents the "correct," the "right," or the only perspective but it does offer a view too often ignored by those concerned with "the big picture," the macrodynamics of macrosystems, a vantage point usually held by those who accept that the appropriate, indeed, the sole way to address issues, implement change and even attempt to ameliorate social problems, is from the top down. This volume is a healthy antidote to that particular form of hubris.

The next few decades may prove crucial for traders and for the state. Though the state in its various guises would seem to be the odds-on favorite, the accounts recorded by the contributors to this volume show that the adversaries are not as unevenly matched as one might assume. We can be sure, however, that we will hear more not less of the informal economy.

NOTES

1. See, for example, the wide range of positions held by the various contributors to the volume edited by Ferman, Henry and Hoyman (1987).
2. Note the growth in the staff of U.S. congressional leaders which has increased dramatically in the last decade.
3. Such information is also required if the state managers are to make informed decisions about economic matters, e.g., favoring or restricting imports/exports.

...APHY

...Pierre
Society against the state. New York: Urizen
Books.

Duvignaud, Jean
1970   Change at Shebika: Report from a North African
village. New York: Vintage Books.

Ferman, Louis A., Stuart Henry and Michele Hoyman
1987   The Informal Economy. Special Issue of The
Annals of the American Academy of Political and
Social Science 93 (September 1987). Newbury
Park, Ca.: Sage Publications.

Foucault, Michel
1971   The Order of Things. New York: Pantheon Books.

Friedmann, Harriet
1978   Simple Commodity Production and Wage Labor in
the American Plains. Journal of Peasant Studies
6:71-100.
1980   Household Production and the National Economy:
Concepts for the Analysis of Agrarian Formations.
Journal of Peasant Studies 7:158-184.

Hart, Keith
1973   Informal income opportunities and urban
employment in Ghana. Journal of Modern African
Studies 11:61-89.

Poulantzas, Nicos
1978   State, power, socialism. London: New Left Books.

Smith, M. Estellie
1988   We teach our people to be good citizens:
Persuasion and the morally defective.
International Journal of Moral and Social Studies
3: 59-93.

Tax, Sol
1953   Penny capitalism: A Guatemalan Indian economy.
Smithsonian Institution, Institute of social
anthropology, No. 16. Washington, D.C.: U.S.
Government Printing Office.

Watts, Michael
1988   Review of Stephen Bunker's Peasants against the
state: The politics of market control in Bugisu,
Uganda, 1900-1983. Urbana: University of Illinois
Press (1987). American Anthropologist 90:201-2.